Logs Wind and Sun

Handcraft your own log home . . .
then power it with nature

Rex A. Ewing and LaVonne Ewing

AN INSPIRING, HANDS-ON GUIDE TO SELF-SUFFICIENCY

PIXYJACK PRESS LLC

Logs, Wind and Sun

Published by PixyJack Press, LLC PO Box 149, Masonville, CO 80541 USA

FIRST EDITION 2002

ISBN 0-9658098-3-8

Publisher's Cataloging-in-Publication
(Provided by Quality Books, Inc.)

Ewing, Rex A.
Logs wind and sun : handcraft your own log home--then power it with nature / Rex A. Ewing and LaVonne Ewing. -- 1st ed.
p. cm.
"An inspiring, hands-on guide to self-sufficiency."
Includes index.
LCCN 2002092471
ISBN 0-9658098-3-8

1. Log cabins--Design and construction. 2. Log cabins--Energy conservation. 3. Renewable energy sources. I. Ewing, LaVonne. II. Title.

TH4840.E95 2002 690'.837
QBI33-645

Printed in the U.S.A.

Design, photography and illustrations by LaVonne Ewing (unless noted).
Illustrations by Sara Tuttle on pages 190-192, 209, and 267. Back cover photo of authors by Mike Fox.

To John and Gretchen,
and Roger and Glee
without whom neither this book—nor its authors—
would have been possible.

TABLE OF CONTENTS

PROLOGUE 10

1 ~ **LOGS, WIND AND SUN — A SUSTAINABLE TRIAD FOR A WORLD WITH DIMINISHING RESOURCES** 13

Beginning Thoughts and Considerations for Living Well

Placement and Orientation of the House | Designing for Efficiency and Comfort | Sound Propagation versus Heat Efficiency | Floor Plan Considerations | Interior Design | Non-Living Spaces | Should you do the log work yourself? | Buckhorn Camp's School-Built Log Home

Build With Logs

2 ~ **SITE SELECTION** 25

Where O' Where Does This House Want To Be?

Access | Southern Exposure | Other Considerations: Water, Wind, Rock

LaVonne's Logbook 1

3 ~ **PLANS AND PERMITS** 33

Paper Dreams and County Hoops

First Steps | Concerns Unique to Log Home Blueprints | Pier Foundations for Off-The Grid Homes | Solar and Wind Power Considerations | Hang in There!

4 ~ **LOGS** 39

Dead Trees and Great Expectations

Buying Logs | Green or Seasoned Logs? | Cribbing | Getting to Know Your Logs

LaVonne's Logbook 2

5 ~ **TOOLS FOR CONSTRUCTION** 47

Essential Tools for Pre-Log Construction

LaVonne's Logbook 3

6 ~ **EXCAVATION AND FOUNDATION WORK** 53

The Indelicate Art of Replacing Rock and Dirt with "Mud"

Excavation | Foundation | Where is North? | Making it Square | Making it Level | Footings | Walls | Damp-proofing & Backfilling | Concrete Floors

LaVonne's Logbook 4

7 ~ **THE FLOOR** 71

Toward Building the Flattest Place on the Mountain

Supporting the Subfloor | Rim Joists | Floor Joists | Installing the Subfloor

LaVonne's Logbook 5

continued

8 ~ **PEELING AND LIFTING LOGS** 79
At Long Last, Let the Real Work Commence
LaVonne's Logbook 6

9 ~ **TOOLS FOR LOGWORK** 87
Essential Implements of the Log Builder's Craft
LaVonne's Logbook 7

10 ~ **BUILDING WITH LOGS: PART I** 93
Scribing and Notching the First Course
Marking the Floor for Openings and Square Corners | The First Log | Second and Third Logs, First Notches | Making it Square (and Keeping It That Way)

11 ~ **BUILDING WITH LOGS: PART II** 103
Building the Walls and Tying-in Second-Floor Beams
Choose Your Logs Well | Scribing | Splicing Logs | Interior Log Walls | Spiking the Logs | Door and Window Openings | Measuring Wall Height | Tying-in Floor Beams | Installing the Second Floor | The Last Log
LaVonne's Logbook 8

12 ~ **GABLES AND DORMERS** 115
Design Ideas to Accent Your Roofline
Full Log Gable Ends | Vertical Log Gable Ends | Framed Gable Ends | Dormers
LaVonne's Logbook 9

13 ~ **ROOF FRAMING: BEAMS, PURLINS, RAFTERS & MORE** 123
Taking It To The Top
Overbuilt and Loving It | Roof Pitch | A Basic (Standard Frame) Roof | A Roof Using Log or Timber Rafters | A Roof With Structural Log Purlins | Roof Trusses | Roof Beams | Log Accents with a Simple Roof | Eaves | Rain Gutters and Rafter Tails | Making It Dry | Roofing Material Options
LaVonne's Logbook 10 & 11

14 ~ **WINDOWS, DOORS, LOG ENDS AND WIRING** 149
Letting Light Into A Shrinking House
Calculating the Openings | Allowing for Log Shrinkage | Marking and Cutting the Openings | Installing the Bucks and Windows | Adding Trim Boards | Cutting Log Ends | Frame Walls and Plumbing | Electrical Wiring
LaVonne's Logbook 12 & 13

15 ~ **SETTLING ISSUES** 163
When Things That Don't Shrink Meet Things That Do
The Big Picture | Frame Walls | Stairs | Plumbing | Chimneys and Stove Pipes | Vertical Support Posts | Kitchen Cabinet Considerations | The Benefit of Experience

continued

16 ~ **CHINKING AND FINISHING** 171
Keeping Weather In Its Place
Good Design = Good Protection | Cleaning the Logs | Finishes, and Finishing | Chinking
LaVonne's Logbook 14 & 15

Power with Nature

17 ~ **A NEW PHILOSOPHY OF FREEDOM** 181
Notes on Developing an Off-the-Grid Mentality
Starting With Nothing | The First Precious Amenities | Moving Up | Learning the System | Changing with the Weather: A Metaphor
LaVonne's Logbook 16

18 ~ **THE EVOLVING SYSTEM** 189
An Unlikely Tale of a Pond Pump

19 ~ **SIZING THE SYSTEM** 193
A Short, No-Tooth-Pulling Course on Practical Electricity
Beyond Ohm's Law | 12, 24, 48 Volts, Or More? | How Many Batteries?

20 ~ **SOLAR PHOTOVOLTAIC MODULES** 197
How to Capture Rays of Sunshine
Types of Solar Modules | Finding a Place for the Array | Tilt Angle of the Array | Mounting the Modules | Wiring the Array | Leaving Room to Grow
LaVonne's Logbook 17

21 ~ **WIND GENERATORS** 209
Making Good Use of the Stuff of Clouds
How Much Wind is Enough? | Old Technology Versus New | AC or DC? | Towers | Looking Deeper
LaVonne's Logbook 18 & 19

22 ~ **CHARGE CONTROLLERS** 221
Processing Your Batteries' Diet
Battery Charging | Equalization of Batteries | A Charge Controller for the Wind Generator | Other Uses for Charge Controllers | Look Around
LaVonne's Logbook 20

23 ~ **BATTERIES** 227
Care and Feeding of the Beasts that Hold Your Sunshine
The Right Batteries for the Job | Pampering Your Batteries | The Battery Box | Wiring the Batteries

continued

24 ~ **INVERTERS** 235
The Last Stop on the DC Trail
Sine Waves and Inverters | Inverter Functions
LaVonne's Logbook 21 & 22

25 ~ **PUTTING IT ALL TOGETHER — SAFELY** 243
Protecting You and Your System from Nature, and Each Other
Grounding & Bonding | Lightning Protection for Home, Well, Solar Array and Wind Generator | DC Disconnect | Wiring It Safely

26 ~ **HEATING OF HOUSE AND WATER** 251
Staying Warm Without Busting the Energy Bank
Propane Wall Heaters | Forced Air Heat | Heating with Hot Water | Wood Stoves | Domestic Hot Water | Curt & Kelly's Excellent Solution
LaVonne's Logbook 23

27 ~ **PUMPING WATER** 263
Getting It From the Ground to Your House, Without Overtaxing the System
Should You Install A Cistern? | Well Pumps (AC & DC)

28 ~ **FINISH WORK: MAKING YOUR HOUSE A HOME** 269
Running the Final Mile, In Style
Hanging and Finishing Drywall | Wainscoting | Interior Doors, Kitchen Cabinets and Countertops | A Custom Log Stair | The Deck | Railings | Log Accents | Many Uses for Tile | Stonework | And Finally...

ACKNOWLEDGMENTS 285

APPENDICES

Appendix A: Costs to Consider 286
Metric Conversion Factors 286
Notes on Appliances 287
Appendix B: Comparison of PV/Wind Quotations 288
Appendix C: System Sizing
Insolation Maps 289
Your Electrical Needs Worksheet 290
Solar Array Sizing Worksheet 291
Battery Sizing Worksheet 291
Appendix D: Electrical Formulas & Helpful Information 292
Wire Size/Line Loss Tables 12-volt 293
24-volt 294
48-volt 295
Appendix E: Resources 296
Appendix F: General Bibliography 298
Appendix G: Recommended Reading 298

INDEX 299

PROLOGUE

the contagious dream

Years ago, in a past that seems far more distant than it really is, I owned a small spread with a rich, verdant pasture, a hay field, and far more Thoroughbred horses than any man in his right mind ought to own. I was a rancher and a businessman— a manufacturer of nutritional supplements for horses. And I was a farmer.

My father, driven man that he was, took precious little delight in any of my antics, but even after I was grown he enjoyed telling new acquaintances the dialog he and I used to have when I was four or five. "Rex," he'd say, way back when, "what're you gonna do when you grow up?"

I'd stand up straight as a rod (so he'd say), stick my lip out resolutely, and answer with a certainty that would make anyone believe I could fly, if I so intended, "I'm gonna get $500 and be a mountain man."

Anyone who ever heard this story would laugh at the little boy in rolled-up Levis and red cowboy boots who seemed to know his mind so well. But not me. I was serious. I was serious then, and I was serious later, when I bought a small acreage and build an octagon log home and a small log guest house. It cost more than $500, but it was worth every penny. Then, as fate would have it, it was all whisked away to the four winds, and I returned again to the flat, dusty plains of eastern Colorado.

There I raised horses, made supplements, wrote articles for horse magazines, and harvested hay. And fought back a yearning to return to the mountains. Finally, when I could fight it no longer, I bought more land than I ever thought I'd need, in a place I rarely ever had the chance to go. But, whenever I did get the chance, I'd head for the hills and enjoy a day or two of heaven. I built a small frame cabin that encouraged the faraway dreams I nurtured, and when I wasn't there, I daydreamed of the wonderful things I would do, if I were.

It wasn't until I met LaVonne, however, that I even dared to rekindle the long-held dream of a life far above the hay fields and horse pastures. There was so much to leave, it seemed, that I could never in a lifetime leave it all. But lifetimes, I've since learned, are far more expansive than the petty things that somehow seem to cling to the mind's coattails, demanding—though hardly deserving—constant attention.

Besides, the baler was getting moody, the hay swather was held together with good intentions and questionable welds, and the horse herd was in serious need of thinning.

And whenever LaVonne was alone and outside, her eyes would drift to western mountains.

I knew what was going through her head.

She was dreaming about getting $500 and becoming a mountain woman……

Dreams; it always starts with dreams.

Every beautiful thing ever wrought by the hands of humankind began as a dream, growing of its own volition from formless and fluid places, where things can exist, without contradiction, in impossible relationships to one another.

Dreaming is something we all do too little of in a tight-minded society, where the rules simply must be followed, even though no one is quite certain why. Dreams are, after all, just intangible wisps of errant energy. How ironic, then, that dreams—most of which are never nurtured to fruition—are exactly what keeps the lid from blowing off the pressure cooker we call humanity. If we can entertain, in our minds, the possibility of better days and better places, then the rat race becomes a little less ratty, and the rays of tomorrow's sun can find a way through, to brighten the gloomy environs we inhabit today.

If you are reading these words, it's because you are a dreamer. You dream of living where you don't, and doing things you've never done. Compelling as it is, it's a frightening thought. But so is life; it's a risky business. And yet you push on, regardless. You weren't born knowing how to run a chainsaw, set a log, or wire a solar module to a charge controller. But neither were you born knowing how to run a computer, or thread your way through rush hour traffic in a rolling steel cage at 100 feet per second. If you can do the one, you can do the other, as long as you hold tight to your dreams. The trick is in not letting your self-prejudices hamstring your abilities.

This is a book for dreamers, it's true, but only those who are ready to cast their airy aspirations to the fertile earth and nurture the seeds with sweat and toil. You may end up doing all the work yourselves, or you may simply use this book as a guide for determining the best way for others to proceed. Whichever path you follow, once you make the commitment, you're halfway there.

LaVonne and I created this book with one idea in mind: to write the book we wished we'd had before beginning our adventure into uncharted territory. And what an adventure it's been! I thought I knew a thing or two about this business before we set out on this latest foray into the unknown, but I was mistaken. If *Logs, Wind and Sun* were a comprehensive personal memoir of the knowledge we've picked up in the past three years, it would not come close to fitting within these pages.

But, though we unabashedly relate a number of personal experiences—the good, the bad, and the comical—throughout the book, *Logs, Wind and Sun* is certainly not a memoir. It's much better than that. It's a hands-on, dirt-under-your-fingernails guide to making your dreams a reality.

This won't be the only book you'll buy to help you through the journey ahead, but with enough common sense and practical knowledge, it could be. It was written to be used by skilled people whose experience allows them to fill in the gaps, as well as those less steeped in the trades who want to know how it all goes together, and what to expect of the crews doing the actual work. We can't all be builders, plumbers, roofers, cement workers, solar and wind installers, or electricians, but we can—and should—know enough about each of these facets of construction that we can direct those who are doing the work.

Logs, Wind and Sun was written and compiled in a logical, orderly fashion. For that reason, it can be used as a reference book. But it's more than that. I find writing to be too much fun to restrict myself to the same, plodding style used in all the boring text books I so despised in school. So, while this book was designed to be used, it was written to be read; to make learning a pleasure, and knowledge a joy.

Logs, Wind and Sun covers all the major aspects of building a log home and powering it solely with electricity derived from the wind and the sun. This is the how-to part. By the time you finish reading it, you will know how everything works together as a cohesive whole, and how to make it all come about. Some things are covered in greater detail than others. The sections on foundation and log work, as well as those on wind and solar energy, are described in detail. By reading those sections, you will know how to build a home log by log, and how to install your PV/wind system, component by component. You will also know what's hard, and what's easy, and why. And, just in case you might feel left out in the woods all alone, you'll learn about many of the successes and foibles LaVonne and I have experienced, walking the same path you are about to set foot on.

Other areas are less comprehensive. Heating and water pumping are covered in a way that presents the systems you may want to consider, and those you definitely want to avoid, without actually telling you how to install any of them. These subjects are both too expansive to be covered in detail within the scope of a single volume.

Plumbing is a can of worms we peek into from time to time, without giving any of the worms a chance to slither out. It's not that I don't know anything about plumbing; I actually know quite a bit. Mostly, I know enough to discourage anyone who isn't already a plumber from trying their hand at it. Just the same, plumbing issues unique to log homes are clearly addressed.

The point is, I don't drone on about things I'm not good at, or things I know little or nothing about. It wouldn't be fair to you. I wouldn't be able to write it with authority, and even if I tried, you wouldn't enjoy reading it. No one knows everything about this business, and if they did, I'm sure they wouldn't be any fun at parties.

So, take a breath and get ready for the adventure of a lifetime. By the time you finish your new home, you'll be satisfyingly amused at the person now reading these words.

And that's the way it should be.

(photo by Mike Fox)

CHAPTER 1

Logs, Wind and Sun

A SUSTAINABLE TRIAD FOR A WORLD WITH DIMINISHING RESOURCES

Beginning Thoughts and Considerations for Living Well

(photo by Ken Jessen)

Nobody packs up, heads for woods and builds a log home, far away from the nearest power line, on a whim. We've all got some pretty good reasons. The nearly-universal appeal of living in a handcrafted log home is easy enough to understand. There is something deeply and profoundly instinctual about the look and feel of natural logs; they hearken to the spirit in a way nothing else can. To gaze at a home solidly built with natural logs is to trigger within the psyche a sense of warmth and strength unrivaled by any other building material. The grain and texture and individuality of logs strikes within each of us a resonant chord of kinship with Nature; a kinship often restrained, but never defeated. A log home invites us, in whispered overtures, to seek the source of the natural rhythms that sough so melodically through our souls.

The desire to live off-the-grid, however, is not so universal in its urging. For some, it's an extension of our natural passion for self-reliance and simplicity; for others, it's simply the most cost-effective solution to a nagging problem. Most of us fall somewhere in the middle. We know people living within a stone's throw of a utility pole, that refuse to be hooked into the power grid. Our hats go off to them.

For LaVonne and I, it was probably cheaper to go with wind and solar than to tap into the neighbor's power line, 2000 feet away. But we'll never know, because we never asked the power company what it would cost to run power to our new house. We figured we'd already given them enough money for one lifetime, and suffered through enough blackouts to last through eternity. It was time for something new.

Three years ago, we didn't realize the serendipitous nature of our decision. We just thought it was a cool idea. We didn't know that log homes require far fewer natural resources to build than conventional homes, or that they are warmer in the winter and cooler in the summer. We only knew we wanted to build our own from the ground up, and live in it.

Nor did we know that every time a kilowatt hour of electricity is produced at the local (faraway) power plant, 20 pounds of carbon are released into the atmosphere; or that, for every watt used in the home, 9 watts are wasted getting it there. We just liked the idea of creating our own electricity.

We've both come a long way since then; this type of enterprise has a way of changing a person. We've learned a lot about the efficiency of logs, and the utter practicability of homegrown electricity. We've learned new skills, and new ways to think about old problems. We've learned how to conserve when there is little, and how to better use whatever is in abundance. Best of all, we've learned that two people, working alone, can build a beautiful log home, power it with the wind and sun, and live in it as though it were a palace.

BEGINNING THOUGHTS

Whenever I hear or read anything about the pyramids of Egypt, I marvel at the abilities of the people who created this planet's greatest monuments with crude copper tools, and techniques abandoned so long ago we can only guess at what they might have been. I find it especially ironic that we moderns, with all our fine steel and impressive horsepower, would be severely taken to task to reproduce what the ancients have already done.

I then look at the snugly interlaced walls of the log home LaVonne and I built, and I smile. It's good that some knowledge gets passed on.

I doubt that the first people who ever stacked logs together to build a house believed, in their wildest fits of fancy, that the building style they were initiating would prove more heat-efficient and less resource-depleting than the most prevalent building practices of their descendants, thousands of years hence. But I'm sure they would have found the thought amusing.

Anyone who has ever had the pleasure of spending a winter living in a log home will tell you—log homes are warm and comfortable. The reason they are has very little to do with their intrinsic R-value; in fact, logs have a relatively low resistance to the passage of heat. But what logs *do* have is a tremendous amount of thermal mass. They soak up heat like a sponge, then radiate it back into the house as the inside temperature falls. (To learn more than you'll ever want to know about this subject, read *The Energy Economics and Thermal Performance of Log Houses,* by Doris Muir and Paul Osborne.)

This is very good news for people living back in the woods, past the last utility pole, since it will take less energy to heat their log home, than a similarly designed frame house in town. Since all central heating systems require *some* electricity to operate, the more heat-efficient the house, the more solar and wind energy there is left over for other things.

With proper design and placement of the house, the inherent resource-conserving properties of logs can be maximized to warm the house in winter, and cool it in the summer. Although creating a comfortable living space is vitally important, it's not the only design issue that needs to be considered. You also want to protect your house from the elements, and provide for the extra non-living space you'll need for heating and electrical components. And, of course, you will want all the elements of your home to flow together into an aesthetically pleasing whole.

While most of these issues will resurface in pertinent places throughout the book, it will certainly be helpful to corral them all together now, and examine each one, in its turn.

PLACEMENT AND ORIENTATION OF THE HOUSE

For both warmth and solar exposure for your solar array, you will want to place your house in such a way that it has maximum access to midday sunshine. An east-west orientation of the long axis is best if you plan to roof-mount your solar array. Many people, however, prefer ground-mounted arrays.

Plan to put your house on high ground, rather than in a hollow or dip, if at all possible. Building on a hill, or a knoll, will greatly increase your chances of having usable wind energy, and it's much easier to plan for water drainage when the ground slopes away from your house in all directions. Besides, you'll have a better view.

You should also design your foundation so there is plenty of room between the ground and your first course of logs. The building inspector may let you get by with 6 inches, but plan for a bare minimum of 12 inches, and more if you live in a particularly rainy area. It's a thousand times easier to replace a piece of rotted siding, than it is to replace a rotted log.

Our solar array faces due south, with wind tower off to the east. *(photo by Ken Jessen)*

DESIGNING FOR EFFICIENCY AND COMFORT

Many of the older log homes you see back in the woods are little more than fortresses, with tight, economic floor plans, low-pitched roofs, and conspicuously few windows, all barely big enough to aim a rifle through. They were built back in the days when windows were considered to be a necessary—but barely tolerable—source of heat loss. These old homes were well designed to conserve any heat produced within the walls, but woefully deficient at allowing in heat from the outside.

The advent of efficient double- and triple-glazed windows has changed that myopic view of home design. Realizing the potential of free solar heat in the winter, most homes today—outside of those built in cheesy developments—take ample advantage of the sun's gifts. Log home builders have followed suit. Prow-like projections, with giant windows set between towering support posts, adorn the southern faces of many modern log homes.

This is all well and good, but like everything else, it's possible to get carried away. Too much glass will certainly keep a house warm on sunny winter days, but it will also allow an excess of heat leakage at night, or when the weather turns cloudy. You should strive for a balance. Design your house to allow ample sunshine on the south side, with as few doors and windows as possible on the north. Large windows, glass doors, and dormer (or gable end) windows that follow the contour of the roof all allow plenty of sunshine while enhancing the home's appearance.

If winter is a long, cold ordeal where you are planning to build, you might want to consider using triple-glazed, or super-insulated windows. They allow as much light to enter as conventional double-glazed window, but will retain appreciably more heat when the sun sets. Insulated window coverings are also helpful for nighttime heat retention.

You might want to consider tile floors for rooms with large south-facing windows. Tile floors—like log walls—can add to a home's comfort levels, by absorbing solar radiation during the day, and releasing it back at night. Nor is tile adversely affected by sunlight; it won't fade like wood or carpeting.

Big eaves are a must for log homes. They keep direct sunlight from hitting the windows in the warmer months, as well as protecting the logs from rain and snow. Big eaves are especially important for keeping moisture off the log ends that stick out past the walls. As a general rule, the eaves should extend at least one foot past the log ends, for each 8 feet of vertical wall height.

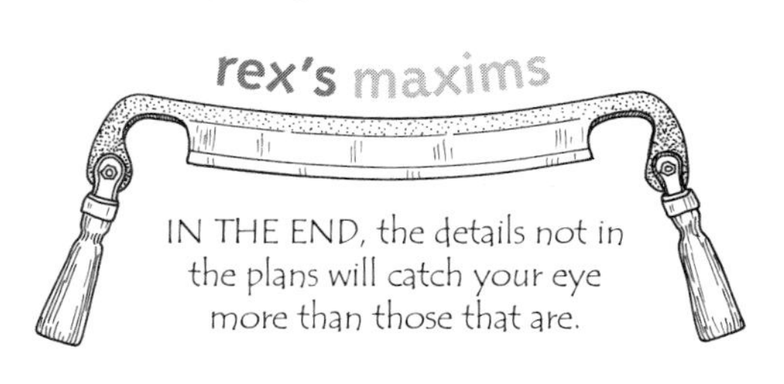

What about cooling? Standard air conditioning is far too power-hungry for a home powered by solar and wind-generated electricity. Fortunately, the same windows that heat your home in the winter can help cool it in the summer. The key is to provide adequate cross-ventilation, preferably of a type that allows air to enter near the floor, and exit through the roof. Double-hung windows, or windows designed with built-in vents at the bottom are perfect for letting air into the house. To provide an exit for hot, rising air, skylights—the ones that open—can't be beat; they are perfect for maximizing airflow through the house. Skylights also help to bring additional, natural light into a house, something that is often needed in lofts with few windows. Just don't install too many of them, or you'll defeat their purpose. Unlike windows under big eaves, skylights are great for letting *in* summer sunlight and letting *out* hard-won winter heat. (Fortunately, this problem can be minimized by purchasing skylights with blinds.) For those living off-the-grid, ample natural light is a must. LaVonne put a small skylight in the loft walk-in closet, and very rarely needs to turn on the light.

Sound Propagation versus Heat Efficiency

Log homes have great acoustics. Our neighbor, Dave, likes to play his flute in our great room, since the logs do such a splendid job of reflecting the instrument's melodious and eerie notes back to him. That's good; except that sound carries so well in our house that LaVonne, from the loft, can hear the crumpling of a cellophane wrapper in the downstairs pantry, every time I have a chocolate cupcake attack in the middle of the night. And that's bad.

Obviously, the best way to dampen sound is to build more interior walls, and insulate them. But, if you rely on a central wood stove for a good portion of your heat, you'll be leaving much of your house in the cold. So it's a trade-off. If you live in a noisy house, efficient, zoned heating (such as radiant-floor heat) is the best solution to supply heat to your "quiet" rooms. But there's one little wrinkle to this solution you should bear in mind: floor coverings that best conduct heat also conduct sound. So, while carpeting may alleviate the noise problem, it will also make the boiler work harder. Tile and wood floors work great with radiant-floor heat, but they can make your house noisy.

Like I said, it's a trade-off. But, since radiant-floor heat is, by far, the best form of central heat for a log home on a PV/wind system, you'll be better off if you incorporate it into your house design, no matter what the acoustic price tag.

FLOOR PLAN CONSIDERATIONS

Whatever dwelling you currently inhabit, there are things you like about it, and things you don't. Incorporate the good elements into the design of your new house, and do away with the bad. Consider the ease with which you can move from room to room, and floor to floor. Leave yourself plenty of room, and design the kitchen and bathrooms for efficient use.

LaVonne wanted (and got) a pantry; a large, roomy kitchen with a central island; more-than-ample cupboard space; and a window over the sink. I wanted (and got) a cozy, carpeted office; a small workshop in the basement; and an extra-wide log stair to facilitate the movement of furniture. Large, walk-in closets, built-in bookshelves, and a handy-yet-hidden location for the washer and dryer are other considerations. Do you have a piano, or a large roll-top desk that you're not likely to part with? Make sure you make space for them.

Interior Design

LaVonne and I see it all the time: someone builds a log home, then goes completely hog-wild finishing the non-log parts of the house with even more wood. Wood on the ceilings, wood on the gable ends, wood on the floor. Please; enough is enough!

An open kitchen design with an island is handy when cooking, and a great gathering place at parties. The pantry (behind the stove wall) stores the awkward appliances, vacuum cleaner, dog food...you name it.

While we'll be the first in line to extol the beauty of natural wood, there is a point at which it becomes excessive. The unique character of logs only becomes truly apparent when it is contrasted with other mediums. A tongue-&-groove wood ceiling may be a nice touch in the cathedral ceiling over the entryway or great room, but if it's used throughout the house you may find it to be too dark and "heavy." Drywall, when it's tastefully finished, greatly enhances the beauty of logs, while brightening the interior of the house. Stone or stucco on the exterior gable ends and foundation walls will give your home a rich, well-balanced appearance.

The same goes for floor coverings. Tile, wood and carpeting all have their places, as long as it's not *every* place. A wood floor works good in high-traffic areas; tile wherever water might be spilled. Carpeting is soft and comforting to the feet in bedrooms and on stairs. (But not log stairs!)

Even in familiar surroundings, the eyes like to explore. The more variety they find, the happier they'll be, so give them a lot to look at. Pick light and plumbing fixtures, and door and cabinet hardware, that will accentuate, without clashing. Every individual element of your home will say something about you—make sure it's the statement you want to convey.

Non-Living Spaces

Every house has a mechanical room, where the furnace, or boiler, and the water heater are located. Since (in all likelihood) you'll be pumping your water from a well, you may also need to allow space for a cistern, or a pressure tank. Basements are great places to hide all the stuff you don't want to look at, but if you have a two-story house on top of it, you will have to plan a route for the vent stacks. In a log home, it's not always an easy matter, since flue chases are much easier to hide (or at least to obscure) when they run next to a frame wall.

LaVonne's Verities

ON STORAGE:
You can never have enough storage space.

We thought we had allowed adequate room for the boiler flue to pass on the east side of the office wall, thus missing the dormer upstairs. Then we realized that the eave on the loft dormer was so wide that the stack would have gone right through it. We resolved the problem by building a flue chase on the other side of the main floor office wall and extending it through the inside of dormer. We then adorned the corners of the drywall chases with decorative logs. In truth, it turned out better than we had originally planned, but it's still a good idea to think these things through, ahead of time—too many surprises have a way of turning your hair gray.

Plan on having at least one or two frame walls in your house. It will make life much easier for the electrician and the plumber. Plumbing pipes en route to the second floor should be run through 2 x 6 frame walls (the larger studs are needed to accommodate the main waste pipe). The total number of walls you need will depend on how extensively the upstairs is plumbed.

Your house will also need to have an electrical room. It will have to be big enough to contain all the components of the biggest PV (photovoltaic)/wind system you will ever conceivably build. This includes—but may not be limited to—wall space for the inverter(s), DC disconnect(s), charge controller(s), a 120-240 volt AC transformer, and floor space for your battery bank. Here are few things you'll need to keep in mind:

- Your battery box cannot be located beneath any serviceable component, such as an inverter (according to the National Electric Code). And neither can anything else. It's really too bad, because that's the logical place to put the batteries, since you will want the large cables connecting the batteries to the inverter to be as short as possible. One clever way around this problem is to build the battery box on the *other* side of the frame wall, just *behind* the inverter, and running the heavy cables through the wall.
- Lead-acid batteries—the ones most used in PV/wind systems—need to be in a sealed box, vented to the outside. It only takes a 1-inch PVC vent pipe, but the closer you can locate the batteries to an outside wall, the better.
- Inverters hum. Just how *much* they hum depends on how hard they're working. To keep your sanity, put the inverter in a room that can be sealed off from the rest of the house in general, and your bedroom, in particular.
- For the sake of efficiency, it's best to locate the main electrical panel in the same room with all the other electrical components. That way everything is in one handy place.

Neighbors

You'll hear us talk a lot about our neighbors in this book, giving you the impression that we all live tightly-packed on the same mountain. Actually, we're spread far and wide over many mountains and valleys. It gives the word "neighbor" a new meaning. Practically speaking, anyone we know within 5 miles (as the hawk flies) is our neighbor.

These ideas and suggestion should help you during the planning stage, and all throughout the construction process. By this point, you've probably begun to form a mental picture of what the house is going to look like, inside and out. Now it's time to figure out where to put it.

Should you do the log work yourself or buy a log shell?

There are hundreds of companies out there that specialize in building custom, handcrafted log homes. Most of them do good work, and all of them expect to be paid handsomely for it.

If you haven't yet decided...consider that log work is not the most time consuming part of the construction. Working alone, LaVonne and I completed the rough log work in a little over 3 months. That's less than 20 percent of the time we spent on the whole project. Not only did we save a ton of money, we have the satisfaction of living in a home we built with our own four hands.

If you have already decided... to have one of these companies build your home, here are some pointers:

- Hand-peeled logs are superior in appearance to machine-peeled, or milled logs. They will also repel moisture better, and the finish will have a much more natural look. Insist on hand-peeled logs.
- Before you sign a contract, visit their yard and observe a house under construction. Ask questions about issues of concern raised in this book (such as how they address settling around doors and windows).
- Ask them if you can watch a reset at a home site. It will give you a feel for how the crew works together, how careful they are, and how skilled.
- Get references and talk to their previous customers.

A book to read for more information on contracts is *Log Homes Made Easy: Contracting and Building Your Own Log Home,* by Jim Cooper.

After handcrafting a log cabin years ago, our neighbor, John Benshoof, decided this time around he'd contract a custom, handcrafted home from Log Knowledge of Fort Collins, Colorado. These photos were taken during his 3-day re-set at the site.

BUCKHORN CAMP'S SCHOOL-BUILT LOG HOME

While LaVonne and I were immersed in finish work on our log home, the directors at Buckhorn United Methodist Camp, a few miles to the north, were having their log home constructed by a log home building school. Working from a design by B. Allan Mackie, Gregg and Donna Kernes harvested the trees—stout Ponderosa—from the camp property, then the Lasko School of Log Building came in and constructed the house on-site.

Two volunteers work on a log purlin. *(photo by Bill Youngblood)*

The Kernes used volunteer work groups from the camp to peel the enormous logs, which were then crane-set by students and instructor, Bill Lasko. Gregg and Donna closely monitored the construction, and pitched in to help whenever—and wherever—they could. In this way they ensured that their home was built to their specifications, and learned the valuable skills they needed to finish the house themselves.

Scarfed notches are a must with these large logs. *(above left photo by Jerry Svoboda)*

Framed gable ends support the log purlins and ridge beam. The 2 x 10 roof rafters are being set by a group of volunteers. *(photo by Bill Youngblood)*

Build with Logs

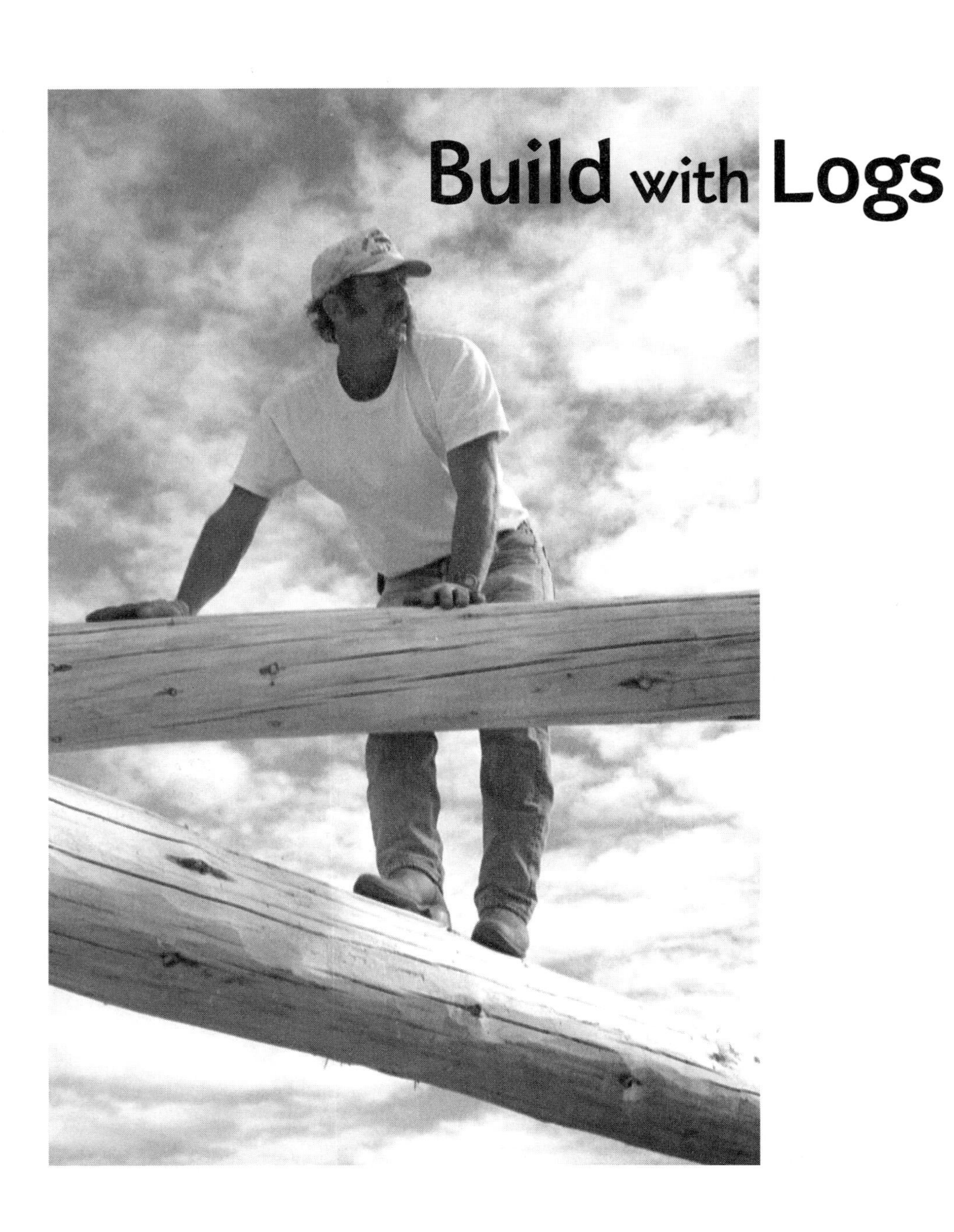

SITE SELECTION

Where O' Where Does This House Want To Be?

Our grassy, wildflower-laden home site.

A high-mountain plateau, where a small brook filled with crystal clear water gently tumbles down a mild tree-lined slope into a two-acre lake where fish greedily jump for unsuspecting insects near the grassy island in the middle. On the high shore, a rolling meadow sprouting wildflowers of every conceivable hue gradually yields to a dense forest of tall, healthy conifers that hide your retreat from all but the birds gliding effortlessly overhead on invisible thermal currents. The sun rises over high mountains in the distant east, and similarly sets in the west. During the day your southern exposure in vast and unimpeded. Your sense of peace and solitude is perfect and complete.

If this is your land, then congratulations. You've just found the property we've all been looking for....the kind of place that, for most of us mere mortals, exists only in wistful dreams and—you guessed it—television commercials for log homes.

Most properties will fall a trifle short of the above-mentioned dream place. Realistically speaking, if you intend to build a log home and derive your electricity from the sun and wind, there are only two criteria that cannot be compromised: access and southern exposure.

ACCESS

Like most things, access is a relative concept. Since you'll be off the grid, proximity to power lines is unimportant. In most areas, the same holds for phone lines, since cell phone service is getting cheap, reliable and more far-reaching by the day. Television and internet service is readily available by satellite. That being said, you still have to be able to get to your place.

After one of the wettest months on record , the well driller, loaded with water for drilling, must be pulled up our muddy new road by the excavator.

When I bought two 35-acres parcels back in the late 80's, I built a small, pole-frame weekender cabin on the piece farthest from the private road that snakes through the hills. With a stout (and temperamental) '72 Chevy flatbed 4x4, I bullied my way over rocks and bushes on the northern face to the top of a steep hill where I intended to build. The access there can more rightly be called two parallel game trails than a road. But I stubbornly persevered, hauling everything that went into that little cabin (including all the poles, one of which was 29 feet long) on the back of my cantankerous pickup. It was an accomplishment, certainly, but one fraught with limitations. Without a real road—one that rises gently, with no sharp turns; one which can be traversed by large, two-wheel-drive vehicles—the cabin will always remain without plumbing, central heat, or even a source of fresh water.

So, while it's true that with enough heavy equipment and dynamite you can build anywhere you can bludgeon your way to with a bulldozer, unless there is good access for cement trucks, well-drilling rigs, propane delivery trucks and lumber trucks (and—unless your land is laden with tall, straight trees nearby—logging trucks), building there is going to end up being more work than you'd probably care to ponder.

Ideally, your building site should be a reasonably flat area several times the area of your proposed house. This will give you plenty of room to lay your logs out individually, as well as allowing space for big rigs to maneuver comfortably. If there's not already a good road to your site, *don't* hire the kid down the canyon who just picked up a bargain-basement bulldozer and is willing to christen it on the side of your hill for a smile and a handful of crisp greenbacks. As tempting as it may be to save a few bucks, you're inviting disaster unless your road is pushed in by a contractor with several years experience under his belt. Any seasoned cement truck driver can tell you horror stories about sinking into a new, poorly constructed road, and then sliding off the mountain. You don't want your road to be fodder for any new stories. Besides, if a truck gets stuck (or worse) because of *your* shoddily built road, you'll be held responsible for towing or repair costs.

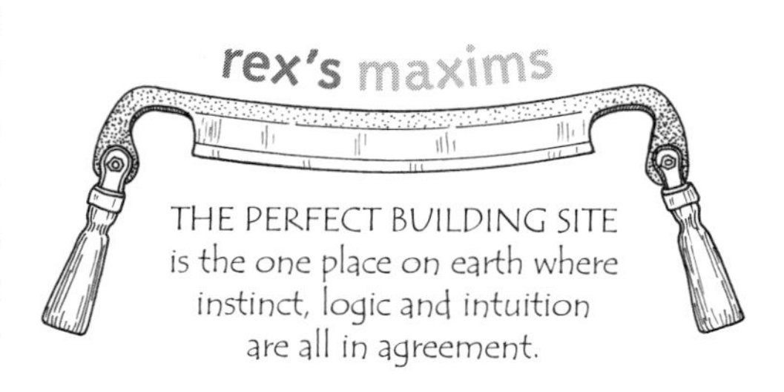

SOUTHERN EXPOSURE

Our house is situated on a saddle, 500 feet above a creek, and surrounded on all sides by mountains. The sun rises here about an hour later than it does on the plains to the east, and sets an hour earlier. It's about as good a spot as you can hope for in this area. Since the solar wattage available from the early and late day

Our ground-mounted solar array is easy to clean, and can be adjusted for the angle of the sun.

sun is only a small fraction of what's available at midday, we lose practically nothing to the surrounding hills. At 40 degrees north latitude we have all the sunshine we need to power our house, even in late December when the days are so short that lunch is the only meal we can enjoy in daylight.

Since your solar array will be a major investment, you'll want as much direct sunlight as you can get. If you plan on building in a valley, be absolutely sure that your winter sun isn't blocked by the hillside to the south. This can be deceptive. In July, when the sun burns high in the sky like a blast furnace ten feet overhead, it's hard to recall just how far south old sol retreats in winter. Several years ago I rented a little place in a deep valley one canyon north of where LaVonne and I now live. It was bright and sunny in August when I moved in, but as fall approached I watched with dread as sun crept ever south. Then, early in November, it just disappeared and didn't offer up a single yellow ray until the following February. The sun's arc was nearly identical to the topography of the mountain to the south; one day the sun was there and the next day it wasn't. Fortunately, I didn't own the place and it was wired into the grid, so I could at least see what I was doing as I shoved copious quantities of cordwood into the stove to keep from freezing to death during the three-month night.

Plan where you're going to put your solar array. The roof of the house is fine, but modules are much easier to clean and sweep the snow from if they are on the ground. Either way, you won't want them much more than 100 feet from your battery bank, because in low-voltage DC systems the size of wire required to carry the current without substantial line loss increases greatly with distance, and heavy wire can get pricey. It's not much fun to work with, either.

OTHER CONSIDERATIONS

WATER

Unless you get some bizarre satisfaction from driving a gas-guzzling pickup to town twice a week to fill up a big green water tank in the back, you're going to want a well. Talk to your nearest neighbors and the local well-drillers to see what you can rightly expect. In many areas the depth at which good water can be found is fairly predictable. In other areas (such as ours), it's anybody's guess. Our nearest neighbor, 200 vertical feet above us, got 3 gallons a minute at a depth of 340 feet. We drilled 540 feet, but lucked-out with a commendable recharge rate of 5 gallons per minute.

If your area is like ours, you'll just have to talk to everyone you can and take your chances. The two people we know with truly abysmal water wells (700+ feet, 5 gallons per *hour*) both built on knolls much higher than the surrounding terrain.

It's something to keep in mind.

Ingram Drilling drills for water.

WIND

The wind, of course, blows where it will. Some states are windier than others, and every point within each state is different from every other. Secluded valleys are generally not good places for wind generators; mountaintops are great. You could get a ton of expensive equipment and monitor the wind at your site over the course of a year to determine if it blows enough to justify the purchase of a wind generator, or you could follow my simple rule of thumb:

> *If the wind blows hard enough, and often enough, to annoy you, you can probably make good use of a wind generator.*

Placement of your wind tower is a little trickier than finding a spot for your solar array. Ideally, the generator should be mounted at least 20 feet higher than the highest point within a lateral radius of 300 feet. This isn't always possible, but it's a starting point.

Depth to "The Rock"

Composting Toilets

In many areas, there is simply no place to put a large leach field. An indoor composting toilet is a viable alternative for such places. The newer, solar-operated models are quite efficient. You'll still need a small leach field for the "grey water," of course, but the restrictions will be far more relaxed. Besides, you'll save thousands of gallons of water per year.

In our neck of the woods, there are three categories of rock. First, there are the kind you can pick up or move aside with a bar or a bulldozer. Plain old rocks, in other words. Then there is what we simply call "rock," which is a variety of decomposed granite bedrock that is soft enough to chip through with the right equipment. Finally, there is "THE rock," a dense unyielding class of gneiss, firmly and stubbornly bound to the core of the planet. Attack it with a jackhammer—or even a backhoe with a hydraulic rock chipper—and it will laugh at you, defiantly. When we excavated for our basement we ran into a chunk of "the rock" the size of an RV. It took thirteen sticks of dynamite to convince it we weren't kidding around.

The point is, rock is troublesome, and "the rock" is downright recalcitrant. For your foundation you will, at minimum, have to dig below the frost line (30 inches in Colorado, up to 6 feet farther north). And don't forget the water pipes and electric lines that have to be trenched in. Or the leach field for your septic system; for good absorption, you will need a large, fairly flat area below your house (a minimum of 100 feet away from your well) where the bedrock is at least 8 feet down.

Travis Kitchen (on the left) prepares a stick of dynamite for one of thirteen holes.

None of this is particularly easy if all you have is 18 inches of dirt over a ubiquitous expanse of "the rock." Of course, you don't really know how deep bedrock is until you start digging, but if the ground around your building site is studded with chunks of granite protruding from the earth like so many weathered teeth, it's a good indication that the process of digging may soon give way to the process of blasting.

AND FINALLY....

While every consideration mentioned above is important, there is one other criterion that should not be neglected, for even if you have good access to a beautiful, secluded spot with plenty of sunshine, an occasional stiff breeze, good well water and a deep cover of topsoil, the place has to *feel* right. Because if you are going to invest thousands of hours of your time—and gallons of your blood, sweat and tears—into the construction of a one-of-a-kind log home, it would behoove you to build it on the one piece of earth that feels truly kindred.

Cast reason to the wind for a moment; it won't help you. Walk the land and let it flow through you. Does the thicket of trees nearby hearken to your childhood fantasies of being alone in an enchanted forest? Does the rock outcropping on the hillside below resonate in your bones when you stand on it and gaze into the distance? Is the hawk overhead speaking to *you*?

Be happy. You're there.

It's a winter wonderland when hoarfrost covers everything.

LaVonne's LOGBOOK 1

Having never built a home, I find myself questioning the amount of work it will take, especially a handcrafted log home. I ask Rex how this will all be possible...how we can do it ourselves, and his ambiguous answer is not altogether reassuring. But my dream is to live in the mountains, surrounded by wildflowers and birds. So I'm ready. I think it was Henry Ford who said, "Whether you think you can, or think you can't, you're right."

2

Summer 1998

We walk the home site and mark the corners with blue flags. House plans have not been drawn, so we are free to dream. It is truly difficult for me to imagine a house rising from the tall grass and bountiful wildflowers. We won't need anything too complicated. Maybe a modest living space above a garage.

September 1998

The soil engineer came from town to examine the big inspection hole and smaller perc holes (that Rex dug by hand), for the leach field. It turns out our soil is fine. Check that off the list. Now Gary can push in the road. He walks the steep sloping meadow and says the road should go "here and up along there." A good route we had not thought of. Soon his big bulldozer inches up the road, pushing rock and brush out of the way. Wow. We are really going to do this! Neighbor Curt fires up his old backhoe to dig the two culvert trenches, under the close supervision of Micky, our ever curious dog [1]. All Rex needs to do is jackhammer rocks along the edges for better drainage [2] and we'll be ready for log delivery, and rain runoff.

1

CHAPTER 3

PLANS AND PERMITS

Paper Dreams and County Hoops

You've got the perfect piece of land, and there is a wide, firm road pushed into your building site. Long nights at the kitchen table have yielded a pile of pages roughing out a house you both agree is *the* house; the one you *will* build. Maybe you're not sure about the foundation specs, or just how beefy your joists, rafters, beams and purlins need to be, but no matter. The essence is there; all that's left is to face the devil in the details.

So what now?

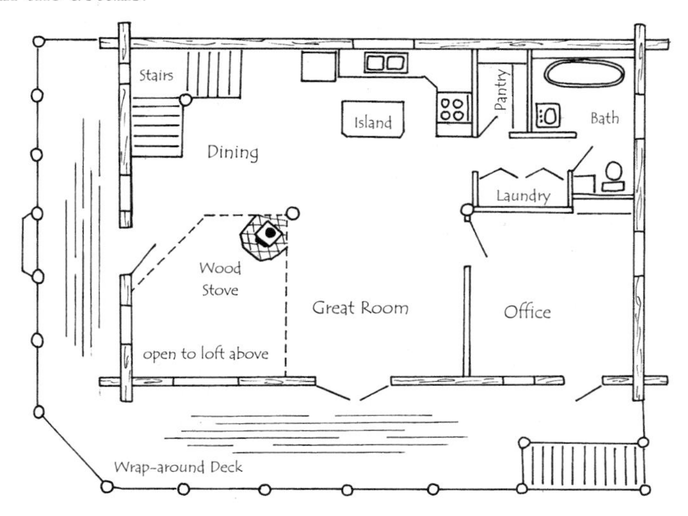

LaVonne and I have very different ideas on how to proceed on a project. I like to make things up as I go along. I plan everything in my head and only resort to paper and pencil when the math exceeds my powers of rumination. LaVonne, on the other hand, is not happy until the minutest detail is addressed. While I was picking out viable prospects for the third course of wall logs, LaVonne was trying to decide what kind of tile design to use in the downstairs bathroom.

Even though it can get a little distracting at times, I have to admit that I admire her attention to detail. Much more so, I suspect, than she appreciates my cryptic spontaneity. And, while I still maintain that a formal blueprint is a waste of time for a garage, tool shed, hay barn or even a small cabin, it's absolutely necessary on a project as complex as a log home.

FIRST STEPS

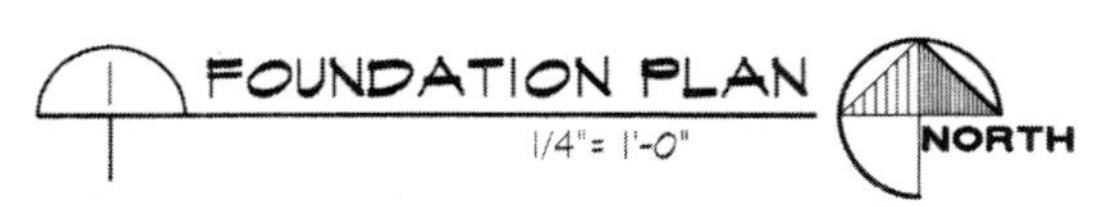

Where to go? Your first stop should be your county planning/building department. They can provide you with a list of their requirements for everything from road specifications to leach field types and sizes for different homes (usually, this is based on the number of bedrooms). They will tell you what they need to see in a blueprint before they can issue a permit.

Armed with this information, you can then decide on how to go about obtaining your formal plans. If you have building experience and managed to make it through high school drafting with a grade sufficient to keep your parents smiling, you might want to take a stab at it yourself. Mostly, the county just wants to make sure your roof won't collapse with 4 feet of snow on it, your floor won't sag under the weight of a bathtub or piano, or that your foundation isn't going crumble from the weight of your house. If something isn't up to specs they'll dutifully mark it in red to make sure the field inspector knows there's been a change.

Permits Required
We were required to get a permit from the county health department for the septic system; another permit from the county Building Department, and an electrical permit from the State of Colorado. Each permit required numerous inspections before we could receive a Certificate of Occupancy.

Most of the extraneous lists you see on blueprints (window, electrical and plumbing schedules, for instance) are for the builder, not the county. While they will want to know where you intend to put your sinks and toilets and tubs—and if your egress windows are large enough to stuff yourself through—for the purpose of issuing a building permit they could care less about your plumbing fixtures, the locations of your wall outlets, or if your windows are hung right or left. (Of course, you or your subcontractors *will* need to know these things at some point.)

Generally speaking, if you make a genuine attempt to show the county what your house is going to look like and how it's constructed, they will probably be willing to play ball with you.

Another option is to buy blueprints from one of any number of vendors that sell them. The cost will be minimal compared to having custom plans prepared by an architect, but if it's not exactly the house you wanted, you will be limited to making only superficial changes in the course of construction, since the county will, by and large, expect your house to look like the plans. Providing you are able to find a plan that suits you, it's a cheap and easy way to go.

Should you end up hiring an architect, be prepared to spend some money. Many architects won't touch a log home, and those that do reckon it's worth a premium. There are non-architect log home designers around, but they aren't much cheaper. Talk to the log home builders in your area and see who they recommend. Then talk to the county again and see what they'll let you slide by with. Like us, you might be able to find a drafting or architecture student or apprentice willing to draw up your plans for thousands of dollars less than a professional.

And remember: if you are in doubt about the structural integrity of any part of your house, a few hundred dollars spent to have an engineer review your concerns is money well spent.

Blueprint Plans

We submitted the following plans to the county building department. Upon approval of these plans, we were issued a permit.

- Site
- Foundation
- Floor & roof framing
- Floor plans for each level
- Exterior elevations
- Wall sections

Each state and county will have different requirements, so check before starting.

CONCERNS UNIQUE TO LOG HOME BLUEPRINTS

Unless your county is even more persnickety than ours—which is hard to imagine—you shouldn't have to worry about details such as sliding jambs and floating walls on your blueprints. These things will all be examined by the field inspector and, unless they present a structural problem (if, for instance, you try to float a bearing wall), they should pass inspection with ease.

The county's biggest concern will be your structural log members. Unless there are a lot of log homes being built in your area, the folks in the plan check division may not be all that familiar with the load bearing capabilities of logs of varying length and thickness. You can avoid this problem, of course, by presenting them with professionally prepared plans. Or you can talk to them beforehand and ask what they require. The book, *Log Span Tables*, (Mackie, Read & Hahney) may be helpful, both to you and the county, in determining how thick your beams and purlins should be.

Our two structural floor beams (shown above), plus two log support posts had to be graded by a certified log inspector.

Site-built log trusses will (rightly) be viewed with far more scrutiny than simple linear load-bearing members. Trusses present such a complex array of opposing stresses that they will probably require an engineer's stamp of approval.

Depending on the design of your house, there may be one more option available to you. In *most* log homes, *most* of the structural support members end up in the roof. And *most* of the time these members are overlaid with rafters of dimensional lumber. If this is the case with your house, you just may find that by either increasing the size of your rafters (from 8-inches to 10-inches, for instance) or placing them 16-inches OC (on-center), instead of 24-inches OC, that they, alone, will be sufficient to support the roof. If so, then your beams and purlins become, from a structural standpoint, "decorative," and their size, grade and placement will no longer be of concern to the county.

PIER FOUNDATIONS FOR OFF-THE GRID HOMES

If you're going to be building on rocky ground, you might be tempted to go with a pier foundation to save concrete and facilitate excavation. While it's true that pier foundations are often used successfully for log homes, they can be a problem if you plan to produce your electricity from the sun and wind.

Why?

Unless you live in an area of the country where the mercury rarely dips below 30 degrees, you won't want to give up the energy it will take to keep the single water pipe than enters your house, from your well or cistern, from freezing. It terms of raw wattage, the least efficient way to use electricity is to produce heat with it. Toasters, hair dryers, coffee makers, slow cookers—and heat tapes—are all notorious energy pigs. And since outside water lines in pier foundations are customarily wrapped in heat tape and then enclosed within an insulated chase, you will end up using electricity to heat a pipe that would not need to be heated with a conventional foundation.

But even if the heat tape takes a minimal amount of electricity, there will still be a lot of heat loss through the floor, especially if the floor is exposed to cold, winter winds. Don't get me wrong, here. I'm not saying it can't be done; only that it should be avoided, if possible. If, on the other hand, a pier foundation turns out to be the only practical way to go, you can minimize your energy loss by completely enclosing your foundation with rock or cinder block, then building a chase around your water (and sewage) pipes and insulating it to the *n*th degree.

SOLAR AND WIND POWER CONSIDERATIONS

In the house where you are now living, there is a single conduit with two heavy wires running into your main electrical panel. This conduit runs from the utility grid to the outside of the house, through a wall, to the panel. It's hidden in the

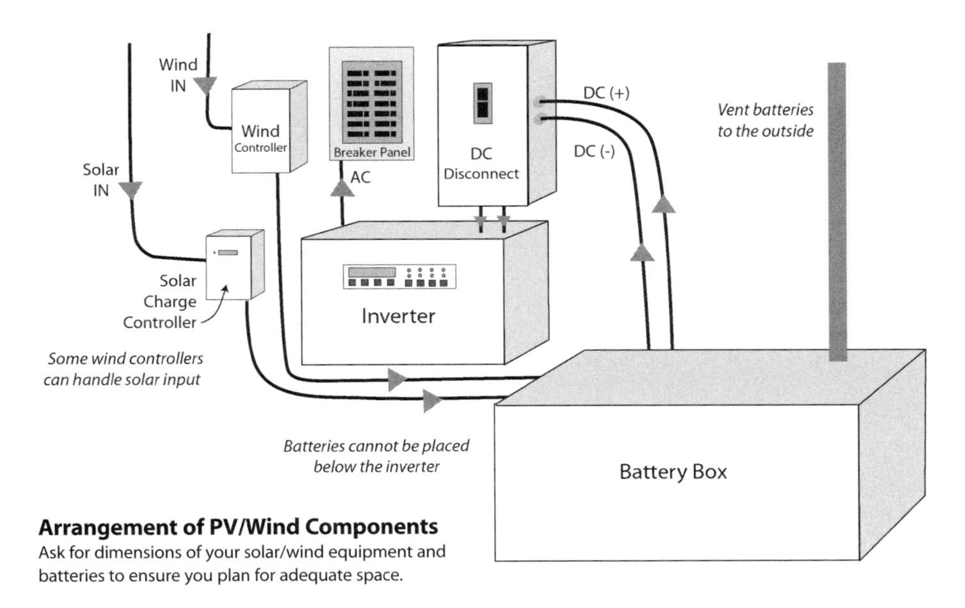

Arrangement of PV/Wind Components
Ask for dimensions of your solar/wind equipment and batteries to ensure you plan for adequate space.

wall and takes up no living space. In the house you are about to build, things will be much different. You will either have to plan for a separate room to hold your batteries, and wind and solar components, or at least allow sufficient space within a storage or similar room. It's a good idea to design your solar and wind generating system before you design your house; that way you'll know how much space to allow.

A Helpful Reminder
If you plan on using a propane refrigerator (due to large energy demands of an electric fridge), be sure to run a gas pipe for it to your kitchen.

To give you a rough idea of how much space everything takes, our electrical room is 9-feet by 4-feet, with a 7-foot, 4-inch ceiling. Our 20 golf cart style batteries fit nicely in a space 48 inches by 40 inches. By squeezing components closer together, we probably could have gotten by with a little less space, but not much. If you can, leave yourself plenty of extra room. In particular, allow yourself space to expand the size of your battery bank, should you want to add more batteries later on.

Most wind and solar suppliers/consultants will be more than happy to help you design your system, and their catalogs give precise dimensions of every component you'll need in your electrical room, including the batteries. So, once you familiarize yourself with the essentials of a photovoltaic solar and wind system and understand what's what, it's a simple matter to draw a diagram detailing where everything will go. *For an interesting comparison of what three consultants/suppliers recommended for our home versus what we actually use, see pages 288-289.*

HANG IN THERE!

It's easy to get dismayed with the seemingly endless list of requirements the county will hand you, even if you are familiar with the permit process. A lot of it may seem like no more than bureaucratic nitpicking. But if it is or isn't, there's really no way to get around it. (Ruffling their feathers, I learned long ago, only marks you for misery later.) So, give them whatever they want—most of it's just a lot of legwork, anyway. And once you pay your fees and get your permit, you can say goodbye to the desk jockeys and start dealing with the inspectors in the field. You will find that, for the most part, they're friendly, reasonable people who will cut you a little slack from time to time, providing you treat them right and don't try to sneak anything past them.

The best part is, you will then be officially cleared to break ground and get busy building with the logs you've been dreaming about all winter.

CHAPTER 4

LOGS

Dead Trees and Great Expectations

It's a crisp, cool morning in early October. The hummingbirds have long since trekked south, and most of the songbirds have followed in their wake. Only the sparrows remain; the sparrows and the ever-present Stellar Jays, ceaselessly announcing their coming and going with throaty squawks and disapproving glances.

A good morning to sit on the deck of our little pole-frame cabin, sipping coffee and warming slowly with the day as the sun inches over the mountain to our east. But not today. Though the winds are calm and the sky is clear, and it appears to all the world that utter peace has settled over the mountain like a calming vapor from a sorcerer's cauldron, we are both buzzing with nervous excitement.

Today is the day. Our logs are coming.

The logging truck arrives with our load of trees.

I check my watch. It's time. We load the dogs in the back of the pickup and head down the mountain to meet the logger at the county road. He's a little late, but not much. He sees our pickup and casually parks his truck in the middle of the road, as if it were his own private parking space. Tall and self-assured, he is completely unconcerned. Anyone who doesn't have the wherewithal to drive around him has no business being on a mountain road in the first place, he figures.

Before we take him on an inspection tour of our calamitous road, we take a walk around his truck. What we see is a little intimidating. Logs—or, more precisely, dead trees—all 50 footers ranging, we figure, from 500 to 1600 pounds apiece. Some are straight with little taper, most fall short of that ideal by varying degrees. The butts range from 9 inches to 15 or better. The tips go from 10 inches to as little as 6. We try to imagine this disparate medley of logs somehow being transformed into a home. But we can't. Not yet.

Even though the road is dry, we keep our pickup locked into four-wheel low for good traction on the winding, washboard road that rises over 600 feet in a little under two miles. With a critical eye, the logger studies every pitfall along the way: the sharp switchback at the half-mile point; the narrow gap between the rocks near the top. The steep, snaking stretch to our building site. We breathe a sigh of relief when he finally says, mirthlessly, "Yeah, I can pull this road."

I dropped LaVonne off at the building site and took him back to his rig. I then drive ahead of him to make sure no neighbors are coming down the hill as he's going up.

Rex ponders how to move our logs over a mile to the building site.

The big truck lumbers up the first hill off the county road, then picks up a little speed on the mild incline approaching the switchback. I go past the switchback and disappear behind the mountain where I drive to the top of the hill and wait.

And wait. And wait.

After 10 minutes I can no longer convince myself that something isn't wrong. A drive back down the mountain confirms my fears....he's in the chair on the back of his rig, indelicately unloading our logs onto our neighbor's property with the hydraulic arm of his loader. "Sorry, Ol' Son," he says. "This is the end of the road."

Apparently, the big, overloaded truck's rear differential was no match for the steep switchback a mile below our building site. The feeling I felt was like that of driving into a brick wall on the way to my own birthday party. Later, LaVonne and I drove down the hill, and stared blankly at our mountain of logs as though it were a tomb for our dreams. We knew of no conceivable

Our log-moving solution involved two homemade trailers. The top photo shows unloading the back end of a log. Then the front log end is lifted off the first trailer (photo on the left); the truck is moved forward; the log let down and rolled off to one side.

way to get them to our building site. We hadn't even broken ground yet, and already things seemed hopeless.

But, there's always a way, if you want something bad enough and, boy howdy, we did. After a few days of exploring a parade of increasingly desperate options—up to, and including, helicopters—I finally hit on a plan.

Sometimes LaVonne thinks I'm a little crazy, and sometimes she's right, but not this time. From some old I-beams and a couple of mobile home axles I had lying around our farm, I fashioned two small trailers. One rode on the ball of our Toyota pickup, the other rode just behind the balance point of the log. Using a high-lift mechanical bumper jack and chain, we proceeded to lift each individual log, one end at a time, and move the trailers under them. One by one, we wheeled our big 50-footers up the hill, where we jacked them up again, and then down, and rolled them onto old corral poles to keep them off the damp ground. It took several weekends, from dawn till dusk, but in the end we had our logs where we wanted them with time to spare before the snows hit.

We popped a cork and celebrated; we had survived our first of many tests.

BUYING LOGS

I rest my case about the importance of access.

Assuming that your road is better than ours—and for your sake, I sincerely hope it is—you'll want to know where to get your logs and what to do with them, once they're delivered.

Unless you are fortunate enough to have a few acres of tall, straight, accessible trees growing on your land, you'll be buying your trees from a logger. As a rule, loggers don't advertise in the yellow pages, but log home builders do. Check with companies in your area that build log homes and find our where they get their house logs. Get as many names as you can; log prices and delivery can vary greater from one logger to another. Then visit their lots and see what they have; buying logs over the phone is a really bad idea.

If the plans for your house are completed, you will have a schedule of the lengths and thickness of the logs you need. You can meticulously try to pick out the individual logs you need or, like we did, you can buy a truckload of long, thick trees and cut them to length later. We found that our logger was willing to offer us a much sweeter deal on a full semi-load of long trees he didn't have to cut to length. In this way, we were able to take what we needed from each log and save the rest for deck supports, steps, benches or any of 1000 other things. (If all else fails, log ends are nice to heat your house.)

Either way, buy extra—it's nice to have a selection when you get near the top and you're trying to keep your walls the same height. Besides, you'll always find a place to use them, even if they don't end up in your house. We bolted a 20-foot log between two left-over 50-footers, then set the whole contraption upright in the meadow below our house. Result? The most awesome rope swing in the canyon.

Species of trees vary from place to place. Our house is mostly Lodgepole Pine, with a few spruce and fir thrown in for spice. Unless you're willing to pay exorbitant trucking costs, you'll have to settle for whatever is native to your area. Straightness and uniformity are more important than what kind of tree it is. The less taper from end to end, the better. For structural members, such as beams, purlins, or upright supports, straightness and lack of taper are critical, as is an absence of knots and twists (especially if the county requires your structural logs to be graded). Besides, endless days of running a drawknife over scores of kidney-jarring knotty logs can really dampen one's enthusiasm.

Log Twist

All types of conifer trees have a tendency to twist, giving them a spiral grain. Odd as it may sound, the direction of the twist is critical, since logs with a left-hand twist tend to become "unraveled," over time.

To determine if the twist is left- or right-handed, place your right hand on the log (pointing toward either end; it doesn't matter) with the middle finger running along the long axis. If the grain spirals in the direction your thumb is pointing, it's a left-hand twist.

Logs with a left-hand twist should not be used as support logs (purlins, beams, etc.) and should only be used as wall logs if the grain deviates less than one inch from the log's long axis, over a distance of 20 inches.

Left-hand Twist

Right-hand Twist

GREEN OR SEASONED LOGS?

There are pros and cons for each. Green trees are certain to be free of rot and insect infestations, there is less cracking and checking, they're more flexible, and they have a nice, pristine look about them when freshly peeled.

On the other hand, you will have to allow for several inches of shrinkage and—this is my biggest bugaboo—they're too heavy! No matter what kind of equipment you have to move your logs around, there's still going to be a great deal of manhandling involved. Why lift, pull, roll and spin 1000 pounds when the same log dry weighs less than half that much?

So, as far as I'm concerned, it's a no-brainer: if you can get dry logs (but not too old), by all means do it. It will greatly facilitate construction, both from a tactical (moving logs from place to place) and a strategic standpoint (it's much easier to design, build and finish a house that isn't going to be 6 inches shorter in 2 or 3 years). In many states there are vast tracts of forest that have been killed by pine beetles. If you can find a logger working a contract in one of these areas you'll have all the seasoned trees you need.

If you use green logs, the longer they can cure before you build with them, the better: 9 months is good, but longer is better, up to 2 years (in which case, of course, they won't be green logs anymore.)

No matter what state of dryness your logs are in when you build, if you can let the structure sit for a season after the log work is done, your finish work will be easier. Unless your logs are dry when you begin building, and you are able to let the house settle for a few months when the shell is completed, you should plan to put jack stands beneath your vertical supports, and leave settling gaps above doors, windows, and interior walls.

Our logs were well-seasoned before we began construction, and we were able let the house settle over the winter after drying-in the roof. As a result, we were able to avoid a lot of the tedious procedures one normally has to take to allow for a spontaneously shrinking house.

CRIBBING YOUR LOGS

Green or seasoned, your logs will have to sit for some length of time before you get around to putting them in your house. They should be laid out individually, several inches above the ground, to allow for the movement of air under them. Old corral poles make good dunnage; culled trees or logs are even better. Longer dunnage poles are better than shorter; the reason will become obvious, once you begin rolling your logs with a bar and a peavey.

Don't let the logs sag in the middle. Use enough dunnage to support each log every 8 to 10 feet. Even then, you will want to roll them every so often to keep them straight. And, since it's doubtful that you'll know which log you intend to use next until it's time to use it, lay them in such a way that they are all equally easy to get to.

Many books will tell you to peel your logs immediately. But unless it never rains where you live, I would strongly advise against it. Ma Nature put bark on trees for a reason, and it wasn't just to make them easier to climb. Leave it on until it's time to use the log! Any staining you get from the bark will be nothing compared to the discoloration you'll see on naked logs after a couple of hard rains. The only caveat to this would be if you live in an area where log-boring insects are so severe that you have to peel the logs to keep them from being destroyed by bugs. Most areas are not this bad. As long as your logs are above the ground and laid out loosely enough that they don't trap moisture, the few bugs you do get under the bark won't do enough damage to worry about.

GETTING TO KNOW YOUR LOGS

Okay. It sounds funny, but it really isn't. If you've never built a log house before, a vast field of rough, unpeeled logs can look pretty intimidating. Even though we had all of our logs laid out above our building site in late October, we didn't get around to building with them until the following September. Eleven months is a long time to convince yourself that what you are attempting is fundamentally impossible. *Can I really take all of these unwieldy trees and turn them into a home I'll be proud of?* You'll ask yourself this question more than once. The answer is: of course you can. But if you just lay them out and forget about them until it's time to start building, you'll be shocked at what your imagination has done to your logs after a long winter's hiatus.

No, I didn't talk to our logs (and I'm happy to say they didn't talk to me, either.) But I did spend a lot of time walking them, picking out which logs would be best to start with, and which would be better for the top of the wall. I'd find artistic irregularities I wanted to be sure to place in highly visible interior walls, and others not so artistic I planned to cut out of door or window openings. Mostly I just dreamed about how good all those logs were going to looked peeled, notched and spiked into a wall.

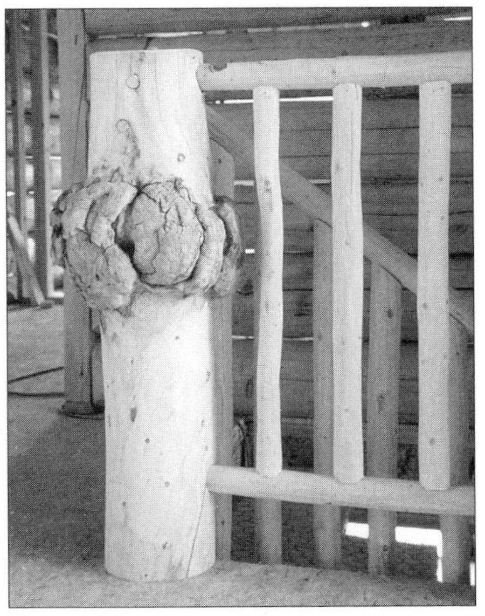
A unique log will adorn Benshoof's stair.

However you do it is up to you, but believe me: the more time you spend with your logs on the ground, the friendlier they're going to be when it comes time to use them. And the less likely they'll be to sneak up on you in the middle of night and hiss in your ear that you're an idiot if you think they're going to agree to being part of your house.

LaVonne's
LOGBOOK 2

October 1998

We waited anxiously this crisp fall morning for the semi load of trees to be delivered. After a road inspection by the driver, I park myself up high on a rock and, with binoculars, I watch his big truck rumble slowly past the first neighbor's drive. I lose sight of him for a moment and then see him stop on the steep, tight corner near the next neighbor's driveway. My heart sinks. Then, in utter disbelief, I watch him unload all 64 trees right there beside the road, and drive away! What a depressing sight. Our heavy house logs set in an ominous pile, over a mile from our property.

Never fear. My handy husband has a solution. I watch him as he cuts, torches and welds steel and axles into two trailers [3]. The black spray paint is a nice touch, but I'm very dubious of this whole thing. The newly made log-moving transports are ready. Me?? That is questionable. But why lose sleep over it. If I know Rex, it's going to get done one way or another.

3

November 1998

Well, we did it! After many weekends of jacking up each log end [4]– chaining it to a trailer – driving slowly up the road – jacking up the logs to offload – rolling each log into a new pile – and going down for the next log....we are done. Every time I'd say how much work this was, Rex would laugh and say, "this is nothin', Honey." Lucky for him I don't have to touch those logs for 6 months.

4

February 1999

We apply for a building permit, house plans in hand. Only a few questions from the engineer to be answered and we can have the permit.

April 1999

Yea! We sold our house and 20 acres down in the flatlands. We (us, 2 dogs and a psycho cat) will move to our small cabin (temporary living space of about 500 square feet, complete with an outhouse) in the mountains in May, providing we can pack, store, throw-out and haul decades of belongings. Hopefully the rain will slow down. Moving is exhausting, but the dream is getting closer.

CHAPTER 

TOOLS FOR CONSTRUCTION

Essential Tools for Pre-Log Construction

There is no substitute for good tools. The price paid for a durable, well-built tool will be paid back several times over the course of building a house by the countless hours of aggravation you'll avoid by not using bargain-box specials. This holds true for every type of tool, from expensive saws to relatively cheap hammers and tape measures. A tool that feels comfortable in your hands and stands up to the repeated punishment of daily use is an ally you cannot afford to be without.

Tools, like friends, should be chosen wisely.

GENERATOR

A generator will be a big ticket item, but since you'll be off the grid, it's no place to start cutting corners. You'll want a generator with at least twice the capacity needed to run your biggest load. This could be a welder, air compressor, or a well pump. A 1.5 hp submersible well pump draws around 11 amps at 240 volts, or a little over 2,600 watts. If that were your biggest load, you'd want at least a 5,000 watt generator to run it effectively. And most importantly, you'll want to be able to get that much power out of one individual circuit, which means you may need an even higher watt-rating.

Our generator is rated at 10,000 watts surge/8,500 watts continuous power, but the actual output is less than that, since it's running on the rarified air at 7,000 feet above sea level. Just the same, I have yet to find a tool that it can't run, and that's the way it should be. I can pump water from the well, and run an air compressor and a circular saw, all at the same time.

But beyond tools and well pumps, you will, on occasion, use your generator to charge your battery bank via the power inverter. This is the best reason among many for having a reliable, well-maintained, easy-to-start generator, since tinkering with a cantankerous generator in freezing weather when the battery bank is about drained isn't anyone's idea of a good time.

Most of the high-end sine wave AC power inverters on the market have an auto-start feature built into their circuitry. If you choose to use it, the inverter can automatically start the generator whenever the battery voltage drops below a preset level. Some people—mostly those who are away from home for long periods of time, or who have inadequate wind and solar generating capacity—think it's the bees knees. Most off-the-grid people (us, included) use their generators so seldom they don't bother with it. If you choose to take advantage of this feature you should make certain that the generator you buy is wired for remote start. And, since gasoline engines, as a rule, need to be choked to start in cold weather, you will probably have to buy a generator than runs on either diesel or propane.

Look for a generator manufactured by a reputable company that stands behind its products. If it's a big generator (6,500 watts, or better) you'll want it to have an electric starter. Make sure it's mounted on a frame with pneumatic tires so you can move it around. And again, be certain it has multiple circuits, one of which is sufficient to power your biggest load.

CIRCULAR SAWS

I went through about a cubic yard of cheap circular saws until I broke down and bought a Sears 7-inch worm-drive saw. That was over one garage, two barns, one cabin and one house ago, and I still haven't had a lick of trouble with it. If it conked-out tomorrow I'd give it a proper burial with honors and go buy another one, just like it. It's been that good of a saw.

It's only drawback is it's unavoidable weightiness. It works fine for cutting lumber and plywood resting on sawhorses, but can be cumbersome for cutting things in awkward places, such as rafter tails. For that reason, I also have a 12-volt cordless trim saw with a 5-inch blade. It's gutless for long cuts in heavy lumber, but works good for everything else. The 18- and 24-volt models are more powerful.

Make sure you have at least one heavy-duty circular saw you can depend on, because you'll be using it a lot. If you're inclined to shell-out the money for a good worm drive saw, you won't regret the decision.

COMPOUND MITER SAW

A compound miter saw is extremely helpful for framing walls, floors, and roofs, and is absolutely essential for finish work, when exact cuts and angle cuts are a must. A heavy-duty 12-inch miter saw can easily handle 2 x 8's. For wider lumber, a model with a sliding blade can cut boards up to 12 inches wide.

DRILLS

You'll want at least two drills; three is better. All of them should be variable speed and reversible. Here's what I suggest:

For screwing-down subfloor plywood, decking, etc., use a 3/8-inch drill. Cordless drills work better for this because they turn slower, making them easier to handle consistently. LaVonne had trouble driving screws with our 120-volt drill, but found it quite easy with a 12-volt cordless model (both were manufactured by DeWalt). The downside to using cordless drills is obvious: without enough spare batteries on hand, you can work yourself out of a job in a hurry. That's why it's good to have both; when you start the generator to run the 120-volt drill, you can plug in the battery charger for the cordless model.

There are some jobs a 3/8-inch drill just can't handle easily; drilling deep holes in log walls for spikes is one of them, drilling large holes through thick rim joists is another. If it's in your budget, pick up a good 1/2-inch drill, for the few times a 3/8-inch drill isn't up to the task at hand. I recommend a 120-volt model for the simple reason that you'll never run out of power, though admittedly there are some very impressive 24-volt cordless 1/2-inch drills on the market.

Odds and Ends
Following is a partial list of other tools you will need to complete the stages of construction prior to the log work:

Basic Carpentry
Tool belt
Framing hammer
Tape measure
Framing square
Combination square
Carpenter's pencils
Handsaws
Chalk box
Utility knives (brightly colored, so you can find them)

Excavation & Foundation
Men's gloves—leather driver's
Women's gloves—leather, purple (6 pairs, please)
Plumb bob
Dry line
Flat bar
Crowbar
Straight bar
Spade
Flat shovel
Pickaxe

RECIPROCATING SAW

A reciprocating saw is one of those tools you don't use often, but when you need it, you really need it. One chore that comes immediately to mind was the time I had to cut two 6-inch diameter holes through 7 1/2 -inch thick, nail-embedded rim joists to install fresh air furnace vents. No other tool I know of could have performed that task.

I've also used a reciprocating saw for trimming floor joists in-place, cutting holes through the roof for vents and pipes, making rounded cuts on roof rafters where they meet the log wall, and cutting the holes for outlet boxes in log walls. Seldom used, but indispensable: don't build a home without one.

BUILDER'S LEVEL

I'll refer to this tool in more detail in the next chapter. Often—and erroneously—referred to as a transit, a builder's level is a tool for establishing grade levels for foundations and floors, but lacks the sophistication of a surveying instrument. A little pricey, it nonetheless falls into the essential category.

LADDERS

You'll acquire several ladders before you're finished. We began with 16- and 20-foot extension ladders. By the time we were finished, we had added a 28-foot extension ladder, plus one 8-foot and two 6-foot step ladders to our collection. And this doesn't include the 32-foot extension ladder we borrowed from a neighbor (and eventually took back, to demonstrate our good faith, when we needed to borrow his scaffolding).

Fiberglass ladders are sturdier, and therefore safer, though they are a little heavier than aluminum. Look for ladders with good grips on the feet; it's no picnic when a ladder slides out from under you.

TOOL STORAGE

At this point, you're probably wondering where to put all of these new and expensive tools. If you're worried about them walking away during your absence (as tools often do) you may want to build a sturdy shed or invest in a tool trailer to keep them from escaping. Otherwise, a portable garage (rubberized fabric over a pipe frame) is inexpensive, easy to erect, and amazingly durable (and does not require a building permit!). In the three years ours has been up, it's endured 90 mph winds and 1-inch hailstones without sustaining any damage.

We built a temporary shed, with zippered doors on each end, to store tools and supplies.

LaVonne's
LOGBOOK 3

5

June 1999

Gary is back, with a huge excavator [5]. Our dog, Newt, thinks such a piece of equipment would be perfect to get those pesky voles! It is a bright sunny, warm day. The grass is unbelievably green, and it's rather a shame to dig up those wildflowers. The first scoop of dirt is huge. No turning back, I say to myself. Then Gary hits 'The Rock'. What an awful sound! Just keep digging around it, says Rex. And so our hole in the ground takes shape, with 'The Rock' in a corner. After a few sticks of dynamite, we have huge chunks of rock outside the hole (and a small spring in the middle of the foundation).

It's raining again, and the dogs [6] have fun in their newly formed lake. Slowly, in all this mud, we are making progress.

Where is that concrete contractor?? When work is plentiful, I guess subcontractors are not obligated to return phone calls. So we wait, while it rains some more.

Ingram Well Drilling can fit us into their busy schedule. This will be the big test. How deep will our water be? The drilling rig makes it up the muddy road and Larry sets up to drill. But the next truck loaded with water to lubricate the drill bit gets stuck. Call Gary. Maybe he and his excavator can help. Lucky for us, Gary is in town, and with lots of chain and teamwork, the truck is pulled to the top. This 'truck-not-making-it-up-the-hill' thing is getting hard to watch.

In between hail and rain, Larry drills and drills for water. I'm getting depressed. Nothing at 350 feet, 400 feet, 450 feet, 500 feet. Finally, water and lots of it at 540 feet. A hefty bill, but it could be worse. We are very relieved.

6

CHAPTER 

EXCAVATION AND FOUNDATION WORK

The Indelicate Art of Replacing Rock and Dirt with "Mud"

THE EXCAVATION

Our land, beautiful though it is, has exactly one building site where the sun shines in abundance and the wind blows often enough to be useful. Before we broke ground, it was a mildly sloping meadow with an occasional granite outcropping rising from the ground near the perimeter. There were no rocks showing within 20 feet of where we intended to dig. Naively, we thought that excavating would be a simple matter; like scooping out quicksand with a spoon.

Then we were mugged by reality.

On the third stab at the soft earth, the excavator shuddered and the huge bucket made a sound like a freight

Excavation begins.

train scraping against the side of a rock cliff. LaVonne looked at me as if to say, "Why does this sort of thing keep happening to us?" I looked back, thinking, *how should I know?* In any event, whatever was happening—and why—was immaterial. It wasn't like we could just move to another spot and try again; it was this site, or nothing.

The man doing the excavating—Gary, a friend who knows a lot more about poking under the surface of these hard old hills than I'll ever know—suggested we keep digging. Maybe it was the only place within the perimeter stakes where the bedrock was so near the surface, he told us. Considering that he had just hit a granite wart on the back of Mother Earth less than 1/100th of the way through his task, we thought he was being a trifle optimistic, but thin on options, we told him to go ahead.

We watched each bucketful come out with anxious curiosity. In a while we actually quit cringing every time the bucket cut into uncovered earth. After a few hours we discovered that, to our relieved amazement, Gary was right. The completed pit was 44-feet by 34-feet, 8 feet deep on the backside, 3 feet on the front. With one gigantic piece of bedrock in the southwest corner; right where we had planned to put a workshop.

Since there was no realistic prospect of removing the rock with a jackhammer (in my estimation it would have taken 10 days, two complete sets of lower lumbar discs and about seven kidneys) there was no choice but to blast.

Dynamite, we happily discovered, was cheap. The greatest cost associated with blasting was in hiring someone to drill the holes to put the dynamite

Rex drills holes with a pneumatic rock drill for placing the dynamite.

in. Giddy with the prospect of having a completed excavation, I volunteered. (However much damage I inflicted on myself in drilling the holes, I reckoned, I was still body parts ahead of what I would have been.)

It went pretty fast, actually. I secured a pneumatic rock drill from a local equipment rental shop, complete with a V8-powered compressor, and attacked the rock that was covering my workshop. After 2 hours (and two carbide bits) I had 13 holes, each 2 inches wide by 2 feet deep.

The explosives expert Gary found for us—his name was Travis—was a mountain man who fit right in with every other guy holed up in these hills. And his pickup was in even worse shape than mine. We hit it off, right away.

One stick of dynamite, Travis told me, has the kinetic energy of a Cadillac hitting a brick wall at 90mph. It sounded like it was going to be quite a show. After the dynamite and blasting caps were placed in the holes and all wired together, Gary covered the whole affair with a couple feet of dirt to keep the debris from flying out like shrapnel from a toolshed-sized hand grenade. Then we all hid behind a juniper tree and peered through the branches as thirteen big Caddies simultaneously converged on our troublesome rock.

I don't know what I expected—maybe something out of a Mel Gibson flick—but what we saw and heard wasn't it. The ground shook from 80 feet away, and a spray of dirt flew up like a dust spout from an earthbound whale, but the ear-splitting *Ka-Boom*! I was braced for was merely a loud, but muffled, *Whump*! Thirteen luxury cars smacking into a brick wall within a tunnel isn't nearly as impressive as on the streets of San Francisco.

The dirt blanket had done its job.

And so had the dynamite.

The rock was now in about a million pieces, ranging in size from sand pebble to dog house. Satisfied, Travis sat on his battered tailgate and wrote out the bill. He figured and re-figured, then shook his head and handed it to me, saying, "This is too cheap." We had to agree; it was under $200.

I can only hope that your excavation goes a little smoother. If not, maybe your explosives expert (or, more affectionately, "dynamite guy") will be as reasonable as ours. Here are a few things to keep in mind:

- Mark your footing perimeter before your excavator arrives. Make sure your corners are square, your stakes are exactly where you want your house to go, and you know at what depth you want the bottom of your footings. Allow for an extra few feet around the footing to facilitate the form work. The excavator should know the rest.

- Before the digging commences, stake out the location of your well, septic tank and leach field, per local regulations. You should also know where you intend to put your solar array and wind tower. Review your plan with the person doing the excavation. If he is experienced, he will be able to point out any problems you may have overlooked.
- You'll want to know—especially if you run into rock—where your water line is going to enter the house, and where your sewage line will leave it, since both will more than likely go under, or through, the footing or foundation wall. This means that the depth of the inlet for the septic tank will need to be determined before the foundation is poured. (Gas and electric lines, on the other hand, generally enter the house through the first floor rim joists.)
- For obvious reasons, it's a good idea to take care of any dynamite blasting *before* you drill a well.

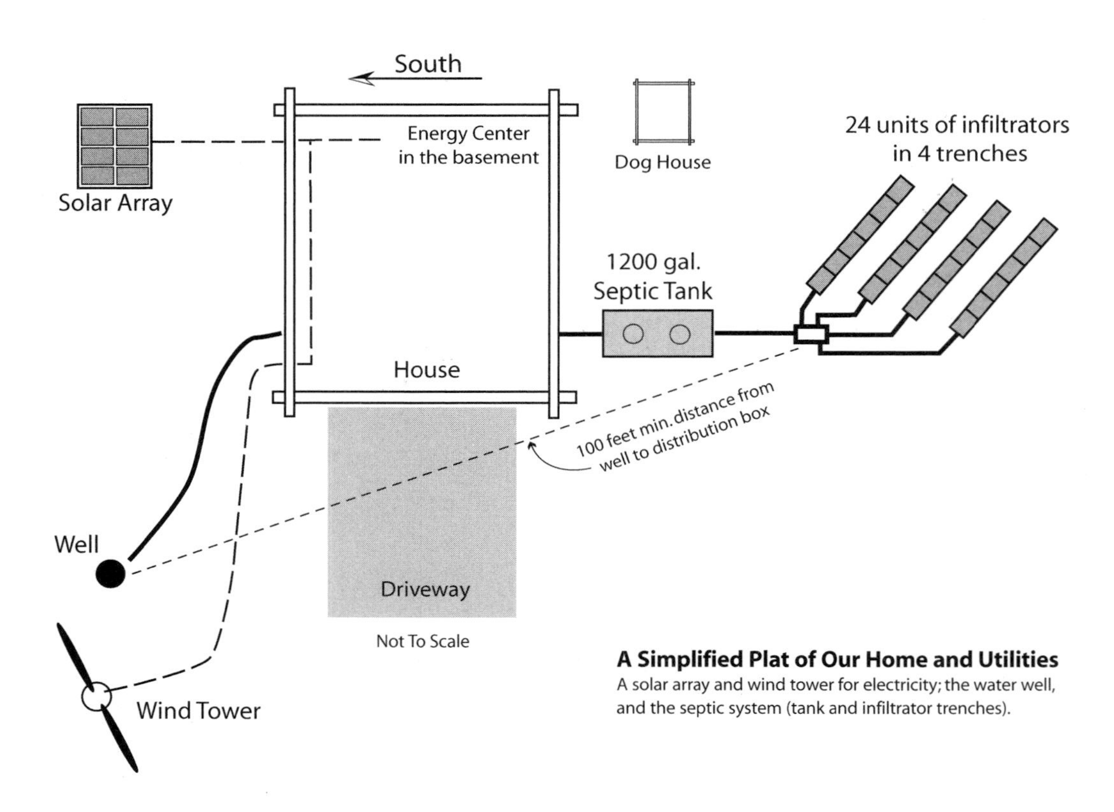

A Simplified Plat of Our Home and Utilities
A solar array and wind tower for electricity; the water well, and the septic system (tank and infiltrator trenches).

FOUNDATION

Whether you hire a contractor or do it yourself, the cost of your foundation will probably be one of the biggest expenses of the entire house project, so make sure it's done right.

We had a concrete contractor lined out months before we broke ground, but once the excavation was complete and we were ready to begin the foundation walls, he kept putting us off. He always had one more big job to complete in town before he could move his crew up into the hills. Then, the day before he was scheduled to come up and look at our building site for the very first time, he hopped on a plane to Mexico for two weeks. So much for Pablo.

It was getting late in the season. We'd wasted over a month waiting for a guy who would never show. And every concrete contractor within 50 miles—at least those with the civility to return our phone calls—was booked solid for several months out. Within this dreary backdrop of betrayal and abandonment, I announced to LaVonne one night that we were going to do the foundation ourselves. The look she gave me was priceless; it was a *you've really lost it this time, Cowboy* look, if ever I've seen one. Even though we were out of options—familiar ground, by this point—it was no easy matter to convince her that we could successfully complete a project as complex and labor intensive as forming and pouring a basement foundation. So, naturally I did what any man would do in a similar situation: I lied. I told her that forming a wall was really no harder than framing a wall; all we were really doing, I explained, was creating a vessel to hold liquid rock (I neglected to mention that the liquid weighed 80,000 pounds). It would probably be fun, I insisted. And, of course, I used the old catch-phrase that the experience would be "character building." She rolled her dazzling green eyes at the last part, and knew I was lying through my teeth about the rest of it, but they were lies she wanted to believe, so after I gave her an (honest) estimate of how much money we would save, she at last consented.

LaVonne's Verities

IF YOU CAN DO IT YOURSELF, DO IT.

At least you'll know when you'll show up for work, and that the job will be done right.

In the end—that mystical place in the unforeseeable future where all seeds at last bear fruit—everything worked out nicely. The thousands of dollars we saved by doing it ourselves was more than just compensation for our labor, and we were both brimming over with newly reconstituted character. Best of all, since we employed a new type of foundation system in which permanent polystyrene is used as the wall form (instead of traditional plywood or aluminum), our basement walls were insulated to R-28, not including interior gypsum board or exterior stone.

It is not within the scope of this book to give detailed instructions on the construction of every conceivable type of foundation. Other writers with far more foundation experience than I'll ever have, have already done that. There are, however, certain methods, techniques and tricks of the trade common to all foundations that bear elucidation here. Also, since many of you will elect to do your own foundation work, I'd like to elaborate (later in this chapter) on the polystyrene system we used for our walls. In our estimation, it's the answer to every do-it-yourselfer's dream.

WHERE IS NORTH?

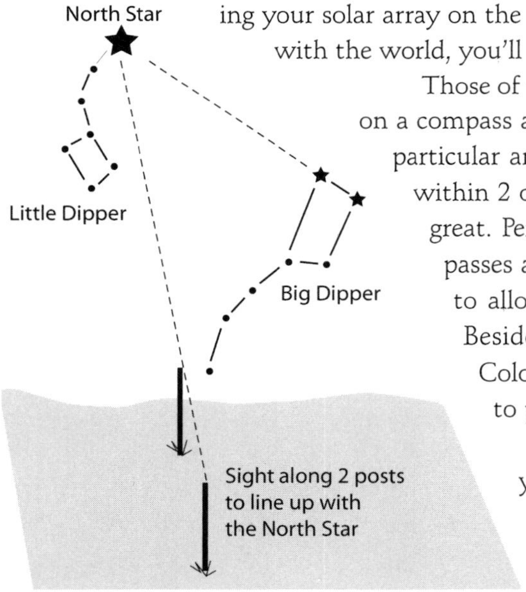

If you plan to build your house along a true east-west axis for the purpose of placing your solar array on the roof, or if you just want your house to be square with the world, you'll need to know where true north is.

Those of us deficient in surveying experience generally rely on a compass and chart giving the magnetic declination for our particular area. With a bit of luck, you might be able to get within 2 or 3 degrees by this method. If that is acceptable, great. Personally, I prefer another way. I own three compasses and a GPS, and I don't trust any of them enough to allow them to dictate the placement of my house. Besides, the magnetic declination for northern Colorado's front range tends to vary from publication to publication.

But why settle for an approximation when you can get a nearly perfect alignment with a couple of T-posts and the ability to locate two of the most conspicuous constellations (the Little Dipper and the Big Dipper) in the night sky? Polaris, the bright, terminal jewel in the handle of the Little Dipper (officially known as Ursa Minor) is the North Star. It is the pivot point around which every other star in the night sky revolves. The two bright stars delineating the outer bowl of the Big Dipper (Ursa Major) point to it from 30 degrees away.

Once you know where Polaris is, all you need to do is to drive a post into the ground, either on your southwest or southeast corner. As you sight directly over the top of the first post, have someone-to the north of you move a second post east and west until a sight line along both posts points directly to Polaris. You now have a true north-south axis to work from, either for your excavation or foundation, or the alignment of your solar array.

Due to a phenomenon known as the ***precession of the equinoxes***, the North Star changes every few thousand years. In the unlikely event that this book is still in print 12,000 years from now, some future editor will have to replace Polaris with the 0.1 magnitude star, Vega.

MAKING IT SQUARE

There are numerous ways to ensure that your foundation is square. Some are easier than others, some more accurate. Here's how I do it:

- Using the measurements for the outside of your foundation wall, drive a stake into the ground to mark one corner.
- Now measure along one wall to find your next corner. Pound nails in the top of your stakes to ensure you have an exact point to work from.
- At this point, we will defer to a clever Greek mystic of ancient times, and the theorem that bears his name. The Pythagorean Theorem, $a^2 + b^2 = c^2$, gives the formula for determining the length of a right triangle's hypotenuse, when the length of the other two sides are known. (Unless you're a whiz at mental math, you will need a pocket calculator with a square root key.) Let's say your foundation is 28 feet by 36 feet. That's a and b. So what is c? It's the diagonal distance from, say, your northwest corner to your southeast corner. To find it, square a, then b, and add the squares together. In this example, $28^2 = 784$ and $36^2 = 1296$. Together they total 2080. Now, hit the square root key, and viola! The answer, 45.60, is the exact diagonal distance in our hypothetical example.
- You'll need two long tape measures for this

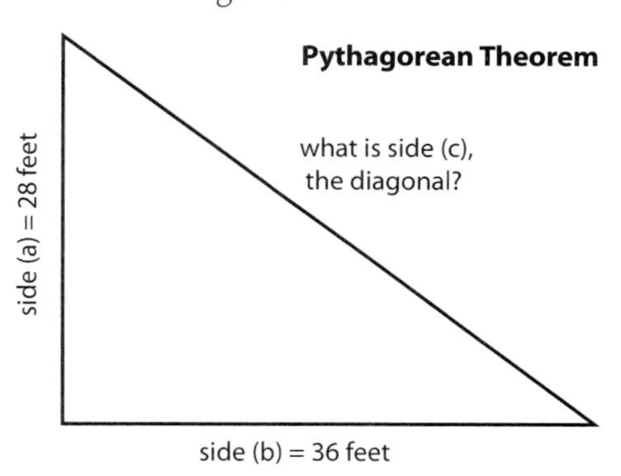

$a^2 + b^2 = c^2$
$28^2 + 36^2 = c^2$
784 feet + 1296 feet = c^2
2080 = c^2
square root of 2080 = 45.6 feet

c = 45.6 feet or 45' 7-3/16"

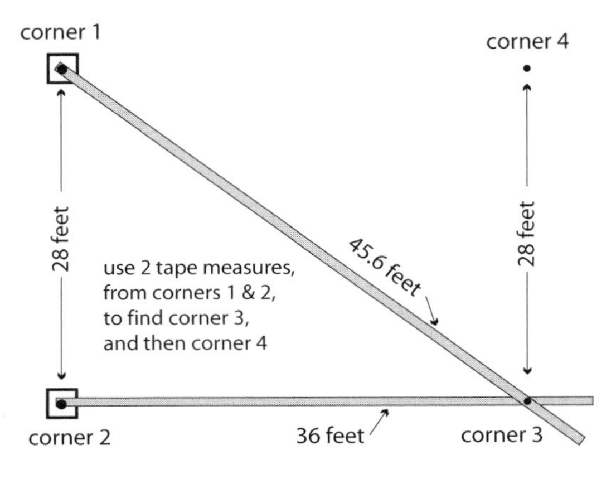

Applying the Pythagorean Theorem to Your Foundation

next part. Put one end of each tape on the nails in each end of your two stakes. Now, pull both tapes until the lengths you want bisect each other (at corner 3). In our example, it would be 36 feet for the long side, and 45.60 feet (45 feet, 7-$^{3}/_{8}$ inches) for the diagonal. Drive a stake.

- Pull the tapes to the opposite corner (corner 4) in the same manner and drive your last stake. Now check and recheck all of your sides and diagonals. That's it.

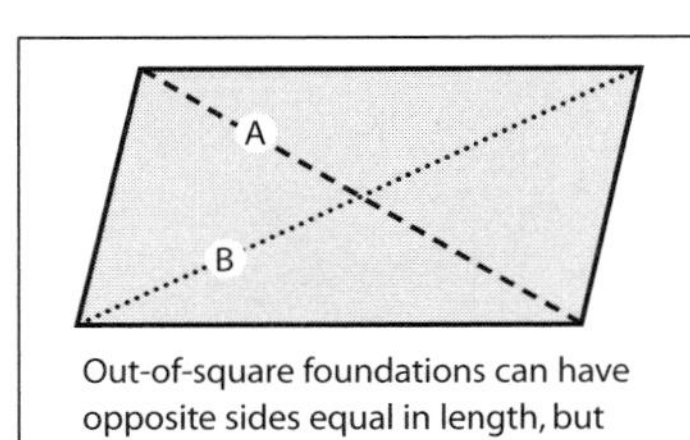

Out-of-square foundations can have opposite sides equal in length, but the diagonals will not be identical. Here, diagonal A is shorter than B.

Many books recommend the use of batter boards, once the corner stakes are in place. These are two boards, 4 to 6 feet in length, nailed to stakes set at right angles, a few feet outside the corners of your excavation. By placing nails along the top edge of the batter boards, you can then run bisecting strings lines to determine the inner and outer perimeters of both your footings and your walls.

corner of house

Batter Boards

While I have found batter boards useful for pier foundations, where it's helpful to know if you've dug a hole just where it should have been, for full foundations they seem to be more work than necessary. Since the batter boards are at least a foot or two above the ground, and your completed excavation is at least 3 feet below it, you are forever dropping plumb bobs from string intersections to determine your corners.

In my estimation, it's easier just to re-square the footing stakes (via the Pythagorean method) once the excavation is complete.

MAKING IT LEVEL

If your excavation is a little out of square, it's no big deal, as long as you have room within the hole to make corrections when you lay out your footings. But if it's out of level, you've got problems. You want your footing to rest on undisturbed ground, and it doesn't work to backfill and tamp if you or your excavator dig too deep over a broad area. Eventually the dirt you put back in the hole will settle and your footing will crack, and then..... Well, just don't do it.

There are many ways to level a foundation, ranging from clever to tedious. I'm going to tell you exactly one: a tripod-mounted builder's level. For under $300 you can set yourself up with a sight level (essentially, a low-power telescope with a spirit level on top), tripod and leveling rod. For a couple hundred more you can buy a laser level. It may sound like a lot of money, but by the time you finish your house, you will have used your level so often that you won't be able to imagine how you could have gotten by without it.

If your house is built into a hillside (as ours is) you'll need it determine the different elevations at each corner. That way you will know how deep to dig in the back of the hole. Once grade (the depth to the *bottom* of your footing) is established, you should take periodic sightings to make sure the hole is neither too deep nor too shallow. No hole is perfect; there will always be a few ups and downs, but try to keep them at a minimum. Remember: the *highest* point in your excavation will be the same grade as the *bottom* of your footing form, so start there.

Once you have formed your footing, take sightings every few feet and raise or lower the forms as need be. What holds true for your excavation is equally true for your footings: if the footing is a little out of square, you can offset the wall forms to bring the structure back into square. But if it's out of level you will either end up doing some fancy form work, or spending a lot of time shimming your sill plate. Neither is much fun.

A sight level and rod are indispensible tools.

FOOTINGS

Most people who form their own footings use 2 x 10's or 2 x 12's (depending on the foundation specs) held in place with stakes and double-headed "duplex" nails. You can either use wooden stakes—which move from where you intended them to go as you drive them in the ground, and will then split as you drive a nail through them—or you can splurge a little and buy metal stakes, with predrilled holes, from a masonry supply.

Either way, all you are really doing when forming the footing is building a continuous channel for concrete. If your footing happens to be the same thickness as your roof rafters, you can buy lumber of the appropriate length and use it later in your roof.

To keep the forms from spreading under the enormous weight of the concrete, you will need to nail 1 x 2 spacers every few feet along the top of your forms. The spacers will ensure that the finished footing is uniform in width, and will provide a bridge from which to suspend steel reinforcing rod (rebar).

If there will be water or sewer pipes going through your footing (or your foundation wall), wedge a PVC sleeve between the boards of your form where the pipe will enter the wall, keeping in mind that the inside diameter of your sleeve will need to be a little more than the outside diameter of your pipe. Once in place, drive a few nails through from the outside of the form to ensure it doesn't slip when the weight of the concrete pushes down on it. When the forms are later stripped, there will be a nice channel for running the pipe.

Some contractors like to install a key way in the top of the

Special framing of the footing is required around a remnant of "the ROCK" in the southwest corner.

LaVonne ties wire around the rebar to suspend it from the 1 x 2 spacers in the footing. The two piers in the center will support the steel posts in the garage, and the wood posts above them.

footing. This a tapered depression made by pushing boards (with sides cut at 15 degree angles) into the wet concrete. It is meant to keep the vertical wall, soon to be poured on top of it, from sliding side to side. If it's in the plans, do it. But unless there are going to be unusual lateral stresses on your walls, you can accomplish the same thing by leaving the surface of your footing rough, and setting vertical lengths of rebar into the wet concrete every few feet. Again, refer to your plans.

Joe screeds the mud to top of the footing boards.

When it comes time to pour, call in all the favors you can. There's no such thing as too much help at a concrete pour. At the very least, you will want two able bodied men (sorry; the cement truck driver doesn't count) for an average footing. Twice as many is much better. Two men working the chute is ideal; that way, one will always be free to motion the driver to speed up the mud, slow it down, or drive ahead. Right in the thick of things should be another man with a shovel, tossing the wet mud forward whenever it piles up and threatens to spill over the side of the forms. If your lucky enough to have a fourth man, he can tap the forms with a hammer to help the concrete settle out, then screed the tops of the forms with a board to level out the concrete before it begins to set up.

However you do it, once the mud starts to flow, no one will be scratching their head wondering what to do.

WALLS

With the completion of the footing there comes a profound sense of accomplishment. It is the first structure to rise from your ragged, unsightly excavation that is truly square and flat. Just imagine, then, how it's going to feel, seeing the completed concrete walls rising up out of the ground. For the first time, you will have a true feel for the size of your house, and an eye level view of the height of your first floor.

Unless you are doing a pier foundation with tubular cardboard forms, you will find the walls several degrees trickier than the footings. No matter how square you have your walls marked out with chalk lines on the footings, they will find a way to twist out of square at the top. And the taller the walls, the more you will need to "rack" them back into square.

But first things first.

If you elect to form your foundation walls using plywood forms, I suggest that you rent them. Plywood concrete forms, though they are no thicker than regular $^3/_4$-inch plywood, are much stronger, since they are made of finer-grained wood, with thinner, tighter laminations, and they have a smooth, waxy surface that repels concrete and makes them much easier to remove than standard plywood. Besides, the only conceivable use you would have for that much $^3/_4$-inch plywood *after* the pour would be in your subfloors. But, since flooring plywood is generally tongue-&-groove, you will find the forms extremely difficult to break down after the walls cure, because the concrete will "glue" many of the tongues to their respective grooves. To make matters worse, you will have done so much damage to your expensive boards—besides damage to the edges, large swatches of board will remain stuck to the concrete—that many of them will be unusable.

Longer lengths of vertical rebar are wired to rebar stubs set in the concrete footing.

As I mentioned above, there is another way. Polystyrene concrete forms, though a little pricey, are easy for one or two people to work with, and the R-value they will add to a basement or crawl space will be more than worth the extra money in the long run, since your basement will cost much less to heat, and the pipes in your crawl space will be less likely to freeze.

There are several different manufacturers of polystyrene forms. Some make a better product than others. I suggest you make some inquiries before deciding on which one to use. While you will, of course, need to talk to the salespeople for the different brands of forms, you should also talk to a few concrete truck drivers, and concrete-pumping drivers. These are the folks out in the field whose job it is to dump wet, heavy mud into these inherently fragile forms. They will be more than

The wall forms go up, one row at a time. Horizontal rebar is added every few rows.

Soon the wall forms are finished, and ready for bracing.

happy to regale you with stories about which types of forms have had disasters. Listen to them—they know what they're talking about.

The system we used is called Lite-Form® (see Appendix E). The individual members are 8-feet long by 8-inches high, by 2-inches thick, with slots cut every 8 inches to allow for the insertion of permanent plastic spacer ties. The local dealer delivered the forms herself, then spent over an hour with us on the job site, demonstrating how it all went together. By the time she left, we were off and running.

It took us about a week—in a constant battle with heavy rain and sticky mud—to form a 28-foot x 38-foot basement with 8-foot walls, and then brace the forms and build scaffolding in preparation for the pour. LaVonne assembled the pieces while I cut, bent and wired the rebar in the walls and around door and window openings. It all went off without a hitch.

Whether you use conventional forms, or one of the polystyrene systems, you will want to brace the walls before the pour. Considering that a 10-foot section of an 8-foot wall, 8-inches thick, weighs in the neighborhood of 6000 pounds when filled with wet concrete, you really can't use too much bracing. If you are pouring a basement foundation, you can run 2 x 4's up the side every 6 or 8 feet, then brace them back in the middle and at the top with diagonal 2 x 4's, and anchor them to the ground with the stakes. The vertical 2 x 4's are also handy to support the scaffolding you will need to work along the top of the wall during the pour. Brace your form walls inside and out, giving special attention to the corners, doors, windows and bulkheads, since these are the most likely areas for "blowouts" to occur.

As you install your bracing, use a level to make certain your walls remain perfectly vertical. Take multiple measurements across your walls and from corner to corner, then use the bracing to push or pull the walls back into alignment.

Before you pour the walls, you should determine if you need to use a concrete-pumping truck. If you are built into a hillside it's a good idea, since the walls on the low end will be higher than the truck's chute. With polystyrene forms, the concrete needs to be poured in "lifts" (a maximum of 3 feet at a time, for our forms). At the very least, a pumper will save you the trouble of having to guide the driver on multiple trips around the foundation.

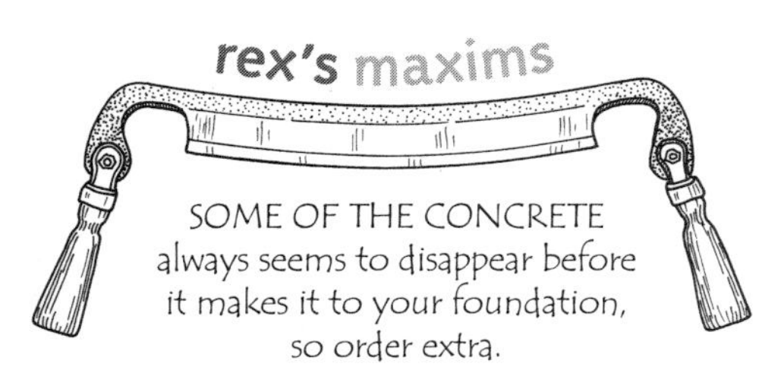

If you still have any friends left after pouring your footing, call them up when it comes time to pour the walls. Entice them with whatever it takes to get them to help, because you'll need them. During our wall pour, we had two men on the pumper nozzle, two trading off on the concrete vibrator, and another smoothing the tops of the walls with a trowel. We could have used more.

Ufer Grounding System

A Ufer grounding system uses the rebar and concrete in your foundation as an extra grounding system for over-current protection. Developed by Herbert G. Ufer during WWII to protect bomb storage vaults from lightning strikes, a Ufer grounding system is simple and inexpensive to install before the walls are poured. It is an especially good system to use in areas with dry (non-conductive) soil, and/or frequent lightning strikes. Any good electrician should know how to install a Ufer grounding system. If not, there is a wealth of information on the internet.

A pumper truck was the only method for us. Two men manhandled the nozzle and directed the mud into the walls; two men operated the vibrator; and one guy made sure there were no blow-outs. He also screeded the top edge, and set the anchor bolts.

Anchor Bolts and Beam Pockets

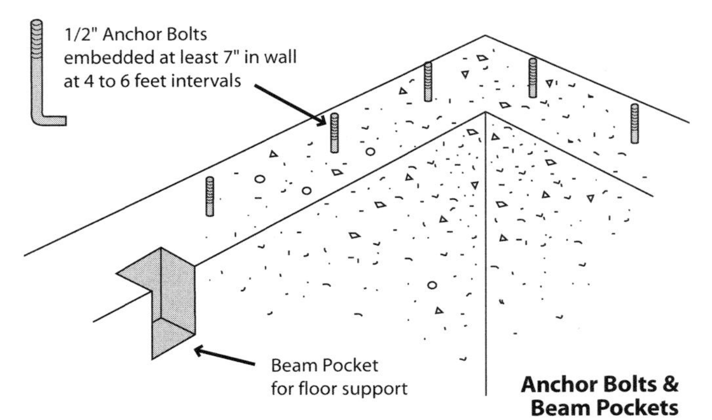

Anchor Bolts & Beam Pockets

The size and placement of the anchor bolts will be determined by local building codes, and should be specified in the plans. Examine your floor plan, then place the anchor bolts in such a way that the floor joists won't rest on top of them. It's a little trick that will save you a lot of work, later.

Beam pockets are simple to make. All you have to do is fashion blocks of dimensional lumber the same height and width of the beam, and screw (or nail) it to the inside of the form. Just be sure to leave yourself a little extra room—it's a lot easier to add metal shims later, than to chip out the sides of a beam pocket.

DAMP-PROOFING AND BACKFILLING

Damp-proofing is a good idea, whether or not your county requires it. The damp-proofing material is simply an emulsified asphalt applied to the foundation walls, to keep ground water from seeping through the cracks that may eventually appear. A glance at the phone book should direct you to a professional applicator, or you can buy it at the lumber yard and apply it yourself, with either a roller or a brush. Be sure and wear grungy clothes—the stuff will never wash out.

Rex damp-proofs the outside of our foundation walls.

The amount of time the walls

need to cure before backfilling the foundation is dependent upon several factors: the length and height of the wall, the wall thickness, the ambient temperature, and the nature of the soil. The longer you can wait to backfill, the better. Ten days for an average wall in normal conditions is usually acceptable. Two weeks is even better.

CONCRETE FLOORS

Concrete flatwork is an art that takes months, if not years, to master. If you've never done it before, nothing I could possibly say here would make it any better for you. Flatwork is not the kind of thing you can learn by reading a book; it takes hands-on experience, and lots of it. Besides, it would be hypocritical of me to try to tell you how to do something that I'm not particularly comfortable doing myself.

Whoever does your concrete floor, you'll need to decide how soon after finishing your foundation walls you intend to pour it. Of course, your below-ground plumbing will all have to be in place and inspected, and that will take some time. If you are planning radiant floor heat in your garage or basement, that will take a while to install, as well.

As much as you would like to have your floor poured as soon as possible, in many instances there is no technical reason it needs to be done right away (we waited almost a year after the completion of our foundation walls). So, before you get gung-ho to pour the floor, ask yourself how you intend to move your logs around, as you build your log walls. If you don't have the luxury of using a boom-truck during your log wall construction, you may want to consider using a gin pole. This is a sturdy log that stands vertically. It will go through a hole left in the middle of your first floor, and rest in a hole dug in the dirt below. With a boom at the top from which you can suspend an electric winch, it will greatly facilitate the handling of wall logs. But it will be impossible to anchor into the ground if you've already poured your floor.

On the other hand, a concrete floor locks the foundation walls into place, and this is important with certain types of soil. If your foundation engineer insists that the floor be poured before the house goes up, you can still leave an area open for a gin pole, then fill it with concrete later.

LaVonne's
LOGBOOK 4

July 1999
The concrete guy gets the boot and my darling husband says we can do it ourselves. I think he is crazy, but we pick a corner in the muddy pit, and start forming the footing. I prefer graphic design, and Rex would prefer that I didn't ask so many questions. Our friend Joe shows up to help with the pour, and of course, it rains. We work in the freezing cold rain of the late day to smooth out the "mud," while getting the other mud up to our knees. Another day to remember (or not remember, which is it?).

Before you know it, we have huge piles of foam boards and plastics ties, waiting to be assembled into our basement walls. A simple demonstration from the dealer, and I'm on my way [7]. It's really pretty simple and enjoyable after the dirt-and-mud of the past few weeks... it's clean, dry and above ground. Reminds me of Lego toys. It is easier to work on the house when you can see measurable progress.

7

August 1999
It's a good day. We've finished assembling the forms for our foundation...complete with two windows and a walk-in door. Two garage doors will fill the east side. The big pour is scheduled for Saturday, so the neighbors can help. We are praying the rains stay away, just for a few days, so the trucks can make it up our road.

The pumper arrives early. What a sight to see that huge vehicle coming through the trees. The driver suggests we add more bracing, so everyone scrambles for the 2x4's, cordless drills and hammers. Then we wait and wait for the mud. Finally the mixer shows up and the pour gets underway. My job is to take pictures, and to keep the dogs out from under the wheels. A second load of concrete arrives too soon and it is getting way too crowded up here on top of the hill. (Actually, the second truck was to be the first truck...but he took a wrong turn. That flustered driver will probably refuse to drive in the mountains again.)

The pour took all morning, but we survived without any blowouts. The guys worked hard. We couldn't have done it without them. Thanks, Errol, Dave, Joe and German [8]! Time to relax.

8

CHAPTER 

THE FLOOR

Toward Building the Flattest Place on the Mountain

It wasn't too long ago that building a log house or cabin meant building with logs throughout. Log beams under the floor, supporting log or heavy timber joists. If the nearest lumber yard was 50 miles away over invariably rough terrain—and your WWII vintage truck was liable to break down half the way there—it was a lot easier just to use the tall, straight trees obstructing your view of the distant, snowcapped peaks.

Today, with reliable vehicles, good roads and easy access to straight, strong, graded lumber, the only real reason to support the floor with logs is purely aesthetic: it's done to preserve the purer sense of the tradition. I can respect that. I sometimes dream that, if LaVonne and I were to sell this place and move 30 miles higher up the canyon into a densely forested high plateau, we might just go primitive, eschewing civilization and all modern conveniences. We would build an eminently non-code log house, entirely from the land, just to prove to ourselves that we could do it. We would mill our own boards for the roof planks and floors, and split the roof shingles with a broadaxe. Make all our own doors and windows, and chink the walls with mud and ash. And, of course, our foundation would be massive piers of carefully stacked rock.

The pure, untainted, two-against-the-world romanticism of this notion, I'm sure, resonates deep in the heart of anyone who has ever considered building their own log house.

At the same time, however, I strongly suspect that you did not buy this book because you yearn to express, in its rugged entirety, the primal urge that growls from deep within your id. You want a home out of the city, but not out of world. A grand log structure of rustic majesty that doesn't compromise, to any great degree, the habits of living you've honed since childhood, or the comforts that make living more a pleasure than an ordeal.

Beyond that, you want to finish your log house within your lifetime, and not spend any more time than necessary on matters that, in the long run, are unimportant.

All that being said, let me suggest—you knew I'd get around to it, sooner or later—that you support your floor with steel I-beams and engineered wood I-joists, rather than logs and timbers.

The reasons for doing this are numerous. I'll give you three.

Reason #1: The fact is, no one will see your fancy log work. If you are building on a pier foundation, or a wall for a crawlspace, the admirers of your craftsmanship will have to crawl under the house to see what you've done. And if you're building on a basement foundation, the only thing that will show when you are all done is the log beams which, since your basement is *not* built of logs, will probably clash, anyway.

Reason #2: Log beams are notched into the sill logs, and the joists that rest on them are notched into the course of logs above. That means you will use two full courses of logs before you arrive at the floor's surface. So by building a conventional floor and beginning your log construction on top if it, you will save yourself two entire courses of wall logs, a few notches and a whole lot of peeling.

Reason #3: If you're still not convinced, here comes the *coup de grace*. The modern floor is not simply a flat surface on which to set your chairs and tables; it's a well-planned highway of water, sewer and gas pipes; hundreds of yards of electric wire (in and out of conduits); phone wires and low-voltage wires for thermostats, stereos, and computer systems. If you build your floor with logs, timbers, or even standard dimensional lumber, you will, at the very least, make more work for the plumber and electrician. And you may even run afoul with the county, since building inspectors take a dim view of the practice of drilling dozens of large holes through structural members that were not designed for such treatment.

Therein lies the beauty of engineered wood I-joists. (In our home we used a Weyerhauser product called Trus-Joist® or TJI's.) Consisting of a layer of wafer board set on edge between finely-laminated 2 x 2's, I-joists are designed to allow for the passage of pipes and conduits without loosing their structural integrity. Besides that, they are perfectly straight (which makes for a flat floor), have practically no vertical deflection, and can be ordered in any length that will fit on a lumber truck. For floors, they're a builder's dream.

SUPPORTING THE SUBFLOOR

If you are building a house and not a small cabin, I'll assume that your joists will have to span distances greater than 10 or 12 feet. That means you will need beams (usually steel I-beams) and posts between your walls to support the joists (and probably concrete piers beneath the posts, in the basement or crawl space). The I-beams should rest in beam pockets in the foundation walls, and the tops of the beams should be level with the top of foundation.

Once the beams are in place, it's time to install the sill plate, a continuous board of the same nominal width as your foundation walls. (So, if the wall is 8-inches thick, you will use 2 x 8 boards for your sill plate.)

Before you begin, measure the top of your foundation walls, corner to corner and side to side. If the walls are a little out of square, you can "rack" the sill plate to bring the structure back into square by marking the corners correctly and connecting these corner marks with chalklines.

To mark the sill plate for the hole locations for the anchor bolts poking out of your foundation walls, set straight boards on top of the bolts, making sure the edge of the board is even with your chalk line. Hit the board with a hammer over each bolt to mark the board, then drill your holes in the board. Since it's

LaVonne bolts 2 x 6 boards to the top of steel I-beams.

doubtful that the anchor bolts are perfectly vertical, or your board is perfectly plumb with your chalk line, drill the holes at least $1/8$-inch bigger than your bolts. This will be your "slop factor."

(If your foundation walls are so out of square that you are not able to fix it by racking the sill plate, try instead to run the imperfections to one corner, then begin laying out the floor in the opposite (square) corner. This will make it much easier to lay the subflooring.)

Before bolting the sill plate into place, run a layer of insulation under it. Any lumber yard that caters to the builder will sell rolls of thin, foam-like plastic insulation of different widths. The insulation will create a seal between the sill plate and top of the foundation. More importantly, it will keep the wood from coming into contact with the concrete, thereby preventing the rot that inevitably occurs when wood and concrete get together.

Now run boards along the tops of your steel I-beams, using the same type of insulation to bring them level with the sill plate. Secure them in place with $1/4$-inch carriage bolts every few feet. Unless you're a glutton for punishment, I suggest you buy three or four high-quality drill bits for this operation. Cobalt bits are my favorite; high-speed steel bits, on the other hand, are next to worthless for drilling through I-beams. ***Note:*** *If you use structural, laminated wood beams for floor support, the wood must be separated from the concrete in the beam pocket.*

RIM JOISTS

With the foundation walls and I-beams plated, it's time to install your rim joists. These are the dimensional lumber counterpart of your I-joists (2 x 10's, for example) set on edge even with the outside of your sill plate and toe-nailed in place with 16d framing nails. Since the weight of the logs will be so much greater than the weight of a normal frame house, it is advisable to use multiple rim joists along the walls that run parallel with your floor joists. Ideally, you should have solid wood the entire width of the sill plate. This will be expensive, however, so you may want to simply run 2 x 4 spacers between each course of 2 x 10, or 2 x 12, rim joists. Unless your log walls are unusually high, or your logs especially thick, two 2 x 4's sandwiched between three full-dimension rim joists should be more than adequate. (Some experienced log builders maintain that a single rim joist will support the walls, and build accordingly, using extra support only in the corners. Though it seems contrary to common sense, our county inspectors accept it.)

Rim Joists that Run **Parallel** with Floor Joists

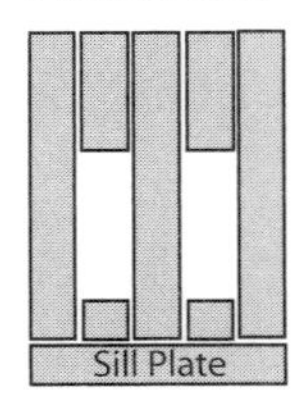

Rim Joists that Run **Perpendicular** with Floor Joists

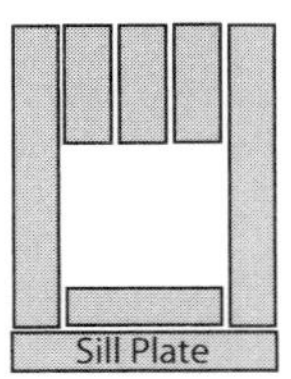

For the walls running perpendicular to the floor joists, run just a single rim joist, for now.

LAYING-OUT THE FLOOR JOISTS

Starting at the most perfectly square corner, mark the tops of the rim joists for the placement of floor joists, according to the spacing noted on your blueprints. Repeat on the opposite wall, and then chalk lines, from point to point, across the wood-plated I-beams. Lay out the joists and toe-nail them into the beams, then drive nails into the TJI's from the backside of the single rim joists. Wherever two joists break on a beam, you will need to put solid bridging perpendicularly between them. This is to keep them from "rolling" side to side.

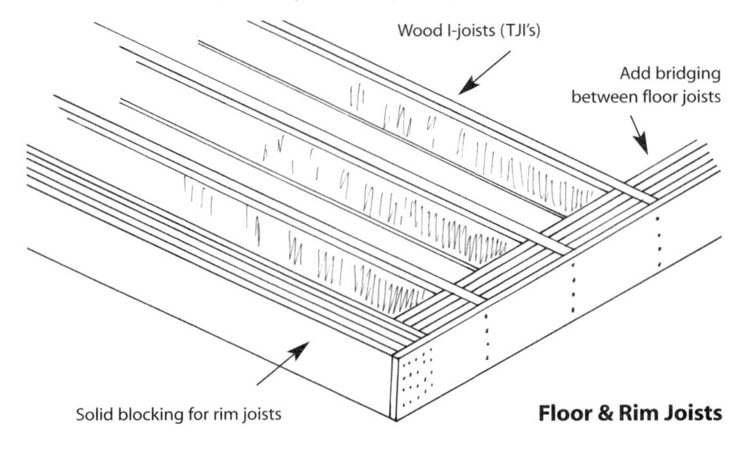

Floor & Rim Joists

After setting all

joists, you can now install bridging between the ends. Since the joists will help support the log wall, you can get by with less support under the log walls running perpendicular with the joists. However, it's important that it be solid across the sill plate, since you will be lagging the first logs through the floor and into the wood beneath it. (Again, some builders only add extra support at the corners.)

The wood I-joists are nailed in place through the outside rim joists.

INSTALLING THE SUBFLOOR

To keep the finished floor from squeaking when you're headed on a clandestine mission to the refrigerator in the middle of night, the subfloor should be glued, and held into place with either screws or 8d ringshank nails. Epoxy-coated square-headed screws are the best, since they strip out less than Phillips-head screws, saving you a ton of aggravation and at least a handful of screw bits. Do not use drywall screws; they're too brittle for flooring. There are several brands of flooring adhesive on the market. I have no particular preferences; they all do the job.

Starting from the squarest corner, chalk a line across the joists, 4 feet from the outer edge of the rim joist. The chalk line must be perfectly perpendicular to your joists, or you'll shortly run into trouble. Lay down a bead of adhesive on each joist and around the rim, then lay down a full sheet of $^{3}/_{4}$-inch tongue & groove plywood (T&G particle board is less expensive, but it won't stand up to rain and snow as well as plywood). Put in enough screws to hold it firmly in place, then move to the next sheet and complete the row. Start the second row with a half-sheet, to avoid having two consecutive joints on a single joist.

Never hit a tongue or a groove with a hammer. If you do, you'll wish you hadn't. Instead, find a length of 2 x 4 long enough to lay across two joists, and use it to drive the plywood home.

After the first two rows are in place, go back and finish screwing down the plywood. Use seven screws on each edge and five screws in the field. Chalk lines are helpful for finding the joists below.

Finish the subfloor just as you did the first two rows. As long as your joists are square with the sill plates—and you didn't leave any gaps between sheets of plywood—the operation should go off without a hitch.

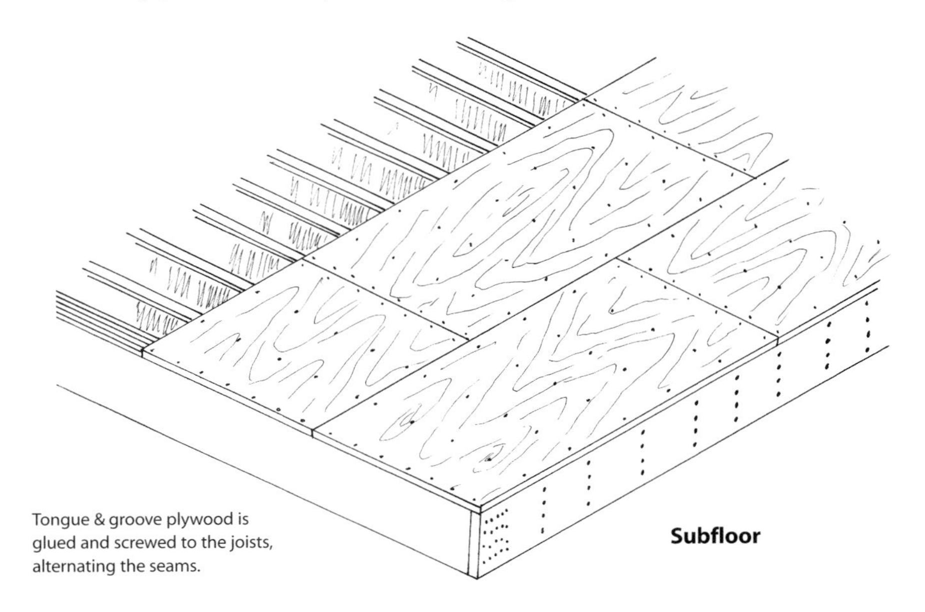

Tongue & groove plywood is glued and screwed to the joists, alternating the seams.

When you're all done, give yourself a pat on the back. Not only have you just saved eight or ten logs, you've made the plumber and electrician happy, and will keep the building inspector from busting you for hacking-up your floor supports.

Walk around the floor and look into the distance. This will be the view you'll see from your windows. Enjoy the flat, clean expanse below your feet, while you can. After today, it will be covered with bark, sawdust and tools, pencil marks, scratches and gouges. So, if you ever wanted to have a dance, now would be the time.

August 1999

The steel beams and posts arrive. Rex maneuvers the old farm tractor into position so he can lift each beam onto the basement walls [9]. After a slip of the chain that almost costs Dave his pickup, Rex and Dave manage to lift and scoot each beam-end down the side foundation walls and into the beam pockets [10]. They are very glad the beams are not any bigger or longer!

Soon the sill plates are on the foundation walls and beams, and next up are the TJI's and rim joists. (Women...it really impresses your husbands if you learn these terms.) After some careful measuring, the joists are in place and the subfloor is glued and screwed down. I can't quite get the screws in far enough half the time, but I make a good attempt at it.

What a nice flat floor! And it definitely looks out of place on this rocky, steep mountain.

Since the weather is good (and trucks can make it up our road), Rex orders the septic tank [11] and infiltrators for the leach field. Gary fires up the excavator (still parked in our trees) to backfill around the foundation, and then digs the trenches, and the hole for the tank. The trenches must be level, so my job is to hold the leveling rod while Rex takes readings through the level and directs Gary with a thumbs up or thumbs down.

CHAPTER 8

PEELING AND LIFTING LOGS

At Long Last, Let the Real Work Commence

LaVonne peels log #45 on a sunny fall day.

PEELING THE LOGS

Ask anyone who has built their own log house what they thought was the hardest part, and chances are they will say "peeling the logs." That may be so—especially if the logs are overly well-seasoned—but it's a necessary step in the process: if you want to join the club you have to pay your dues. But more than that, peeling the logs yourself will help prepare your mind for the next step. You will come to know every knot and hollow in every log, and by doing so you will develop a kinship with your logs that will never waver.

When you remove the bark, you transform a lifeless tree into a unique element of your walls or roof, ready to take on new life in the grand organic gestalt that will one day be your home. Peeling logs, therefore, is a task that should be approached with resoluteness, rather than a sense of dread.

It does not take a great deal of strength to peel logs, though strength is certainly helpful. LaVonne, whose graceful, lithe stature belies her simmering endurance, peeled most of our logs as I notched and set them in the walls. Whenever she ran across a log that was particularly vexatious (of which there were more than a few), I would climb down from the walls and give her a hand. She never gave up on a log, but she certainly appreciated the help whenever she needed it.

I like to remove the knots before the log is elevated for peeling; it's easier on the shoulders and elbows. Some builders like to use an axe for "knot-bopping"; I prefer a small chainsaw. Cut the knots as close as possible to the body of the log to avoid elbow-jarring jolts when the drawknife catches on what you didn't cut off. If you use a chainsaw, wear eye and ear protection. If you don't, you'll soon wish you had.

LaVonne's father, Roger, gets a short lesson before being turned loose with the drawknife.

The peeling environment should be as comfortable as possible. To avoid a chronic backache, elevate the logs to a comfortable height. I made a pair of 34-inch high, heavy-duty sawhorses to set the logs on for peeling. We'd hold the logs in place with cleats or log dogs and peel as much of the log as we could before rolling it. Most logs we could peel in four quarter-turns. Since our home site is on a gentle slope, we moved most of the logs onto the floor for peeling, with one end protruding through the door opening. The level surface kept the logs from sliding as we peeled, and gave us a surefooted surface to work on. After the loft floor beams were set, we had to peel the logs outside of the house.

By the virtue of their added inertia, big logs will slide a lot less than smaller ones as you peel them. To facilitate the peeling of smaller logs, I built another pair of sawhorses with sawbucks (a V-shaped wedge from 2 x 4's) on top. I ran a stout board between the sawhorses, then held them fast to the ground with stakes. For added grip, I affixed an arm to each sawbuck—with a 10-pound lead diving weight on the end—that would drop across the top of the log. This method worked great for purlins, railings, and spindles.

Peel the logs as you need them; you'll avoid spending hours bleaching and sanding off the rained-on, weathered surface.

By the time you're finished peeling, you will have accumulated several cubic yards of peelings. And since you will have run your drawknives over several miles of log surface, they will be begging for a little R & R at the local sharpening shop.

LIFTING LOGS

We began our house with no concise plan of how to move our logs from the ground to the tops of our ever-growing walls. At first we used a pickup to drag the logs in front of a loader-equipped, 60's vintage farm tractor, which we then pressed into service to lift each log onto the wall. This worked well enough until the walls grew higher than the tractor could lift. At that point, we had to do some planning.

I'd used a gin pole before, in the small cabin I built in the 1980's. It was crude, at best: nothing more than a straight pole with a chainfall fastened to the top. But the logs were fairly short and right next to the foundation, so it was enough.

The boom is bolted onto the gin pole

The electric winch, chained to the gin pole boom, pulls in a log to be peeled.

(For my first log house, by contrast, I needed no equipment, since all the logs were short and I had full use of a whole crew of tough, labor-seasoned roofers.)

After a day's deliberation on the matter, we decided to place a gin pole through the center of the floor, like I had years before. The problem before us, however, was not a small one: how can one man and one woman raise a 30-foot pole, 8 inches in diameter, from the horizontal to the vertical? Deliberately, cautiously, and inch-by-inch, we concluded.

I cut out a hole in the plywood between two joists (considerably larger than the diameter of the pole) and boxed the hole with 2 x 10's. I then dropped a plumb bob to the basement floor, marked the spot directly below the hole, and dug down a foot or so into the dirt. Next, I made a chute from three 2 x 4's, fastened together at 45 degree angles, and ran it between the hole in the floor and to the one in dirt below.

We moved the gin pole into position on the main floor, then lifted the top of it as high as we could with the tractor, while the butt of the pole dutifully snuggled against the 2 x 4 chute I'd fashioned to guide it's descent through the floor.

It is a psychological fact that the human mind cannot look at a pole lying flat on the ground and fully grasp just how much longer it will appear when pointed toward the sky. Although the tractor had only raised the pole 35 or 40 degrees, it was beginning to look ominous. But, at that point, there was nowhere to go but up.

Next, I took six of the long 2 x 4's left over from bracing the foundation forms, and nailed them together in long, offset X's. I then nailed 2 x 4 cleats into the floor to keep the X braces from sliding back as we pushed the pole ever higher. By the time we pushed as far as we could with the third set of braces, the log grudgingly slid into the hole.

Admittedly, it wasn't the smoothest operation I've ever been a part of, but it worked. In the end, our gin pole rested in its earthen nest in the basement, and rose 20 feet through the hole I'd cut in the floor.

It worked, yes. But I really can't recommend this method to anyone, without a few modifications. Even though we got the job done, it was a little too risky for comfort. At the very least, two more people should have been placed at offset angles on the backside of the pole, working strong ropes secured to the top of the pole and dallied to trees, or truck bumpers. That way, if the bracing had given out with LaVonne and I under it, neither of us would have been hurt.

However much trouble the gin pole was to erect, it was worth it. Our crude contrivance worked perfectly for us. After adding a well-braced boom to the top of the pole—from which we hung a heavy-duty 120-volt winch—we could easily handle any log in our pile.

Here's how it worked:

I used the loader tractor to lift one end of each log onto the wall. Then, by securing the cable from the winch to the elevated log end, we pulled the log a little past halfway into the house and set the end gently on the floor. At that point, we could hook the winch on the gravitational center of the log and lift it.

Once suspended, it was a simple matter to spin the log onto the wall and roll it into place. I should mention here that this takes a little bit a planning, since the log will have to go to one side of the gin pole, or the other. Just *which* side depends on where you want the log to ultimately end up (right or left; butt end to the east, or to the west, etc.) It's often necessary to pull the log onto one side

A peeled log is lifted onto the house with the tractor.

of the pole and spin it a full 180 degrees to the other side. If this isn't quite clear, don't worry—you'll only do it wrong once.

For those of you not fortunate enough to have access to aging farm machinery with whimsical hydraulics and questionable brakes, there are other methods to pull your logs onto the wall. One way is to erect a second gin pole near the wall where your logs are laid out, with the boom extending out over the wall. The only drawback to this plan is that you will need to move the winch from one gin pole to the other, three-fourths of the time.

Alternately, if you have a door opening on a short wall facing your logs, you can drag each log through it and into the house. From there, simply lift one end onto the wall, then the other.

If all else fails, you can build a log ramp to roll your logs onto the wall. This is achieved by securing two strong logs at low angles to either end of a wall, then attaching a rope to either side of the inside wall. By hanging the rope over the wall and looping it around each end of the log you want to move, the log can be rolled up the ramp by pulling the ropes with a winch. (The one drawback to this system is obvious: with each new course of logs you will have to reset your ramp.)

Variations on this method are possible. With enough help on either side of the rope, you can pull the log up the ramp by hand and possibly dispense with the gin pole altogether. Or attach the winch to a tree—or some other stationary object—on the backside of the house. Without the gin pole, however, each log will have to be manually pushed, pulled, rolled and cajoled into position, once it's on the wall. It can get tiring, after awhile.

If you're fortunate enough to have stout trees on either side of your house, you may want to consider running a steel cable between them, then attaching a winch to a pulley that glides along it.

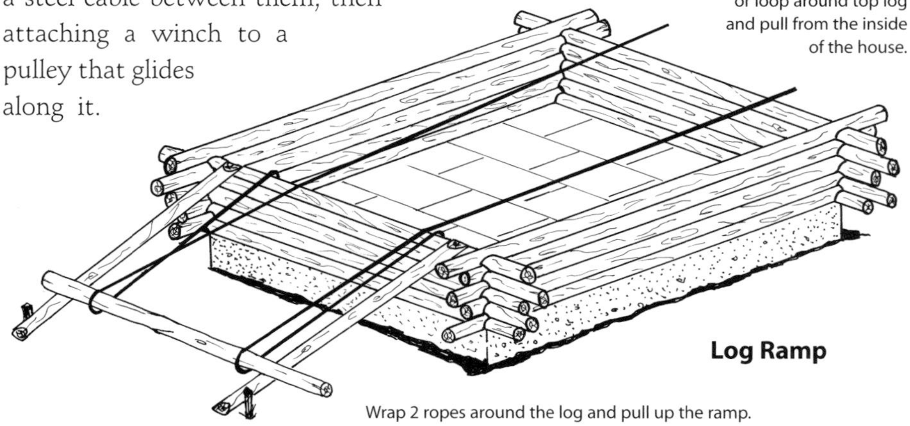

Log Ramp

Called a skyline, you can use this system to lift logs from the pile and safely pull each log over your wall with two ropes attached to the pulley (one for pulling, the other for braking.) If there are no suitable trees nearby, the same thing can be accomplished with a pair of well-secured poles. I would not advise erecting this apparatus, however, without the use of a boom truck and lots of help from someone who truly knows how to do this sort of thing.

Whatever method you use to raise your logs, be careful! Chains break, ropes snap, cables slip and booms shatter under enough stress. Every system ever devised has it's weakest point, and you *don't* want to be in harm's way when it fails. At every moment you should take stock of where you are in relation the log you're working with. What would happen if suddenly the chain broke, or the boom snapped off the gin pole? Never walk under a suspended log, and never stand on the downhill side of a log that's being moved; once a log starts rolling under gravity's tug, there's nothing you can do to stop it.

By way of illustration, in the course of building our house we had one log get away from us as we were fishing it out from between two others. One of our two dogs—the fastest and most agile, thankfully—was walking among the logs on the downhill side at the time. I yelled out, she looked up and saw the huge log barreling her way and—without a moment's hesitation—scurried to safety like a rabbit with its tail on fire. Knowing that neither LaVonne or I could have moved that fast, we were—from then on—humbly sobered into a more acute sense of caution whenever we were moving logs.

Though the process of moving logs may seem disconcertingly arduous at this point, once you settle on the system that's right for you and you set a few logs in place, you'll be amazed at how smooth the work proceeds. With every log, you'll discover a new trick or shortcut that will make this log easier than that one. And by the time you set the last log into place you'll wonder why you ever thought moving and lifting logs was so difficult.

Our neighbor, Josh French, used a boom truck to lift and maneuver his logs.

LaVonne's

LOGBOOK 6

August 1999

The last day of August: Log work has begun, finally! Rex has been anxiously looking forward to this time; I just stare at the big pile of unpeeled logs, wondering, "How long will this take?" Rex cuts the first log in half [12] and bolts each half to the floor. Then we peel and set logs #2 and #3 in position, scribe the notches and cut them. Here we go!

12

September 1999

Log work begins in earnest. The first few logs are easy to maneuver and lift up on the house with the tractor [13]. Peeling logs is, well, work. It helps to have a beautiful fall day to work in...not too hot because you are burning lots of calories. Good music helps. The occasional easy-peeling log is a nice break. But I found that the most important item is a well-designed drawknife. My very own arrived in the

13

mail after Rex got tired of me using his drawknife. Thank goodness we found a good knife from Bosworth, a log home builder in Montana who happened to be on the internet. The ones I bought at antique stores and flea markets can now decorate the walls.

Scribing and cutting notches are Rex's job. I'm worthless with a chisel after 10 minutes, so my job is peeling [14]. I've never been so weary in all my life.

14

CHAPTER 

TOOLS FOR LOGWORK

Essential Implements of the Log Builder's Craft

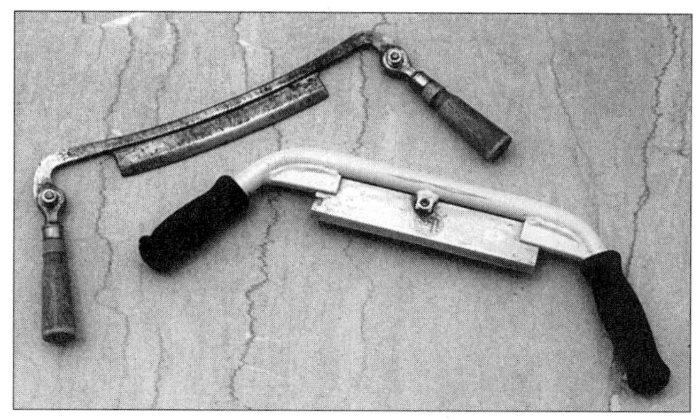

Over the next few months you will personally get to know every one of the dozens of logs in the pile next to your foundation. Some you will like, others you won't. Some you will swear sprouted from the forest floor, years before you were born, for no other purpose than to cause you grief.

Some you will threaten to reduce to cordwood and cast into the stove.

In the end, though, you will love them all. You will love them because each log will have found its special place in your home and—by virtue of that fact—will have become irreplaceable.

Log work is not difficult; at least not in the sense that writing complex software, or rebuilding a car engine, is difficult. But it is physically demanding. Just *how* demanding depends on two things: how much experience you have in working with logs, and how well you have chosen your tools.

While the experience may take a little time, the tools we can address right now.

CHAINSAWS

A log dog on each end holds the log in place and prevents rolling when chainsawing the notch.

Before we began our house, I had three chainsaws: two middle-aged Homelites and a geriatric McCulloch. They all ran pretty good and any one of them was fine for felling and limbing the occasional tree, or cutting up firewood. But none was the saw for building a log home. For that I needed a sleek and mean machine; a saw that was both light and powerful, rugged yet sophisticated. A saw that would start hot or cold, or warm, without my having to alternately curse and plead with it.

After spending a lot of time looking at different makes and models of chainsaws, I finally settled on a Stihl, model 036 Pro. At 12.5 pounds (minus the bar and chain) and 4.6 bhp with a 20-inch bar, it's the perfect saw for someone like me: medium height and build, with good, but not extraordinary, upper body strength. Unless you're a bouncer at a biker bar, building with 18-inch logs, you probably won't want anything much bigger.

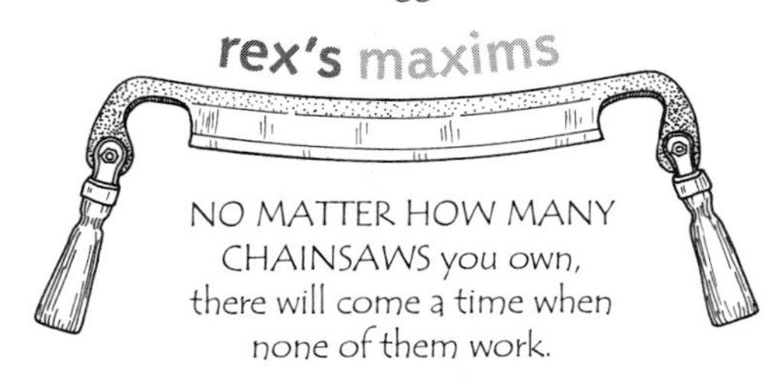

Whatever you buy, don't scrimp. A cheap chainsaw is a world of misery waiting to happen. At the very least, make sure it starts easy and has good anti-vibration buffers. That way your elbows won't ache and your hands won't tingle at the end of the day.

POWER PLANER

Flat-based power planers are useful for everything from planing the treads of log stairs, to giving a smooth, clean finish to cut log ends. Curved-base planers are great for smoothing down knots, knocking bumps off purlins and cleaning up scarf cuts. Though you may be able to get by without a power planer, there will certainly be times when you'll wish you had one. The heavy-duty power planers sold in log home supply catalogs are far better than the cheap models sold in lumber yards, though even they are better than nothing. Compare!—the deeper the cut, the better.

DRAWKNIVES

Next to a junky chainsaw, nothing will cause more needless exertion than a dull, or poorly designed drawknife. It's not easy finding a good one, but once you do you'll think it's worth its weight in gold. Before beginning construction, we perused every flea market we could find, looking for drawknives. We bought three or four that ranged from worthless to passable. Three more knives borrowed from a friend were no better. Then LaVonne found a manufacturer on the internet, a log builder from Montana. He'd finally given up trying to buy a truly good drawknife, and designed and field tested his own. We ordered one, tried it, and quickly ordered another. Our average peeling time for a 50-foot log dropped from a grueling 2 hours, to a relatively smooth 30 to 45 minutes.

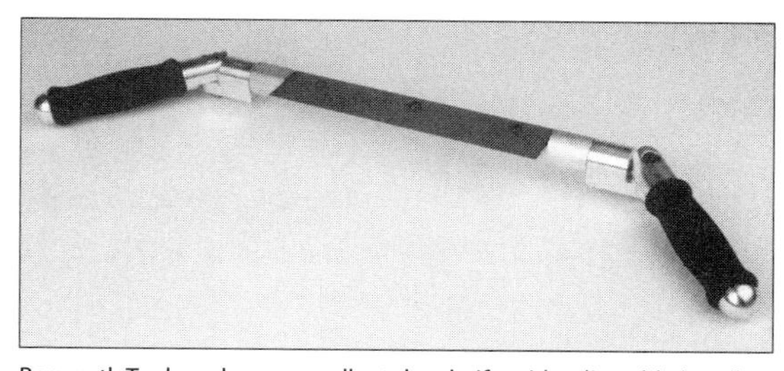

Bosworth Tools makes an excellent drawknife, with adjustable handles. *(photo courtesy of Bosworth Tools)*

Get the heaviest knife you can handle easily, with a long enough blade that you're not constantly running your hands into the log. My knife has a 10-inch blade, LaVonne's an 8-inch. Even her short knife worked fine on 12-inch logs.

CHISELS

A good chisel set is a worthwhile investment. Even if you don't use the whole set during log construction, you will later on when it come times to do the finish work. Get the kind with a steel shank in the handle so you can beat it with a hammer. I bought a set of Stanley chisels and mercilessly pounded the ends with a heavy framing hammer, from the first log to the last, and never did any damage to any of them.

Log home supply catalogs offer a variety of chisels. Most cost more than I'd care to pay, without a compelling reason. So far, I haven't found one.

LOG DOGS AND LOG CLEATS

Log cleat. *(photo courtesy of Schroeder Log Home Supply)*

Log cleats are good for holding logs in the scribing position. Log dogs can be used for particularly stubborn logs that refuse to stay put, and they're more stable than cleats when working with a chainsaw. We made our own inexpensive log dogs from lengths of leftover rebar, and our log cleats with angle and flat iron. If you've got access to a welder and oxy/acetylene torch, it's easy.

SCRIBERS

Veritas scriber. *(photo courtesy of Schroeder Log Home Supply)*

Scribers are used to transfer the shape of one log onto another. Used mainly for notches, you will find them useful for a number of operations. Many commercially available scribers are quite sophisticated and expensive. Most come with two spirit levels to ensure that the contour of the lower log is faithfully traced onto the upper log. Get what you think will work for you. I made my own with pencil rod and a few odds and ends, with a holder at the end for a pencil. To save some hassle next time around, I'll probably buy the real thing.

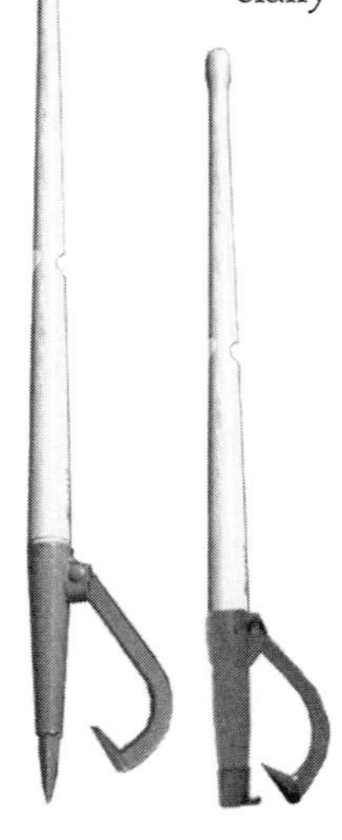

Peavey (left) and cant hook (right). *(photo courtesy of Schroeder Log Home Supply)*

PEAVEY AND STRAIGHT BARS

The peavey and the cant hook are used to roll logs; straight bars to slide, push and lift them. Any hardware store or lumber yard should have a selection of straight bars. Peaveys are a little harder to come by; probably you will have to get one by mail order from a log home supplier. I made my own by cutting a "V" out of a length of pipe, them bending it into a long cone and welding the seam. The hook was made from 3/4-inch rebar.

Admittedly, the shovel handle I used is lighter than the thick handles on commercial peaveys, and as soon as mine breaks I'll probably bite the bullet and buy the real thing.

ELECTRIC WINCH

Logs are heavy, contrary, inertial creatures. Rolling logs is hard enough, but raising them without the right equipment is all but impossible. The mere thought of lifting the wooden beasts has culled many a poor soul who would *like* to build a log house, from the ranks of those who actually do. But the fact is, it's done all the time, and with a minimum expenditure of energy by those who know what they're doing. How? Well, you could lease a boom truck for a couple of months, or hire the Packers' defensive line during the off-season. Or you could invest in a good electric winch. (Of the three, this is definitely the cheapest.) The two manufacturers I know of that make 120-volt winches are Dutton-Lainson, and Dayton, though there are probably others. Find a model that is rated to *dead-lift* your heaviest logs, not just pull them. Spend a little extra for the remote. It will save you the trouble of having to climb a ladder every time you want to lift a log.

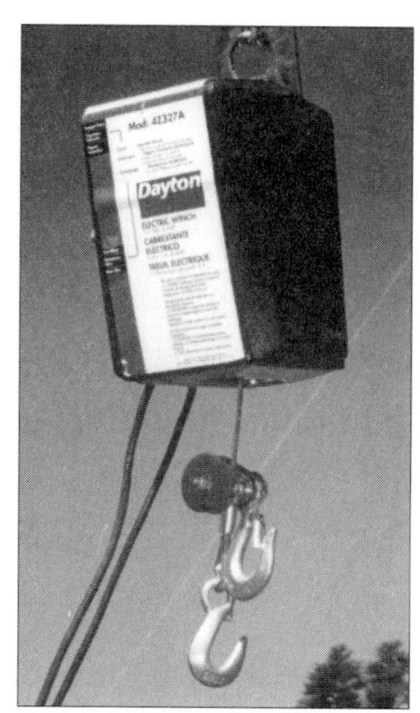

Dayton electric winch.

A logger's tape is handy for measuring the long logs. *(photo courtesy of Schroeder Log Home Supply)*

There are dozens of tools I haven't mentioned here, primarily because I rarely—if ever—use them. Many log builders like to cut all, or part, of their notches with axes. I've personally never gotten the hang of using an axe for much of anything besides splitting firewood, so I can't recommend any particular style of axe.

Bark spuds are used to remove loose bark, thus making drawknife operations easier. On the right logs, a spud would be quite handy, but so seldom do I find a log with loose bark that I've never invested in one.

The same goes for specially-shaped draw knives, adzes, and....well, the list is a long one. I try to buy the tools I *need*, first, and *then* buy the ones that catch my fancy. As long as I actually use the tools I buy, she-who-controls-the-purse-strings lets me slide with a smirk and a sigh.

LaVonne's
LOGBOOK 7

September 1999

Now we need a gin pole. Sounds easy. But I'd rather not repeat this day. I've come to understand that men can deal with the concept of moving heavy things (a troublesome log, in this case) much better than women. I find it intimidating. Believe me...I was very happy to see that gin pole standing upright in the hole at the end of the day!

16

The electric winch on the gin pole's boom is quite easy to use. The tedious part is starting and stopping the generator to use it. A remote starting generator would've been handy. Now we are peeling logs set on saw bucks in the middle of the floor and then lifting them with the winch. The pile of peelings is getting huge, and there is never a shortage of something to sweep when the nieces and nephew show up for an afternoon [15].

Our first, heavy, wet snow is hard to shovel out [16]...up and over the wall it must go.

15

October 1999

I keep peeling and Rex keeps notching. Our future home looks more like a fort than a house. And it will stay that way for many months, since the windows will be cut in after winter.

More logs arrive for the last few wall logs, floor beams, purlins and other roof beams. This log delivery made it closer... only a half mile from the house. Once again we use the home-made log transports for the large logs, and a 12-foot trailer for the purlin logs.

CHAPTER 10

BUILDING WITH LOGS: PART I

Scribing and Notching the First Course

A notch is scribed.

There are two fundamentally different ways to build with full, round logs (as opposed to milled logs, or logs that have been flattened on two or more sides.) The full-scribe (or chinkless) method is preferred by some professional log builders, while the standard practice of simply stacking notched logs and later filling the gaps with chinking is almost universally done by do-it-yourselfers. While each method has its merits, in the end, the method you choose will be based upon your level of expertise, the quality of your logs, the amount of time you have to complete the log work, or simply your own sense of aesthetics.

Not too many years ago, there was no truly durable material available for chinking a log cabin. Moss, mud mixed with straw, dirt and ashes, and masonry mortar were all used with varying degrees of success—or failure. The proponents of full-scribe construction had only to point to the hapless home owner rechinking his house every year to keep the cold arctic breezes out of his bedroom, to prove that their method was superior.

The introduction of synthetic chinking changed all of that. Today's modern chinking materials are strong and pliable, seal tightly with the logs, and last as long as the house. If properly applied, synthetic chinking has excellent insulative properties, and adds an undeniable measure of rustic charm to a log wall.

Our house is chinked. And it's the warmest house I've ever had the pleasure of spending a winter in. It's sealed up so tight we often open a window in December and January, when the wood stove is blazing, just to get a little extra air. I can offer several reasons for our decision to build the way we did. Cutting grooves down the center of each log is time consuming. So is drilling holes in each log for pulling electrical wires throughout the house. Starting late in the season as we did, time was a distant luxury: I don't like shoveling snow out of the inside of a building, and I like roofing in January even less. Nor were our logs the straight, barely-tapered, archetypical logs one admires in million-dollar homes. Far from it. They were an odd assortment that ranged from beautiful to comical. Many had to be straightened with a chain and a come-along before they could be spiked into the wall. Not the sort of logs, in other words, that would ungrudgingly lend themselves to the full-scribe method.

Those are all good reasons for building the way we did, but the *real* reason is not among them. For us, it was a matter of taste, pure and simple. We concluded long ago that we prefer the looks of a chinked house, over a chinkless house. The chinking nicely separates each course of logs, faithfully accentuating every subtle bump and curve, and thus setting each log in its own frame, to be admired as a work of art in its own right.

Even if our logs had been as straight and uniform as utility poles, and we'd had an eternity to build with them, we wouldn't have done anything differently. Except maybe that part about the chain and the come-along.

Chances are, if you're doing all the log work yourself, you will choose to build in the same way we did. I will not, therefore, take the time here to detail the full-scribe method of grooving logs. Not only is it hard to follow a narrative that skips back and forth between differing techniques, it would be dishonest of me to attempt to elucidate a method in which I am not adequately skilled. (For those of you who wish to build a chinkless log home, I refer you to B. Allan Mackie's excellent book, *The Owner-Built Log Home*. As far as I've been able to tell, the word "chinking" does not appear anywhere between the covers.)

MARKING THE FLOOR FOR WINDOWS, DOORS AND SQUARE CORNERS

Before getting to the logs, there are some preliminary details to address. For starters, you'll need to know, within a couple of inches, where you intend to put all the windows and doors in the perimeter walls. That way, you won't run a chainsaw into any steel spikes when the wall is finished and it comes time to cut the openings.

Mark the rough openings for the doors and windows on the floor with an indelible marker (a grease pencil works good for this). Give yourself plenty of room on either side, being sure to allow for the thickness of the bucks you'll install in the openings to hold the doors and windows. Make bold heavy lines that will be visible to anyone straddling a wall several feet up, then connect the lines to clearly define the opening.

(You may not know, with any degree of certainty, where the windows are going until you've set a course or two of logs in place. That's fine. But you'll still need to know where the doors will be so you don't lag a section of log to the floor that will have to be removed later.)

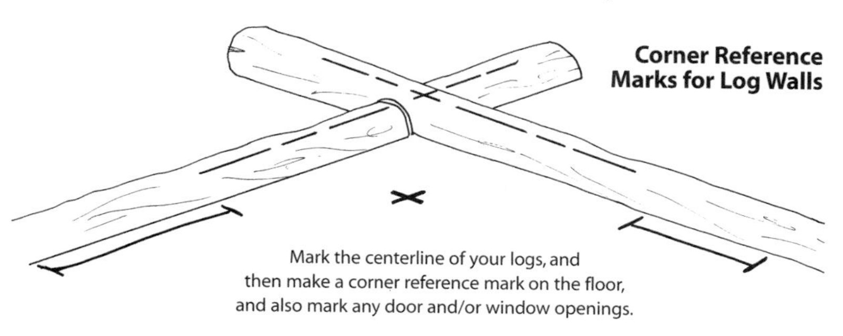

Corner Reference Marks for Log Walls

Mark the centerline of your logs, and then make a corner reference mark on the floor, and also mark any door and/or window openings.

Now, since you won't be able to measure to the outside corners of the floor, once the walls start going up, you'll need new marks inside the log perimeter to use as reference points. To do this, measure perpendicularly in from the edge of floor. (Be sure that your marks will not later be covered with the first course of logs.) Make two intersecting marks in each corner, equal distance in from the edge of the floor. Measure along the floor side to side and corner to corner to make certain the marks are square.

Using a tape measure and a spirit level, you will refer to these marks with each course of logs to keep your walls plumb and square.

The first log is split in half.

THE FIRST LOG

"Log" is singular here, because you'll be cutting it in half, right down the center of the long axis. Since this will be your first log, choose it carefully. Find a log that's straight, with very little taper, and bigger than most.

Set each end of the log on blocks and roll it, looking down the length of it as you do. You'll be looking for straightness. Since you'll be cutting down through the top of this log, any curve that you see should rolled into the bottom position, rather than the side or the top.

When you are satisfied you've found the straightest axis, secure the log with cleats or log dogs, and chalk a line down the center of the log (measure, to be sure).

Using several passes with your chainsaw, cut the log down the center of the chalk line, never going more than a couple of inches deep on any one pass. This will take some time. Use a very sharp chain, and be certain the bar is in good condition, otherwise the cut will veer to one side or the other. Be very careful to maintain a consistent angle with the saw.

If you are not confident that you can do this, I suggest that you buy a bar guide to keep the bar at a consistent angle. Not only will you use it now, for the first log, but also later for steps, purlins, benches, etc.

Before your last two passes, cut the log all the way through in a couple of places on either side of center, and wire the log loosely together at these points. This will prevent the two halves from falling to either side—and breaking where you don't want them to—before you're finished cutting.

When the cut is complete, undo the wire, roll the two halves face-up, and study your work. The cut sides won't be perfectly flat, but they don't have to be; the weight of the house will take care of what the lag bolts don't. Just be sure to level out any irregularities with an axe, adze, drawknife or chainsaw.

Move the two half-logs into position with the butt-ends pointing in opposite directions, and insulate under each one. A thin layer of fiberglass is fine; plastic foam (like you put under the sill plate) is ever better. Find the center point on the end of each half-log and measure across to the other side. Satisfied? Lag the half-logs through the floor and into the beefed-up rim joist below. (Your plans should specify the spacing and size of lag bolts; $^{3}/_{8}$-inch bolts, 4 feet apart should be adequate.)

SECOND AND THIRD LOGS, FIRST NOTCHES

Pick out two nice logs, equal in size and quality to each other, and to the log you've just halved. It's a good idea to mill the bottom side of each of these logs a little, to help them lie flat and to distribute their weight across the floor, though some builders don't bother with this step.

Position each log over the ends of the half-logs and stabilize them with cleats. **Remember: small ends should *always* go over butt-ends, and vice versa.** It is now time to scribe your first notch.

Without a single exception, every hand-hewn full-round log house I have seen built in the last 25 years has been constructed using the saddle notch—or a variation of it—for lacing the wall logs. There are several good reasons for this. First and foremost, the saddle notch is the simplest notch to scribe and cut. In addition, it sheds water as well, or better, than other notches because only the top log is notched. And, since it leaves the logs full-round, and therefore natural, on the ends that emerge from the wall, it's proper execution is a treat to the modern eye that hungers for rustic beauty.

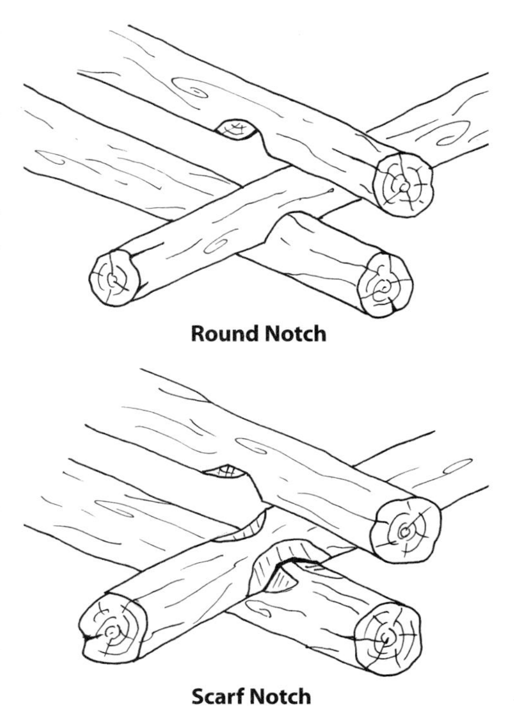

Round Notch

Scarf Notch

The common (round) saddle notch has two drawbacks, however, since there are two conditions that can cause it to open up at the bottom. The first is shrinkage of the lower log. The second occurs when the notch is cut past the widest point of the lower log, since the notch cannot hope to follow the log's curve as it begins to diminish.

For these reasons, some builders prefer to scarf their logs, especially if they're using very large or unseasoned logs. A scarf is simply a cut dished-out with an axe, planer or chainsaw on each side of a log. Incised at a 45-degree angle, it should extend a little below where the top log will rest on the bottom. The scarfs should not meet at the top: leave a couple of inches for the upper notch to settle on. The upper log is then positioned and scribed to match the scarf, taking out a little extra at the top of the notch to allow room for settling. As the log below shrinks, the notch above simply settles, without opening-up. And, with the curve now removed, the notch stays tight, even when it falls below the bottom log's thickest point.

Scarfed notches at the Buckhorn Camp home.

The method you use will depend on the logs you use, or simply your own personal tastes. If you plan to chink your house, it's easy and wise to chink the corners, as well as the walls. In that case—since synthetic chinking materials expand to accommodate joint shrinkage—the reasons for scarfing the logs is not as compelling as it once was.

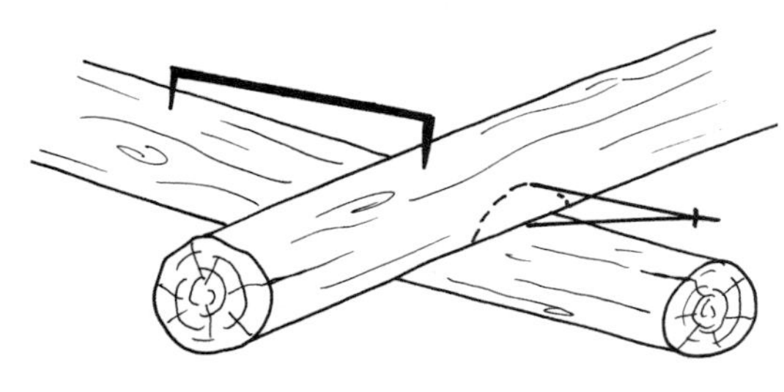

A log dog will prevent the log from rolling as you scribe the notch.

Either way, this is how the scribing and notching is performed:

With the log you wish to scribe resting on the ends of the lower logs, sight along

Setting Scribers for Notching

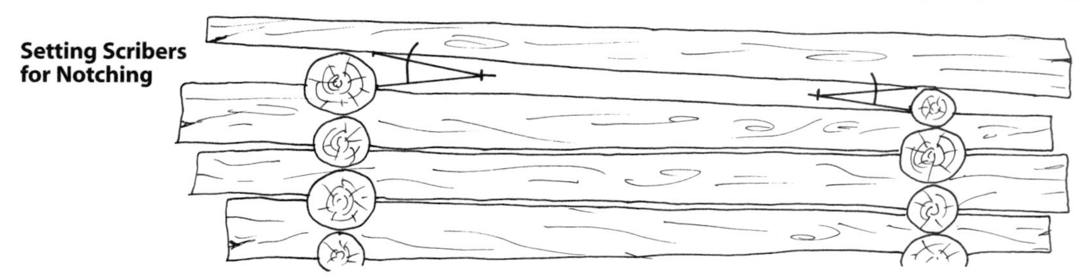

Measure the distance at each cross log to find the setting for the scribers.

the bottom of it to ensure that it follows a straight line from one end to the other. If you milled it, it should. If not, reposition it so that the straightest side is on the bottom (or mill it).

Beginning at one end, adjust the scribers until the points *just barely* slide between the floor and the bottom of the log. Position yourself so the scribers are directly in front of you, and trace the shape of the half-log onto the full one, beginning and ending at the lowest points. Be certain to hold the scribers perfectly vertical as you do this, or your notch will not be true. When you're finished, scribe the outside of the notch, then move to the other end of the log—being certain to reset the scribers, since the space between the floor and the bottom of the log will doubtless be different—and repeat the process.

At this point you will need to decide if you want the ends of the half-log to stick out past the edge of the foundation wall. If there will be a deck directly beneath it, you may want to leave them; if so, cut the full notch. On the other hand, if the half-log end is just going to hang out there, you may consider hiding it for a cleaner look. For this option, cut the notch only to the middle of the log, and then lop off the end of the half-log below, to hide it in the half-notch.

After scribing, the log is rolled over and kerfs are cut with the chainsaw.

Roll the log back 180 degrees (so the notch is facing up) and secure it so it doesn't roll off the end of the wall—and onto the napping dog below—when you start cutting. Before cutting the full notch, the scribe line should be legible all the way around the log. You will probably have to extrapolate on the bottom, where the lines peter-out; just join the two line ends with a straight line and you've got it.

Now the fun begins. Using a chainsaw, make a series of vertical cuts through the area enclosed by the line. Don't try to cut right to the line—you can't do it consistently, and it will make for a ragged-looking notch. Cut a series of parallel kerfs, leaving $^1/_2$ to $^3/_4$ inches of wood in between.

Next, take a hammer and knock out whatever wood

readily breaks loose, then use a chisel (my all-time favorite is the $1^1/_4$ inch) to cleanly incise around the line and an inch or so into the log.

There are several ways to proceed from this point. Sometimes I'll finish the notch with a chisel, other times I'll go back and clean it out with the tip of the chainsaw. It just depends on the log and how big of a hurry I'm in. However you do it, leave the notch a little dished-out in the center to allow some space for insulation and for irregularities in the log below. Bend down and, with one eye closed, sight along the edge of the notch. If all you see is the other side of the notch, then it's deep enough.

Repeat the process on the other end of the log. Lay a thin layer of fiberglass insulation on the log below, and roll the top log onto it. It will fall into place with a triumphant *whump*!

Check to see that the notches lie down snugly on top of the lower log. Modify the curves of the notches, if necessary. (If you use a double-level scriber, it won't be.) If they ride a little high, find any high spots in the log between

After knocking out the wood remnants, the inside of the notch can be cleaned with a chainsaw. Edges are best done with a chisel.

the notches, mark them, roll the log 180 degrees, and flatten them with a chainsaw or adze. Once it fits, cut your notches in the log at the opposite end of the floor. Don't lag down either log until they both fit snugly onto the logs below, and you have made certain your corners are square.

MAKING IT SQUARE (and Keeping it That Way)

One of the reasons we love logs so much is the fact that they are never perfectly straight or perfectly round. This makes them beautiful. Technically speaking, it also makes them topologically unquantifiable. You can't locate the center of a log with the same accuracy as you can measure to the middle of a 2 x 4, but, by the same token, your eye cannot discern geometric irregularities nearly as easily. In other words, if your wall logs veer a *little*, here and there, the overall effect is neither unpleasing nor problematic.

The idea, however, is not to let the walls go willy-nilly, but to keep them as square and plumb as you can, while at the same time understanding that perfection is fundamentally impossible.

Bearing this in mind, it's time to make the first course of logs as square as possible before lagging them down. Begin by marking the center of each end of the notched log with a short line that runs with the long axis, and intersect it with another line representing the center of the half-log below it.

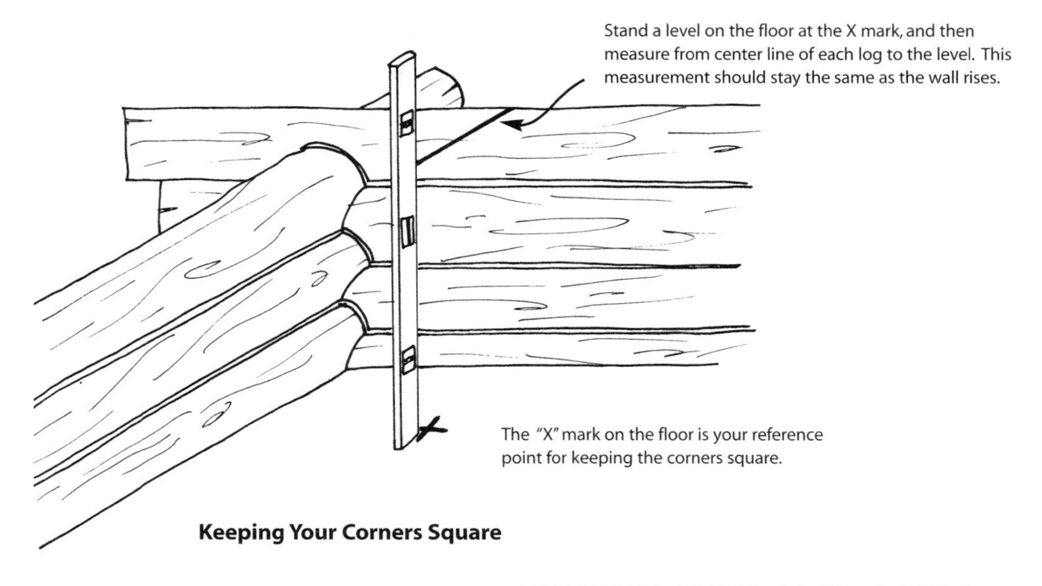

Keeping Your Corners Square

Measure from these marks along all four sides to make sure your distances are equal, then measure corner to corner to make it square. Remember the marks you made on the floor, earlier? You will want to position the logs so the center point of each is equidistant from those marks. When you're satisfied the first course of logs is as square as it's going to get, lag down the two end logs and pat yourself on the back; you're on your way!

STANLEY JOHNSON: CHAINSAW WIZARD

If someone had told me about Stanley Johnson and the way he goes about notching logs, I would have had a hard time believing what I was hearing. It's good then, that I first saw him do it with my own eyes.

Stanley is the crew foreman for Log Knowledge, a well-regarded custom log home company out of Fort Collins, Colorado. He's been building log homes for over 20 years. He and his crew were up in our neck of the woods, resetting a home (for a friend of ours) they had built months before in their log yard. Because of a glitch in the foundation plans, four logs had to be replaced with new ones, notched on site.

Two un-notched logs were set on the wall, and four guys descended on them in a flurry of activity; first with double-bubble scribers, then with chainsaws. None bothered with chisels (too time-consuming, I was told). Three of the four first traced their notches with razor blades, to keep the wood from chipping out as they cut down to the line.

Then there was Stanley. He didn't bother with a razor blade. Instead, he held the saw upside down, so the teeth would cut in from the edge, rather than out. First, he cut out large wedges with the chainsaw, and knocked them free with his hammer. Then he skillfully feathered the edges down to the line with the upside-down saw. He finished off the notch in under 3 minutes. He made it look about as easy as removing the seeds from split cantaloupe with a spoon. And when he rolled the log into place, you wouldn't have been able to slide a piece of paper under the notch.

Stanley Johnson finishes up a 3-minute perfect notch.

Even though it works for Stanley, I've never tried this, and I'm sure I never will. Neither will any of the other guys on Stanley's crew. It's dangerous, to say the least. Not only does it change the whole dynamics of chainsaw operation, it obviates the usefulness of the chain-brake. So, unless you're one-in-a-million with a chainsaw, you'd better plod along with a right-side-up saw and a sharp chisel, like the rest of us.

CHAPTER 11

BUILDING WITH LOGS: PART II

Building the Walls and Tying-in Second-Floor Beams

If you don't feel like a bona fide log home builder after the first course, you will long before the walls are finished. Any hesitancy you feel toward choosing and notching logs will soon be replaced with focused confidence, especially after you've worked your way through a blunder or two. Just don't let the rarified air from the top of fifth course make you giddy; there's always planning to do, and the higher you go the more critical it becomes.

Laying the rest of the wall logs is not fundamentally different from setting the first course, but there are additional considerations and tricks of the trade that will be helpful as you work your way ever higher.

CHOOSE YOUR LOGS WELL

Picking out the logs for each course is a little like playing chess; you need to be able to think past the next move. A log that will solve a problem now may cause a bigger one later. This is especially true if your logs have a lot of taper, since you will always notch the small end over the big end (and vice versa), and big and small are often awkward bedfellows. At times it may seem that you've worked your way into a trap you can't get out of, but it isn't so. If it were, the back-country landscape would be dotted with half-completed log homes and "4 Sale—Cheap!" signs, because everyone feels whipped at one point or another. In the course of building three log structures, I have yet to reject a log, once it's been notched, though there were several I *wished* I hadn't notched. If asked today, however, to point out a single blunder on any of my log work, I'd be hard pressed to find it. In the end, it all works out.

On extremely rare occasions, it may be necessary to run a log in reverse order; that is, to put a big end on another big end, and small on small. Think the consequences through before doing this, however, since it's nothing you want to try unless there is no other way to level the wall.

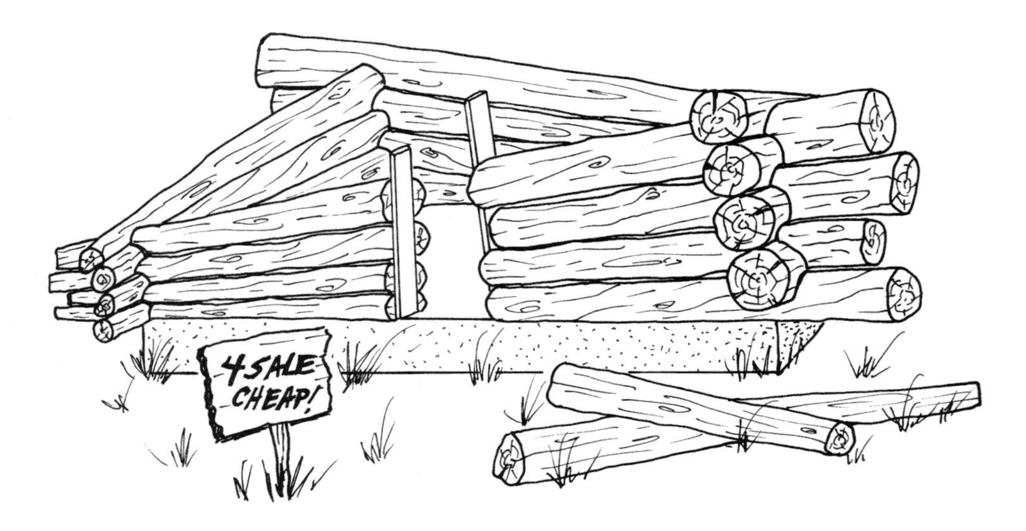

Generally, you will want to begin with your biggest logs and finish with the smallest ones. That's not really a rule, however; it's more of a theme. Often a log will be of greater diameter than the one below it. Again—you'll do what you have to do to make it work.

The most important thing to consider when picking out logs is to avoid extremes—notches that are either too deep, or too shallow—because it will probably get even worse on the next course. If you have to bite the bullet and leave a bigger gap in the wall than you wanted, do it. It's better than the alternative. And when the chinking is all done, you won't even see it.

Whenever possible, hide large cracks (checks) on the downside of the wall. That way, they won't trap moisture, and you won't need to fill the crack with caulking or chinking.

Position large cracks (checks) on the downside of the wall.

SCRIBING CONSIDERATIONS

You will always set the scribers for each notch by adjusting them to the space between the log you are going to scribe and the one below it. But exactly *how* you set them depends on what you hope to achieve. I try to get my logs to fit as close together as possible. If your logs fit so tight you have to climb the walls to see what your dog is barking at, you're doing fine.

Carefully observe the repose of each log as you roll it back and forth on the wall. Every log will have its optimum position, and it's your job to find it. If there is a bit of a curve in the log, roll it to the outside. You can pull all or most of it in, after the notch is cut and the ends are spiked down, by using a come-along secured to the gin pole or a lower log on the opposite wall.

Once the log is in viewing position, look for high and low spots along the gap. If you set your scribers for maximum depth on

A come-along is used to pull in a log that curved slightly outward.

Removing Bumps & Knots for a Snug Fit

For tight-fitting notches and logs, mark the bumps and knots to be removed with the chainsaw.

Knots and bumps can be removed with a chainsaw.

each end, how much chainsawing will have to be done in the middle? My usual self-delusional answer to that question is, "not all *that* much." Then I spend the next half-hour running a chainsaw back and forth between logs until my notches finally lie down. You may not be as militant about tight-fitting logs as I am, and it's certainly not imperative that your logs fit so snugly. But the better they lie down at this stage, the less settling there will be later on.

On the other hand, long, unsupported gaps (and there will be a few!) should be shimmed every few feet to keep the wall from sagging later.

SPLICING LOGS

Long walls are often built with two carefully picked logs per row, spliced at the intersection of an interior log wall. The butt-joints are then hidden by the notches of the intersecting logs. To keep the joints from spreading, you should spike each of the adjoining ends, then connect them together with a piece of steel banding, held in place with 20 penny nails.

A long log wall is spliced in the center of a perpendicular log wall in Benshoof's home.

INTERIOR LOG WALLS

Interior log walls can add a nice touch to any home, and they're a slick way to hide the butt ends of spliced logs on the exterior wall. Curved openings are a particularly eye-catching use of interior logs.

An interior arch in Benshoof's home.

SPIKING THE LOGS

Unlike the first course, where the logs were lagged to the floor, the subsequent courses can be held together with spikes. The length of spike you'll need will vary, depending on the size of the logs, but $^{3}/_{8}$-inch x 12-inch spikes work well for most logs.

Some builders spike the corners, and the walls near the corners, then drive heavy rebar into predrilled holes next to door and window openings, leaving long stretches without spikes. I, on the other hand, like my spikes 3 to 4 feet apart, and staggered with each course. I place a spike near each corner and next to all window and door openings. Some builders advocate placing spikes through the notches, others don't. If there are enough spikes in the walls, it's doubtful the notches are going to shift.

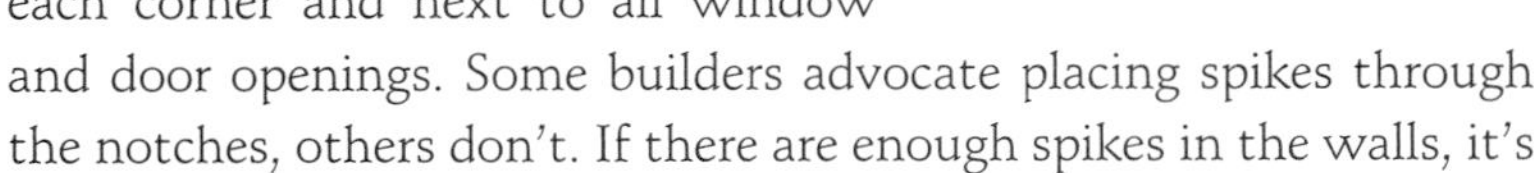

Countersink the wall spikes so that half the spike is driven into the log below. Even if the spike is plenty long, countersinking is still a good idea, since it keeps the spike from pushing into the log above as the wall settles.

Drive spikes with a hand-sledge or a rigging axe; a framing hammer just doesn't command enough authority. Unless you're a glutton for punishment, pre-drill the holes (a little smaller than the spike—you don't want it to be *too* easy). Once you've hammered the head of a spike a little ways into the countersink hole, use a piece of rebar or a bolt to drive it home. And do yourself a favor—hold onto the rebar with locking pliers. There's nothing like hitting yourself in the back of the hand with a 4-pound sledge to muddy the rainbow accents of an otherwise beautiful day.

Spiral or smooth spikes can be used for anchoring logs.

When you think you've built your wall high enough above a door or window opening that you can safely spike the logs, think again, just to be sure. Not only do you have to allow for the thickness of the door or window buck, but also for the distance the house will settle above it. If in doubt, wait until the next course to spike above the opening. A spike can ruin an expensive saw chain in the blink of an eye.

DOOR AND WINDOW OPENINGS

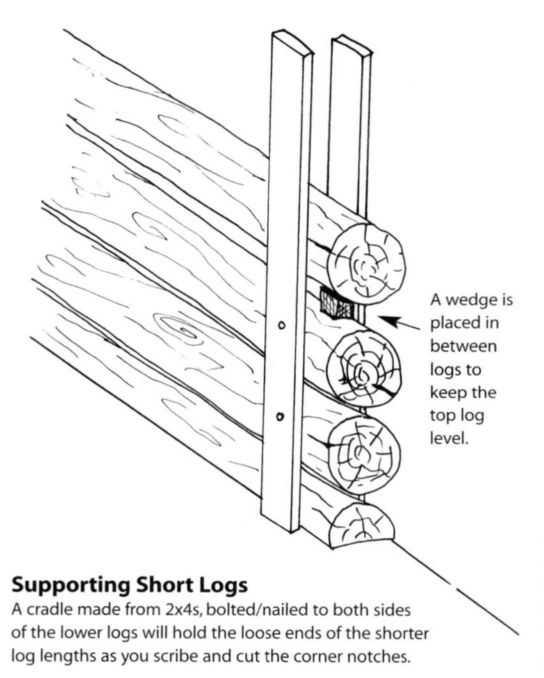

Supporting Short Logs
A cradle made from 2x4s, bolted/nailed to both sides of the lower logs will hold the loose ends of the shorter log lengths as you scribe and cut the corner notches.

It's common to use log ends and short pieces to build the walls segments between window and door openings, but it can also be exasperating, if you're not careful. Differences in log thickness—from one side of the opening to the other—can add up by the time you reach the top and tie-in the two sides with a single log.

If you can, build with logs that run the full length of the wall and cut the holes later; otherwise choose your logs with care. Make sure the grain runs the same direction, on both sides of the opening. If you do resort to piecing a wall together, you will have to find a way to elevate the log end at the opening, and to keep it from rolling off the wall as you work with it. A pair of 2 x 4's nailed to either side of the wall, with a spacer board in between is usually enough to hold the loose log end in place.

Watching the walls grow higher every day is a constant source of pride and wonderment. Each night, as we walked wearily back to the cabin, we'd turn and admire what we'd done, and the sense of accomplishment we felt was worth every sore muscle, every nick and scratch and bruise. And when the walls were at last complete, we knew we had indeed scaled one very high hurdle on the long, arduous path to our dream.

MEASURING WALL HEIGHT

Every log should be set using the method described in the last chapter to keep the walls plumb and square. As the walls become higher than the level, simply wire the level to a long straight board. At that point, it will become a two-person operation to take accurate measurements. If the walls are exceptionally high, or you don't trust a spirit level over such a distance, you can suspend a plumb bob from a stick with the proper distance marked along its length. It will take a little longer, but your measurement will be true.

> **rex's maxims**
>
> IF YOUR WIFE SAYS it is time to quit for the day, dinner will be much more pleasant (and more than peanut butter and jelly) if you agree.

It's also a good idea to monitor the height of the walls frequently—but not incessantly. It's easy to drive yourself buggy by taking constant measurements of the height of your walls, when it really isn't necessary. Even if you manage to do the impossible and get them perfect at some point, you won't be able to keep them that way; the next two courses will certainly undo all your hard work. That's just the way logs are.

Since logs are stacked big end to small, ideally only the even numbered courses will be the same height on either end. Measure the height on each end of every other course, and one or two places in the middle, by resting a level on the top of the log and measuring down to the floor. If you're an inch or two off, either from end to end, or from one wall to the other, choose your next logs accordingly. As you approach the top, all measurements become more critical, and your choice of logs needs to be even more exacting.

Before the final wall logs are spiked down, measure again along the sides, across the ends, and corner to corner. If you've been vigilant about keeping the walls square and plumb, little or no adjustment should

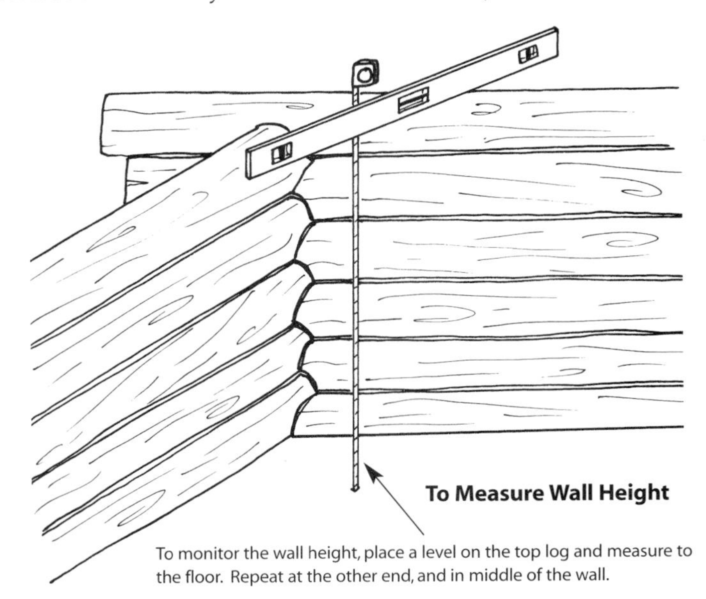

To Measure Wall Height

To monitor the wall height, place a level on the top log and measure to the floor. Repeat at the other end, and in middle of the wall.

be required at the top to bring the walls into alignment.

While you certainly want your height measurements to be equal all around, it is especially important that each wall be the same in height along its length. If two opposing walls are a little different in height, it will easier to adjust than if a wall varies in height from one end to the other. This is particularly true if you plan to construct your roof using conventional framing techniques, since you will need to shim the plate the rafters rest on in ever diminishing degrees to make it level.

TYING-IN FLOOR BEAMS

When it comes time to tie-in the beams that support the second floor, you may need to willfully violate the rule that dictates only the upper log is ever notched, since these structural beams should never be cut more than one-third of the way through. You'll be much better off if you avoid cutting any of the structural beam; instead notch the logs above and below it.

With the second-floor log beam resting on the walls, measure from the top surface of the beam to the first floor on both ends *(see illustration below)*, and

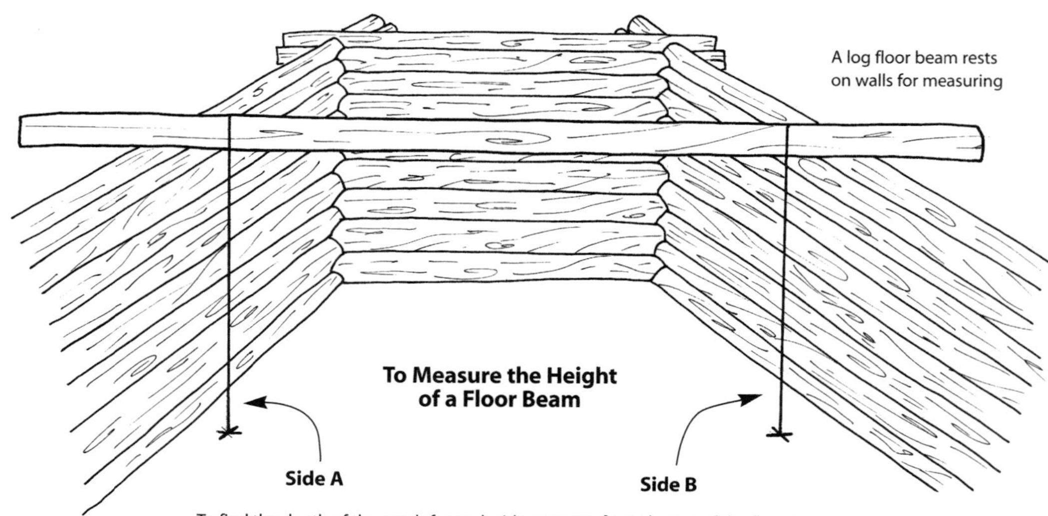

To find the depth of the notch for each side, measure from the top of the floor beam (where the upper floor will rest) to the floor below. Then adjust the notch depth accordingly so the top of the floor beam is perfectly level.

Example: If side A measures 105"; and side B is 106"; the notch will be 5" deep on side A for a finished height of 100"; and notch B will be 6" deep. Set the scribers accordingly.

Two floor beams are leveled and notched into place, and the next log (with 4 notches) is ready to be rolled over.

adjust the scribers to make it come out the same height, once the notch is cut into the wall log. Measure again, after the notches are cut and the beam is rolled into place. If level, securely spike the floor beam into the lower log. Then scribe the upper logs around it, as if it were a corner notch. Simple.

What may not be so simple is deciding which course of wall logs to notch the beams into. There are two things to consider as you ponder this. First, the lower log notch that cradles the beam should never be cut more than halfway through, since there will be a tremendous amount of weight resting on just a few square inches of log. Also, you will need to factor in how much your house will settle after the beams are in place.

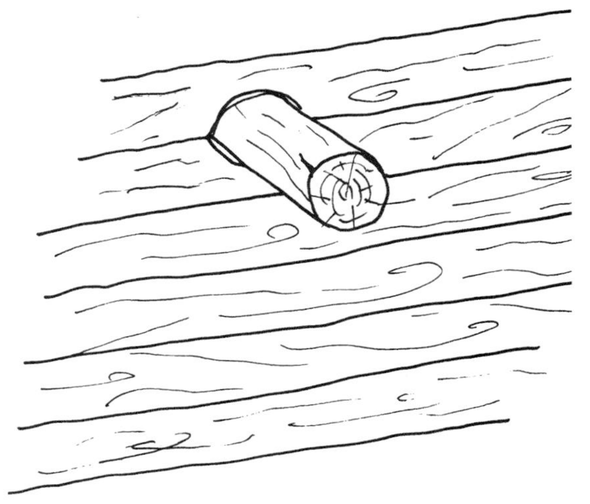
Exterior View of a Floor Beam
The logs below and above the structural floor beam are notched.

How much will your house settle? You can figure anywhere from as much as 3/4-inch per foot for green logs, to as little as 1/8-inch per foot for well-seasoned lumber.

We set our floor beams at a little over 100 inches, allowing for 2 inches of settling (about $1/4$-inch per foot) and another 2-$1/4$ inches for the finished floor ($3/4$-inch hardwood over 1-$1/2$ inches of low-density concrete, in which our radiant-floor heating tubes were embedded). It worked out fine, though we were actually a bit surprised that our dry, tight-fitting logs settled the full 2 inches. The point is, a high ceiling is far preferable to a low one, so leave yourself plenty of latitude.

INSTALLING THE SECOND FLOOR

If the walls will continue a few feet above the floor beams, it's a good idea to take the time to install the second floor, now. It has to be done sooner or later, anyway, and it will make the remainder of the wall-work easier and safer. As with the main floor, you will simplify things for the electrician and plumber if you elect to use wooden I-joists for the floor supports. Otherwise, careful planning will be needed to avoid cutting away the structural support the joists provide.

Square the joists and the plywood subfloor with the points marked on the first floor (the ones you used to keep the walls square and plumb). By dropping a

Second floor joists are set on log floor beams, with shims under any low spots. The ends of the joists are then trimmed even for the loft opening.

The subfloor in the loft is glued and screwed down.

plumb bob on both ends to the marks below, you can run a line to determine where the first joist should be set, then measure all the other joists from it. The plywood subfloor, in turn, can be laid out in the same way.

The butt-ends of the I-joists can either be notched into the wall—deep enough to allow adequate support—or a solid rim joist can be bolted to the wall and the joists connected to it with metal joist hangers. The rim joist method is the fastest, and it provides an extra support for attaching the ceiling below.

THE LAST LOG

Wind passing over a roof tends to lift the whole structure, just like air passing over an airplane's wings. To make sure your roof stays where it is, you should lag the top course of logs to the course of logs below. It may seem excessive, but the first time a 140 mph gus hits your house, you'll be glad you did.

Drip Edge/Flashing

To keep water from coming in under your first round of logs, add a metal drip edge (flashing) to the outside edge of your subfloor that extends over the rim joists. We also chinked on top of our flashing, sealing it to our bottom log.

17

October 1999

We set the two log floor beams [17], and with only a few more rounds of wall logs to go, we must get more creative on how to lift the logs onto the house. The winch can't be used to lift logs from the inside with the loft floor beams in the way, so we peel logs outside the fort and then lift them onto the wall, one end at a time, with the farm tractor...it's questionable brakes make for a couple of dicey moments.

November 1999

Thank goodness my advertising clients are understanding about the wind whistling through the cell phone as I work on the house.

A load of lumber is delivered for the loft floor, which we install before finishing the walls. It is much easier standing on the floor, than perching ourselves on ladders. Rex always tips the delivery drivers, and it pays off in prompt delivery and careful service.

Yea! End of November and I am done peeling logs (for a while). The last two logs were not easy-peelers...they were very green and full of sap. Or maybe they just seemed more difficult than the others because I knew they were the last two logs of the year. (It's the same idea that the last 100 miles of a big road trip are always the longest.)

A most memorable day was the Saturday afternoon when Rex cut his knee with a chainsaw. "Why waste a perfectly good afternoon at the hospital?" he said. "I'll stitch it up myself." Good grief!! Cowboys.

The last two logs are on the house [18], and we are going to town to celebrate (if we don't fall asleep from exhaustion). The celebration continues: we cut the gin pole in half and drag it out. Now we can put in the loft floor.

18

CHAPTER 

GABLES AND DORMERS

Design Ideas to Accent Your Roofline

Long before the walls are finished you'll be thinking about the roof. Having shoveled 3 feet of snow out of our house before managing to get it covered, we thought about the roof a lot. When we weren't dreaming about the time when we no longer had to cover all of our tools and run for the shed every time a pregnant cloud passed overhead, we were thinking of ways to simplify the roof, without sacrificing the rustic, hand-hewn look we'd worked so hard to achieve with the rest of the house.

The technique we used was not original, but it was clever. Original or not, the result was even more than we'd hoped for. We did it for the simple reason that it served our needs at the time, since our blueprints called for heavy, trussed gable ends that would have had to be set with a boom truck; an unlikely prospect at the top of a steep, icy road in the dead of winter.

Invariably, every visitor to our home finds the loft ceiling to be the most impressive part of the house. Though LaVonne and I are a bit partial to the split-log stair, we have to agree that the overhead log work nicely amplifies the hand-crafted character of the rest of the house. It was an effect we achieved by taking a very simple roof design and adding embellishments later, after the structural members were covered and dry. I'll discuss our solution to a vexing problem over the next two chapters.

Rather than cloud a complex issue even more than necessary, this chapter is devoted solely to gable ends and dormers. While it is true that the roof members and the gable ends are woven together into a single structure, it is equally true that any roof system can be made to work with any gable end design, and vice versa. So, by first deciding on a gable end design, you will be able to proceed to the roof with half the problem solved.

The gable ends are one of the first things a person notices when they see a house for the first time. They are, in my estimation, a defining feature of any log house. If they are done tastefully and in concert with the rest of the structure, the gable ends can add an extra dimension of beauty to an already striking house.

There are three basic styles of gable ends: full log, vertical log, and the standard frame type.

A large gable end is set with a crane at Benshoof's home. This south-facing wall will be filled with windows, between the vertical logs.

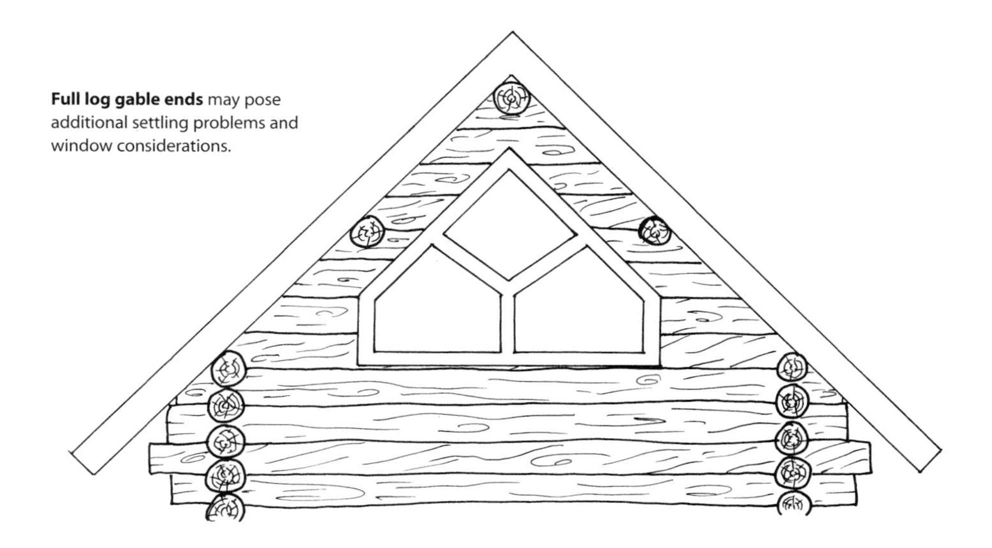

Full log gable ends may pose additional settling problems and window considerations.

FULL LOG GABLE ENDS

Many consider full log gable ends to be a standard feature on any *real* log house. What, after all, could be more natural than continuing the walls right up to the peak of the roof? Nothing, obviously. It's a style that is often used today with very pleasing results.

Before you build with full log gable ends, however, there are a couple of things you need to ask yourself. First, how steep is the roof going to be? Since it is the nature of stacked logs to settle, the steeper the roof the more settling will become an issue. On a modern house, where plumbing vents, furnace stacks and stove pipes emerge through the roof from fixed points below, a roof that changes angle (pitch) appreciatively because of settling can cause a number of problems, all of which need to be addressed. With low-pitched roofs, where the gable ends are not so high, the problems are less severe, but still worthy of consideration.

The best way to deal with settling is to build the gable ends with dry logs, and allow them to sit in place for several months before completing the roof. Any settling that occurs after that should be slight. If this isn't feasible, then you may want to install "floating" rafters or roof beams, with slotted attachments to the purlins that allow them to slide up as the gable ends settle.

Heavy, permanently-fixed window bucks, capable of supporting the roof, are often used with full log gable ends. They will stop all settling wherever the weight of the roof bears directly over them, but not on the unsupported log ends. So, again, they should only be used with well-seasoned logs.

VERTICAL LOG GABLE ENDS

When building the gable ends from vertical logs or heavy, milled timbers, you can avoid the headaches inherent in full log construction. Only the top members will bear any lateral load, so shrinkage and settling are no longer an issue, and with the enhanced support of the vertical members, windows can be of virtually any size. It is, in fact, quite common to build vertical log gable ends and fill every space in between with glass.

The amount of engineering required for the design and construction of vertical log gable ends depends entirely on how the roof will be constructed. If, for instance, you plan to use load-bearing purlins running the length of the roof, the load transferred to the gable ends will be substantial, and a considerable amount of engineering may be required. On the other hand, if you build the roof using dimensional lumber (or T.J.I.) rafters of sufficient strength and spacing to support the roof without the purlins, the load transferred to the gable ends is insignificant. In this case, their design and execution is greatly simplified.

(It's been my experience that building departments are a bit reactionary when it comes to log structural matters. That is, they will either calculate that the purlins [and log beams, if you need them] will support *all* of the roof, or *none* of it. They don't care to assign percentages to any part of a roof system. So, if all you have to do is change the spacing, or the size, of your rafters to swing the pendulum from one extreme to the other, it's probably worth it. Though it may be a little insulting to see "decorative only" red-penciled next to your heavy beams and stout purlins on the blueprints, at least you're off the hook.)

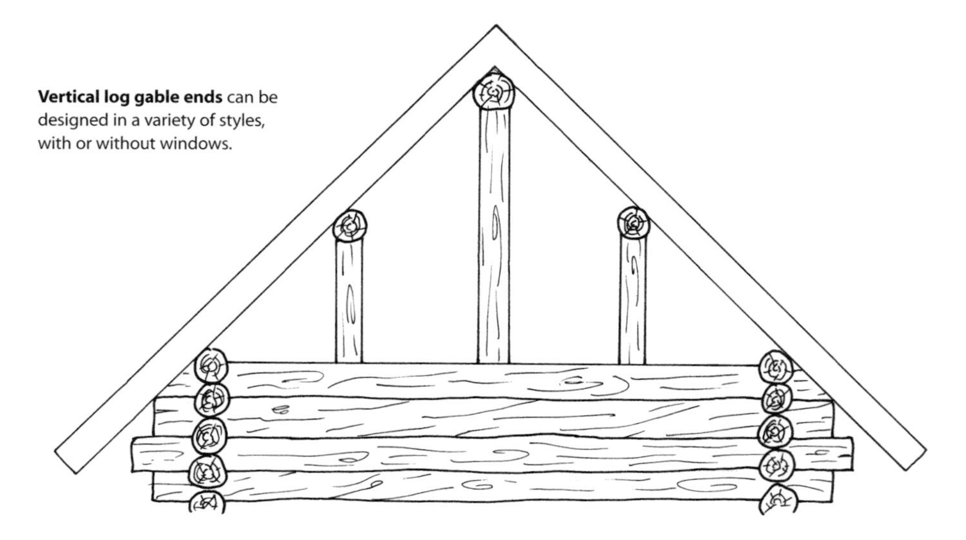

Vertical log gable ends can be designed in a variety of styles, with or without windows.

Vertical log gable ends in another style.

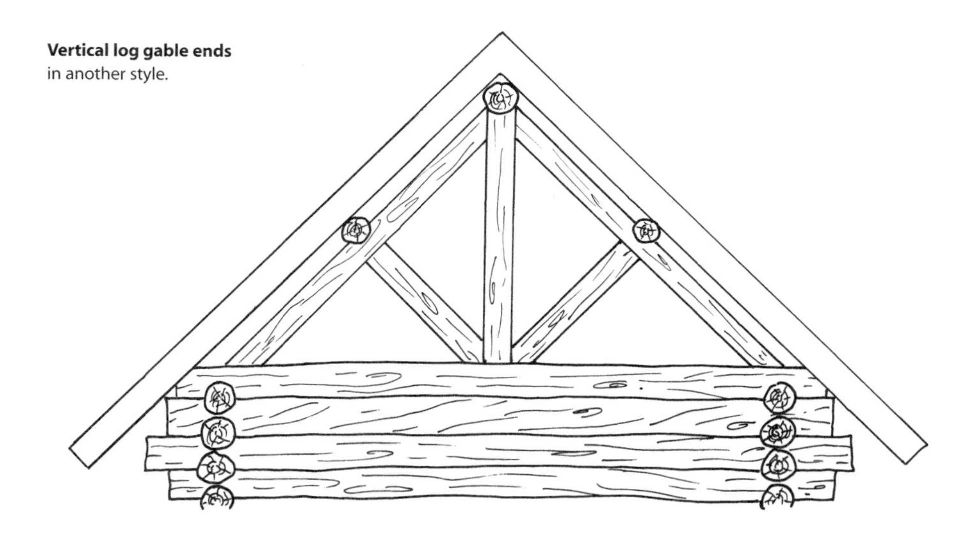

There are two things to keep in mind if you plan to build your own vertical log gable ends: first, it will be much easier completing the gable end if all the log members are milled on two sides. Whether you plan to fill the spaces with windows, logs, or standard framing for stucco or siding—flat, straight sides are a must.

You might be able to pull this off with a chainsaw and a chalk-line. (I did this on my first log house; it worked, to a degree.) But if you have a saw-guide, or a chainsaw mill, or a friend at the local sawmill, you may be happier with the results.

Secondly, you will need to decide how to connect the members together. You can do this with any of a legion of complex notches (which the building department may or may not buy), long bolts, or you can use gusset plates, which are simply pieces of flat steel ($^3/_{16}$ or $^1/_4$-inch thick). Hidden gusset plates fit into slots cut into the truss members and held in place with countersunk bolts. For a nearly-seamless appearance, the countersink holes can be filled with dowel segments.

Setting vertical log gable ends will be tricky if they're being placed on walls several feet above the floor. Your best bet is to build them on the ground and set them with a boom truck. If that's not feasible, you may be able to slide them onto the wall using a log ramp, then raise them with ropes and a winch.

Whatever you do, have a plan before you start; you don't want to be forced to improvise as you go along.

Gusset Plates

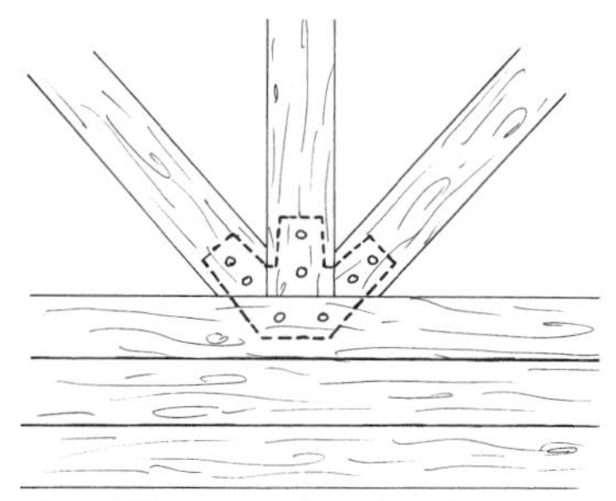

Use hidden gusset plates for a clean look.

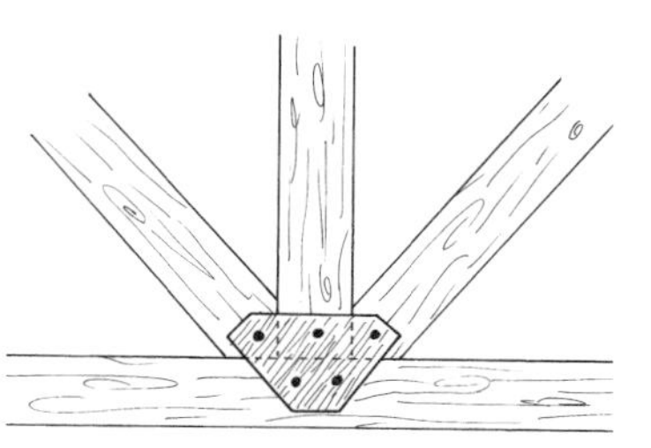

Gusset plates can be a decorative element.

FRAMED GABLE ENDS

At first blush it might seem that framing the gable-ends with dimensional lumber is a cop-out, so inconsistent with the rest of the house that you wouldn't be surprised if the log home police came and hauled you away for even thinking about it. But it just ain't so. It's done all the time, often with spectacular results. Some of the most beautiful log homes ever built have framed gable ends, and your's could be one of them.

Some people frame their gable ends to save time and labor; some do it out of desperation. Others, I've been told, actually plan to do it, all along. Whatever category you fall into, you have lots of company.

By building your gable ends in this seemingly pedestrian way, the sky is the limit as far as the effect you hope to achieve. (The same holds true, of course, for vertical log gable ends.) An exterior finish of stucco, or stucco with stone, can be a complimentary contrast with the logs below. To achieve the vertical log look, split logs can be attached to the wall before the stucco is applied. Wood siding and wood shingles are also widely used with pleasing results. Often vertical logs are inserted within the dimensional lumber walls to accent windows or serve as purlin supports. The point is, wherever your imagination takes you, you can probably find a way to make it happen with framed gable ends; you'll certainly increase your window options by building the gable ends this way.

What makes framed gable ends so versatile is the fact that all the support structure is hidden, leaving a flat, clean surface for whatever embellishments you might choose for the finishing touches. Go wild.

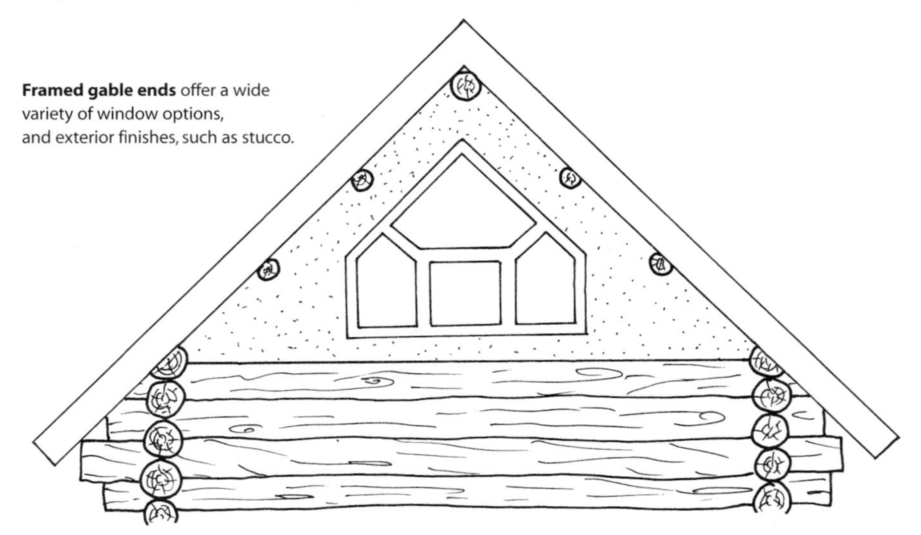

Framed gable ends offer a wide variety of window options, and exterior finishes, such as stucco.

As mentioned above, we designed our roof so the entire load is carried by the rafters, subordinating the beams and purlins to "decorative" status. And, due to practical concerns (and, okay, maybe a little bit of desperation), we decided to forego the vertical log gable ends in favor of the more common framed variety. It was the right decision, and one we certainly don't regret. Not only did it allow us to cover our structure before the deep winter freeze, we were then free to add our beams and purlins whenever and wherever we chose, without any need to address structural concerns.

It was liberating.

In the end, you'll design the gable ends for your house based on the time you have to spend, the amount of work you believe the task is worthy of, and the appearance you want your house to have. No one way is better than any other, as long as you know beforehand the limitations of each. Play with different ideas for awhile, then be pleasantly surprised when you see the results.

DORMERS

Not only do dormers add a degree of charm and complexity to an otherwise boring roof, they also create extra living space in loft areas, and are a pleasing source of extra light. In the winter, south-facing dormers with big windows can allow more warmth to enter a house than they permit to escape it. In summer, with the sun nearly right overhead, a dormer with big eaves will keep out the direct rays of the sun, while providing an extra opening to enhance cross ventilation.

Our south-side dormer is filled with windows.

We originally planned to build a single dormer on the south side, then framed one in on the north side, just opposite the south dormer. The north dormer encloses an upstairs bathroom that wasn't in the plans. (The building inspector wasn't too thrilled about our deviation from the blueprints, but he finally decided to let it slide.)

So, by building two dormers, we added enough room that we could have a full bath under one, and LaVonne could set up a studio under the other. The extra time and material expense was insignificant, compared to the beauty and practical use of space our two dormers provide.

LaVonne's LOGBOOK 9

December 1999

No rest for the weary, yet. Winter is coming and we need to get that roof on. First we frame the gable ends, and thanks to a very complicated window design, it takes a while. It will be worth it, I keep telling Rex.

Thankfully, Joe shows up to help with the roof framing, and nice weather holds for a time [19]. But one morning, the freezing winds arrive and the clouds drop. Men are relentless. They keep working. Me...I stand next to the propane heater whenever possible.

19

Phew!! Another 8" of snow to shovel out.

True to Colorado, the days get sunny and warm again while we put on the plywood sheathing [20] and temporary rolled roofing. Next up, heavy plastic over the framed window openings in the loft, and then plywood on the gable and dormer walls. We also pop in a temporary door on the west side to keep out the snow.

20

Now we can hibernate with the bears for a few months.

Well, I realize that I don't hibernate very well, and I can only do graphic design for so many hours in a day. For a change of pace, I gather up piles moss rocks for the rock veneer that will go on the basement walls. And if I'm <u>really</u> motivated and if the weather is <u>extremely</u> beautiful, I'll peel a purlin. I take my time at peeling these purlins, roof beams, ridge beam and collar ties. But when Rex is done writing that novel, we'll be ready to 'decorate' our ceiling.

On the list of things to do: order windows; pick out tile and wood flooring; and shop for light fixtures and plumbing fixtures, especially that clawfoot bathtub I've always wanted.

CHAPTER 13

ROOF FRAMING: BEAMS, PURLINS, RAFTERS & MORE

Taking It To The Top

The framed gable end was assembled on the floor and is being tilted up, anchored securely in case of high winds.

There are dozens of ways to design a roof for a log house, all working from but a handful of central themes. Of these, only a few variations are used to any extent in modern log homes. In this chapter I'll cover the basic details of the most practical roof designs in use today, and leave the embellishments up to your imagination.

OVERBUILT AND LOVING IT

It is the purpose of the roof covering to protect a house, and its occupants, from the ravages of nature. It is the purpose of the roof support structure, in turn, to ensure that the roof covering stays over your head—rather than on it—through whatever adversity nature is able to dole out. Most of the time, for most houses, both systems do their jobs; other times one or both systems fail, sometimes dramatically and with dire consequences.

You can take heart, then, in the fact that the majority of log homes' roofs are greatly overbuilt. Generally, log beams (or trusses) are overlaid with purlins, creating a structure that, alone, is capable of holding up the roof. But then, dimensional lumber (or T.J.I.) rafters—which provide a space for insulation and a framework on which to attach the sheathing—are installed at right angles to the purlins, adding an additional degree of support not found in conventionally framed houses. With such redundancy, the snow load—or the wind storm—that destroys a standard roof usually won't even faze the roof on a log home.

ROOF PITCH

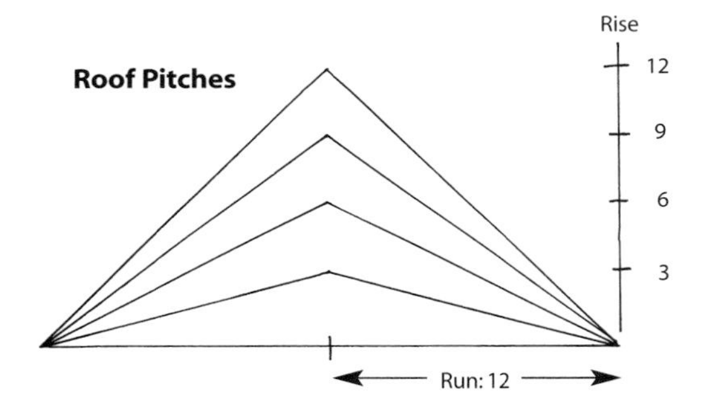

How steep should you make your roof? It's a matter aesthetics, as much as anything, though there are some practical issues to consider. Many of the old-time log builders regarded a low-pitched roof to be a thing of beauty. I won't argue that point, one way or the other; the eye knows what it likes. But it has always been my belief that the faster water can be made to run off a roof, the less likely that roof will be to leak. This is especially true in cold, snowy mountainous regions where snow on the roof melts from the warmth of the house, then re-freezes when it runs down to the relatively colder eave, creating an ice-dam behind which water can pool. And I'm not taking about a little water, either. While doing repair work on a 3:12 pitch roof at a ski resort in the Colorado Rockies, I once unwittingly stepped over an ice-dam and sunk to my knees in cold, slushy water. (As I recall, it was the defining moment of a stupendously lousy day.) I decided then and there that deep snow and low-pitched roofs rate a little below ketchup and ice cream in the go-together department.

During that time in my life (when I wasn't vainly attempting to repair intractable leaks in ill-conceived high-mountain roofs) I did shingle repair in Boulder, a town that lies at the base of Boulder Canyon—a scenic, moody gorge that just happens to be one of the most efficient wind-tunnels ever devised by nature. Boulder is a place where—in the midst of one of its fabled windstorms—you might find an entire roof—rafters and all—lying in the middle of a highway, a half mile away from the nearest house.

What I learned, after examining hundreds of roofs in that windy place, was that steeper roofs were far less likely to suffer wind damage than lower-pitched roofs. Moreover, roofs in the 9:12 to 14:12 range were practically impervious to the hurricane-like winds that roar down the canyon. Curiously, extremely steep roofs, such as mansards, fared no better than 3:12 and 4:12 pitched roofs. The only explanation I can offer is this: on roofs at (or near) 45 degrees, the wind works as hard to push the shingle against the roof as it does to tear it off.

Whatever the physics may be, it's a fact that roofs within a certain range of pitch endure wind better than higher or lower pitches. It's something to consider if you're building on a mountaintop where gale-force winds are a fact of life.

If you happen to live in an area where it rarely snows or blows, of course, none of the above is of much interest. What difference does roof pitch matter, then? In this case, it boils down to a matter of cost- and labor-effective living space. That is, you can increase your living area easier and cheaper by building 12-foot walls—with a floor at 8 feet—and constructing a steep roof over them, than by building 17- or 18-foot walls covered by a low pitched roof.

Roof pitch becomes a practical matter when you are adding a loft. Our loft is 26 feet, side to side, with 3-foot knee walls. At first we considered making the roof a 12:12 pitch, since (as you may have guessed) I'm partial to steep roofs, and it's simple to build a roof and gable ends where all the angle cuts are at 45 degrees. But in our case, it just wouldn't have worked. We would have gained a little more headroom near the walls, but the peak of the ceiling would have been 16 feet high. A 9:12 pitch was a good compromise: we still had plenty of headroom, and the peak of the ceiling came out at 13 feet, 9 inches.

A BASIC (STANDARD FRAME) ROOF

It's unlikely that you will construct your roof entirely by conventional framing methods, without the addition of beams and purlins, but you could, if you were so inclined. Consisting of nothing more than trusses, or rafters, over which plywood decking is then nailed, a standard frame roof is simplicity, itself.

However plain or uninspired this type of roof may be in it's basic incarnation, it's a good point of departure for shedding light on the principles of roof construction, since many of the same methods and procedures will carry through into the construction of more complex roof systems. When discussing other roof types, therefore, I will refer back to this style of roof.

And, just so you know, I'm assuming here that you have some knowledge of basic framing techniques, though you may never have laid out a roof before.

The Wall Plate

Note: *If you are planning to install a tongue & groove ceiling over purlins, the roof design will differ from what is presented here, and there may not be need to flatten the top of the wall logs, or to install a plate. More on this, later in the chapter.*

The beginning point for a conventionally framed roof is the level of the top wall log, or the plate. With a builder's level, shoot both top wall logs (long walls) marking them every few feet at a height far enough below the top that you can create a flat area with a chainsaw, without cutting away too much of the log.

If you level the tops of the wall logs in place, be extremely careful, especially if the saw will be held below your waist! After 25 years of using a chainsaw without so much as a scratch, I finally drew first blood on this operation, and a lot of it. I was using the saw in the one position where the chain brake would not engage if the saw lurched toward me. And it did. It opened a 3″ gash in my knee and made a tidy groove in my kneecap. The wound took a slew of stitches, and I hobbled with a cane for the next two weeks. I considered myself lucky.

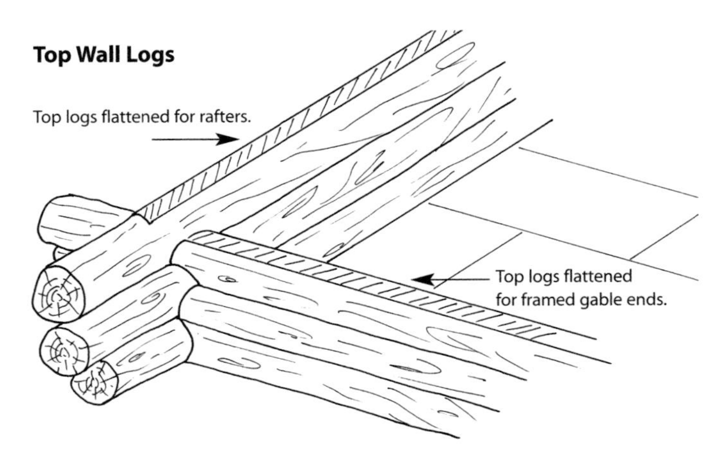

Once both top wall logs are milled, you could notch and set the rafters directly on top of it, but I prefer to install (with lag bolts) a dimensional lumber plate on top of the logs, first. Not only does a wall plate give you a crisp edge to gauge the "bird's-mouth" notches cut in the rafters, the $1^1/_2$-inch edge also provides a solid, vertical surface for attaching the metal "hurricane clips" that help ensure the rafters remain attached to the wall in high winds. Additionally, if there is any disparity in height—either from one end of the wall to the other, or across the walls—shims can be placed under the plate to bring all the walls to the same level.

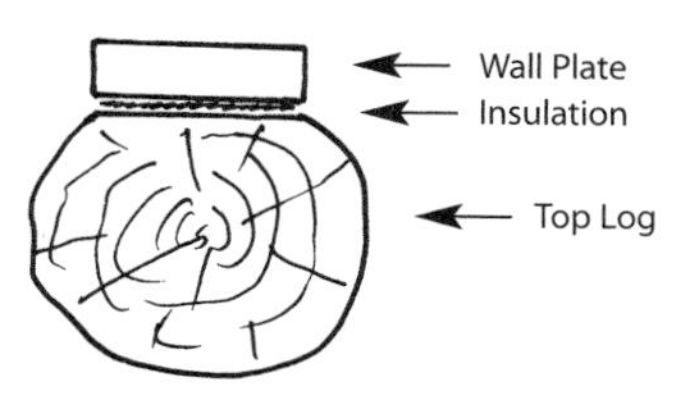

Bolt a wall plate on top of each long wall.

Measuring for the Rafters and Gable Ends

Once the plate is lagged into place on the long walls, you will be able to determine the two critical measurements you'll need to build the gable ends. *Remember that the top plate of the gable end will be on the same plane with the bottom sides of the rafters.* So, before you can build the gable ends, you'll need to determine the length (and therefore the angle) of the bottoms of the rafters. Here's how it's done:

- Measure the distance between the two wall plates, inside edge to inside edge. Then divide by 2. This measurement will be the actual run. *("a" in illustration below)*
- Using the pitch ratio of the roof (9:12, for example, where 9 is the rise, and 12 is the run), multiply by the rise, and divide by the run. Let's say the distance from wall to wall is 28 feet. The actual run, to the center, would be 14 feet (or 168 inches). If the roof pitch is 9:12, we multiply: 168 x 9 = 1512; then divide 1512 by 12 = 126 inches. This is the vertical rise from the top of the wall plate to the inside peak of the ceiling. *("b" in illustration below)*

Calculating Roof Height and Length of Rafters

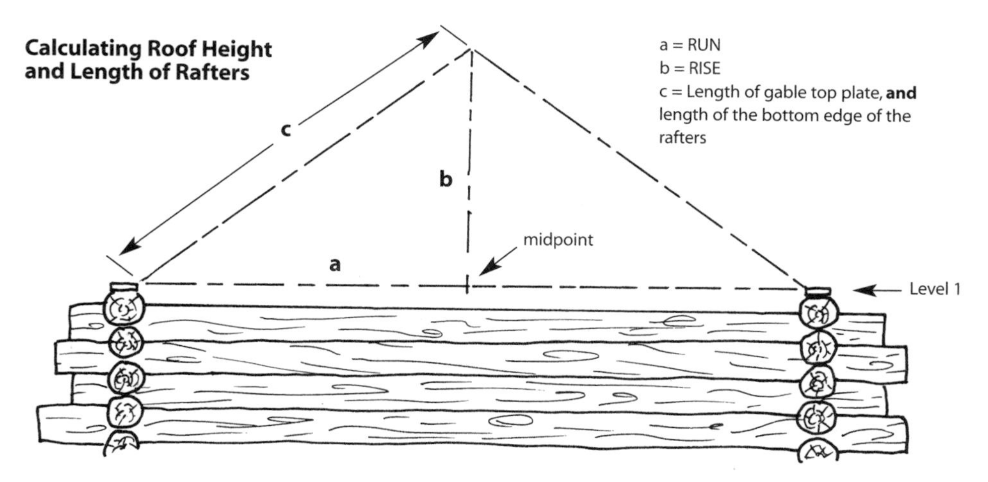

- We now have the two sides of the right triangle: 126 inches of rise, to 168 inches of run. Using now the Pythagorean Theorem, $a^2 + b^2 = c^2$, we see that the exact length of the bottom of the rafters is 210 inches. This is also the exact length of the top surface of each top plate on the gable end. *("c" in illustration above)*

For making bevel cuts on the framing members of the gable ends you will need to know how to calculate the angle of the roof. To do this, find the angle that corresponds to the tangent (rise/run). In a 9:12 pitch roof, for instance, the tangent is 9/12, or .75. The corresponding angle is 36.87 degrees. The quickest and most accurate way to find the angle is to use the inverse tangent key on a scientific calculator. (If you don't already own one, here's the excuse you've been looking for.) Below is a table giving the angles for the most common roof pitches.

If a ridge board is to run the length of the roof, half its thickness must be subtracted from the length of the rafter before cutting. For a $1^1/_2$-inch ridge board, this measurement would be $^3/_4$ inches.

Build and brace the gable ends, and install the ridge board (if one is used), and then lay out the rafters. Unlike the floor joists, begin the layout measurements for the rafters in the middle of the roof, rather than on one end. This will

Roof Pitch	**Tangent**	**Roof Angle** *(degrees)*
3:12	.250	14.04
4:12	.333	18.43
5:12	.417	22.62
6:12	.500	26.57
7:12	.583	30.26
8:12	.667	33.69
9:12	.750	36.87
10:12	.833	39.81
11:12	.917	42.51
12:12	1.00	45.00

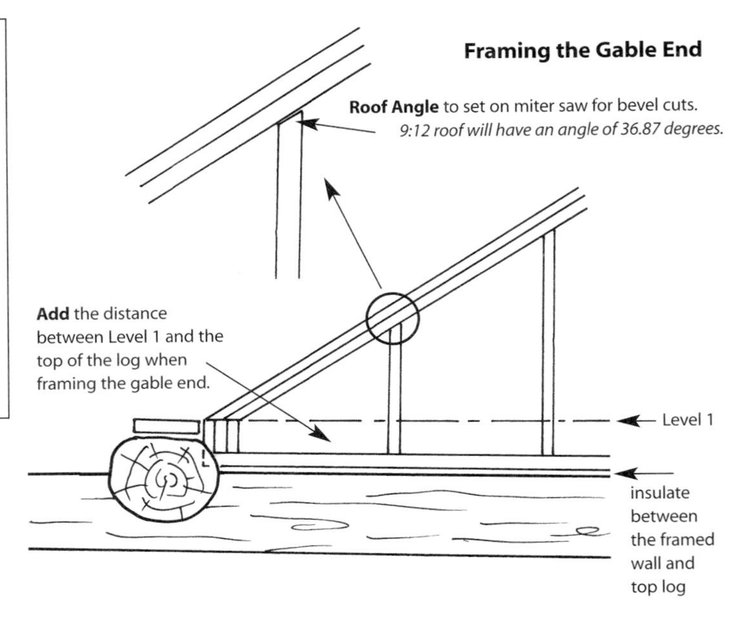

ensure that the end rafters are equal distance from the gable ends, and will simplify the installation of the lookout rafters you'll use to support the eaves.

Cutting Rafter Ends and Bird's-Mouths

The easiest way to mark the cut angle for the top end of a rafter is by using a framing square. Lay it flat on the rafter with the long end perpendicular to the angle you wish to cut. Reading the inside inch marks, set the long end on 12 inches (the run) and the short end on 9 inches (the rise), for a 9:12 pitch roof. This will be the angle where the ends of the rafters will meet at the top of the roof.

The angle for the bird's-mouth, where the rafter rests on the plate, will be laid out in exactly that same way, only in this case we want the run, not the rise, so make a line along the long edge of the square *("Cut Y" below).*

To complete the bird's-mouth, measure along the seat cut line from the bottom of the rafter to a point equal to the width of the plate. Then, using a square, make a right angle. A scriber can be used to mark the rafter if additional cutting is needed to fit around the outside of the top wall log. To save the time of setting each rafter in place, scribing and then cutting, we bent a length of rigid house wire over the log, then traced the shape onto the rafter.

Measuring and Marking Roof Rafters

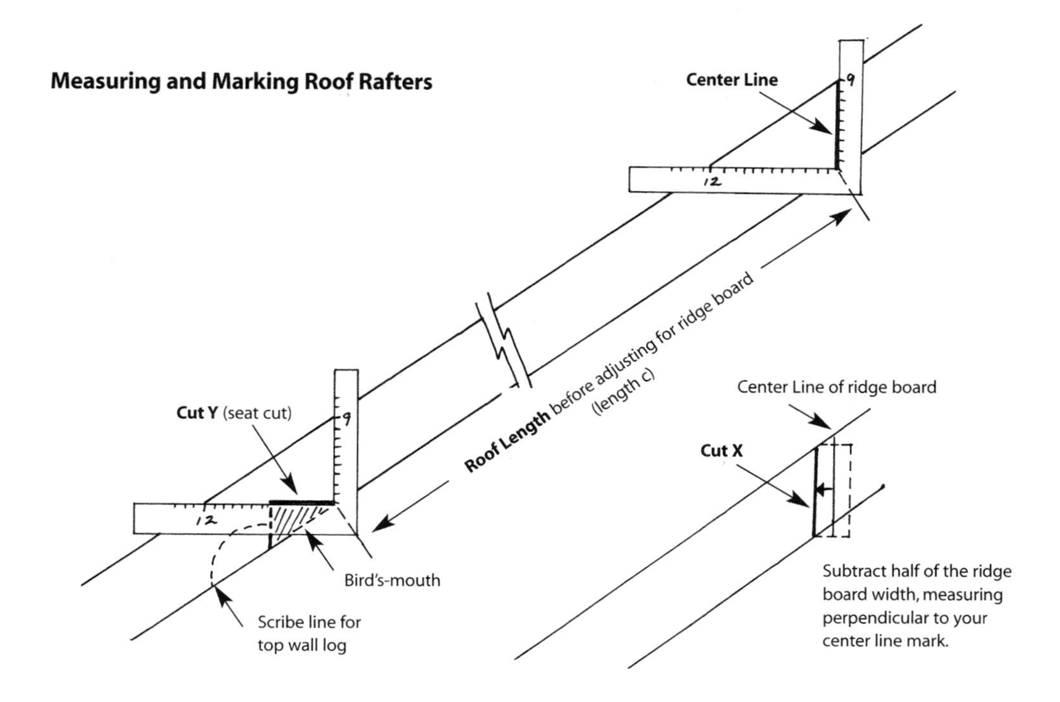

Rather than using a framing square for every cut, it's much easier to make a template, using a short board with the rafter angle cut on one end and the bird's-mouth on the other.

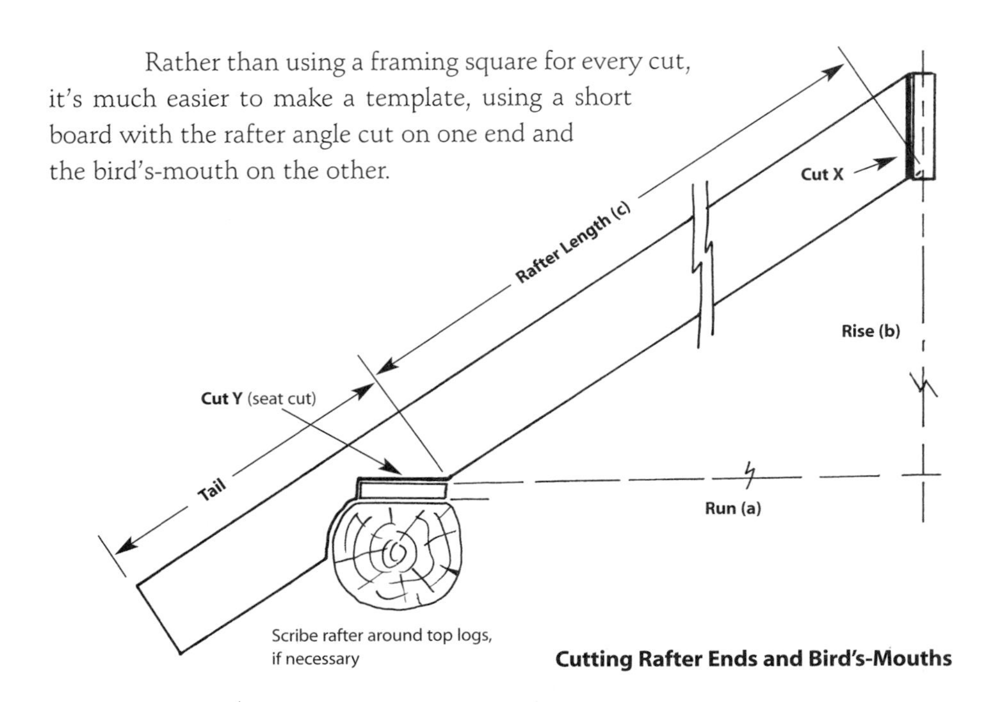

Cutting Rafter Ends and Bird's-Mouths

Main roof rafters are in place; the south dormer is framed next.

Ridge boards are set in place on dormers (left).

Rex secures a cripple rafter to the ridge board (below).

Putting in the Dormers

If you are planning to install dormers, you should leave an opening in the rafters equal to the width of each dormer, then double-up the rafters on each side for added support. You can then go ahead and finish the main roof, and complete the dormer roofs later. In this way, you can concentrate all of your efforts on building the dormers, which is good, because dormers—especially gabled dormers—are just a trifle complicated.

The most sensible way to proceed is to build each dormer in discreet steps. Begin with the gable end, followed by the side walls (if there are to be any) that rest atop the double rafters. With the walls in place, you will know the height of the ridge board, and the double header on the main roof that supports it, so go ahead and install both.

The valley rafters are next. They begin in the corners of the intersection of the ridge board and the header, and end against the double rafters, just before they meet the side wall. A compound angle cut will be needed on both ends.

The angle cuts on the valley rafter ends can be determined with a framing square, using the roof rise over 17 (instead of 12). Example, for a 9:12 pitched roof, mark the compound angle at 9 and 17, and bevel it at 45 degrees. There are complex procedures for determining the length of valley rafters, but they never seem to work on *my* valleys. Consequently, I just take careful measurements and cut the first rafter long, cutting and testing until it fits. With one valley rafter cut, the others are easy.

After the valley rafters, only the jack rafters remain. They, too, are easier to cut by empirical—as opposed to theoretical—methods.

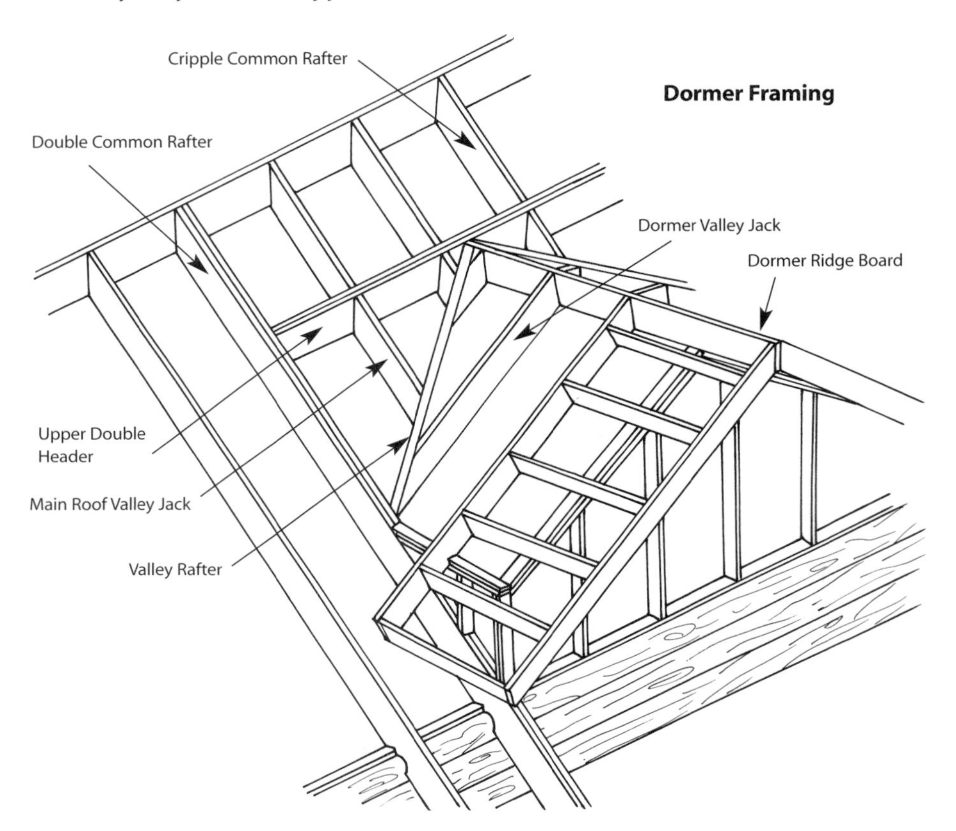

Dormer Framing

Constructing the Eaves

With the gable ends and common rafters in place on the main roof, all that remains is to build the overhanging eaves. Like so many things in construction, building the eaves is utterly simple in principle, but rather tricky in practice, since precise measurements are hard to come by.

To begin, your final common rafter should be further away from the gable end, than the gable end will be from the edge of the eave. (The rule is 2:1 for cantilevers—2 feet inside the structure, for every foot out—though this rule is rarely followed when building eaves, since the plywood sheathing provides extra tensile strength. If in doubt, ask your building inspector.) To save plywood, the distance between the *center* of the last common rafter, and the *outside edge* of the fly rafter should be a multiple of the spacing used for the common rafters. (For instance, if the rafters are spaced 16 inches OC, then the above distance should be calculated at 48 inches, 64 inches, etc.)

Lookout rafters and fly rafters are complete.

Lookout rafters run across the gable ends, perpendicular to the common rafters, and are joined on the outside of the eave with a fly rafter. They are generally spaced 16- or 24-inches OC, measuring from the bottom of the common rafters, or the sub-fascia, if sub-fascia is to be used (I highly recommend it).

Cut the lookout rafters, nail them into the last common rafter, and anchor each one to the top of the gable end. When all the lookout rafters are in place, trim

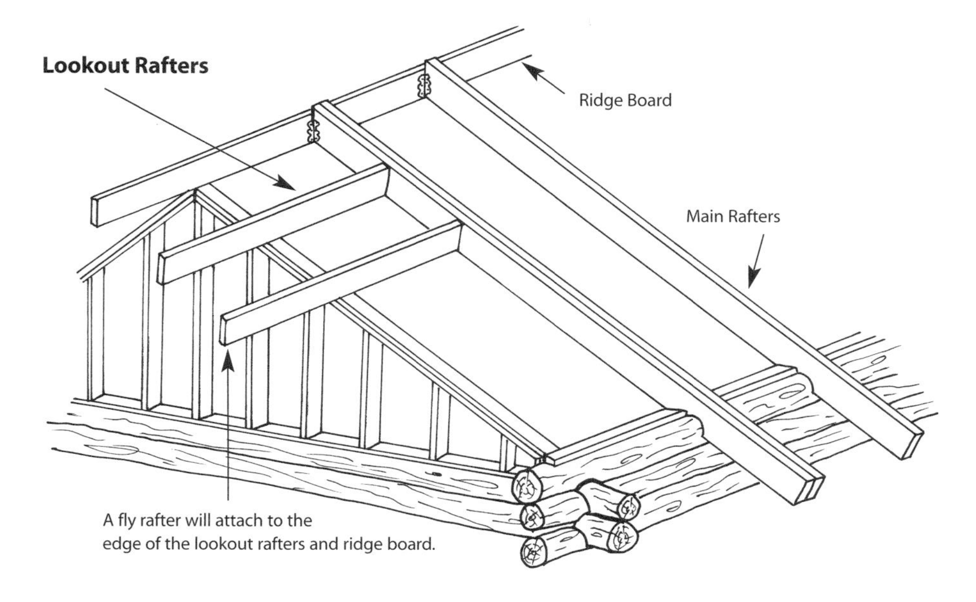

the ridge board and add the outside fly rafter. Not too bad, huh?

All I can add are two simple tips. Deflection in the last common rafter may cause the lookout rafters to hang over the gable end unevenly, so be sure to push or pull the rafter straight, before nailing each lookout rafter to the top of the gable wall. Otherwise, the outside edge of the overhang will follow the deflection, looking at it will cause stomach upset, and thoughts of sheathing the roof will give you bad dreams. Also, you'll want to double-up the last common rafter *after* the lookout rafters are nailed in place (16d nails won't reach otherwise).

A ROOF USING LOG OR TIMBER RAFTERS

Logs, or heavy timbers, can be used in the place of dimensional lumber, or TJI's, for the roof rafters. Though the general lie of the roof is the same as with standard dimensional lumber roof framing, there are some important differences. Since the log rafters will be exposed, the ceiling (usually 2 x T&G planking) is attached to the top side of the rafters, rather than the bottom. After the ceiling

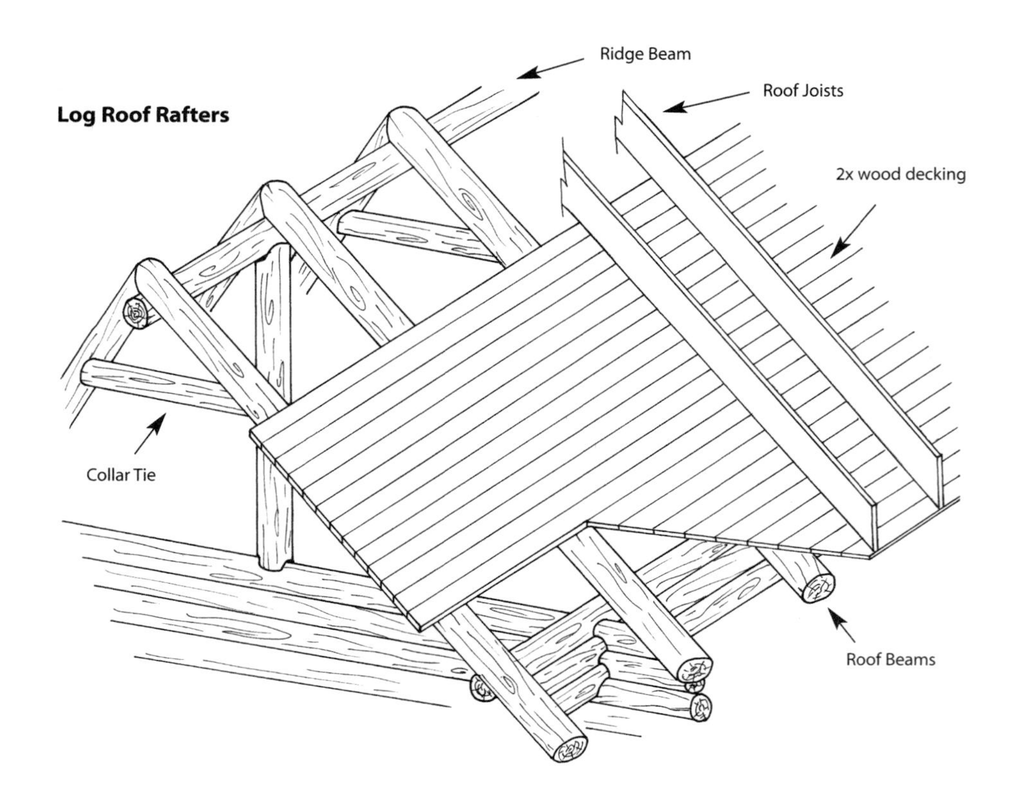

planks are in place, dimensional lumber sleepers are then installed on top of the planking. This will allow a space for insulation, and a surface for nailing on the roof decking, since log rafters are generally spaced farther apart than standard $^{1}/_{2}$ -inch plywood is designed to span.

A ROOF WITH STRUCTURAL PURLINS

If your roof plan calls for structural log purlins, and a structural log ridge beam, they will have to be installed before the rafters. The placement of the rafters, however, depends on what type of ceiling you intend to install.

When installing a conventional, gyp board ceiling—or some other material that will be installed *after* the roof is in place—the placement of the rafters, in relation to the wall plate and the gable ends, will remain unchanged from the basic roof style discussed earlier. This means, simply, that the tops of the purlins and ridge beam should all lie on the theoretical plane defined by the bottom side of the rafters (that is, *if* the rafters were really there, which they aren't—yet).

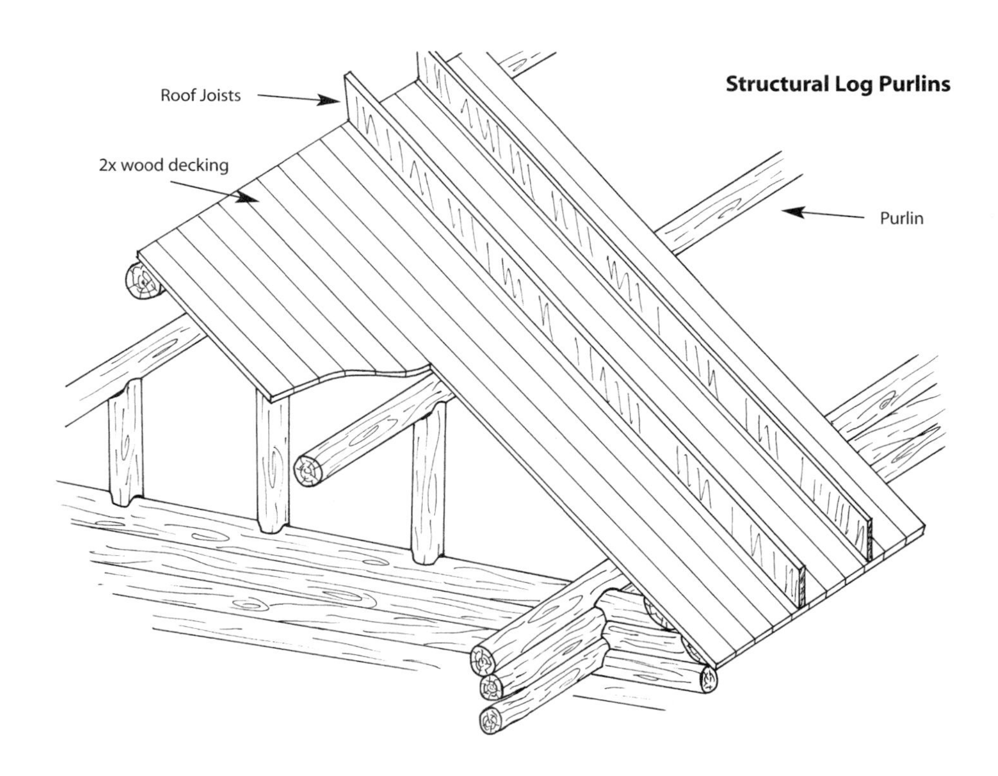

Structural Log Purlins

On the other hand, if you plan to install 2-inch tongue & groove ceiling planks over the purlins and ridge beam, the purlins should be placed on a plane defined by the *outside edge* of the top wall log, since it is customary to extend the planks beyond the wall to serve as the soffit for the overhanging eave. (In this instance, the top wall logs are not flattened and plated.)

This type of roof calls for a great deal of planning—and a stretch of nice weather, from beginning to end. Once the planks are in place, and the rafters are attached (with metal clips) through the planks into the purlins below, any electrical wires for lights, smoke alarms, lightning rods or ceiling fans must be run, followed by insulation.

This is usually the point where towering thunderheads crest the horizon, and the gentle breeze you've been enjoying becomes a stiff wind. This distressing change in weather has been mystically conjured up by the building inspector, who wants to bust you for wet wires and soggy insulation. But there's no time to worry about it, because you can't quit until the roof is sheathed with plywood, and felt paper is nailed into place. So everyone descends on the roof like a swarm of mosquitoes, with the guys installing the felt paper yelling at the guys nailing down the plywood to hurry up and get in gear, which causes the plywood guys—who now, more than anything, just want to aggravate the felt paper guys—to slow it down a notch. And there you stand, trying to smooth over the disputes as the first few drops of rain begin to fall.

Like I said, it takes some planning. Start early, and line up a lot of (compatible) help. If it looks like more than a day's work (and it probably will be), you

French and crew nail the T&G boards onto their log purlins. The smaller roof has been covered with black felt paper.

can always run felt paper over the T&G planks, then finish the rafters, insulation and sheathing another day. And for emergencies, it's a good idea to have a big tarp on hand.

Purlins with Framed Gable Ends

Framed gable ends can either be built with beam pockets (and extra framing support under them) in which the purlins and ridge beam can rest, or they can be built smaller, so that the purlins and ridge beam rest directly on the top plate. In this latter case, additional framing will be needed to fill in the space between the purlins and the ceiling planks.

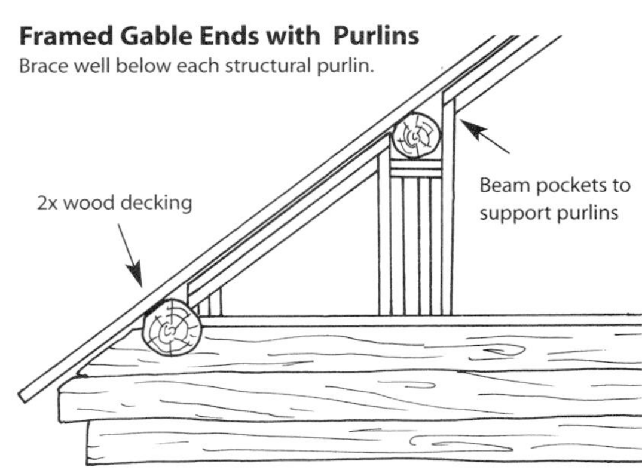

The log home at Buckhorn Camp uses framed gable ends with large purlins, each adequately supported with dimensional lumber. Also showing in this photo is an arched truss.

Purlins with Vertical Log Gable Ends

Vertical log gable ends, on the other hand, must be built to the height of the bottom of the purlins, since there is no practical way to build beam pockets into them. The spaces between the purlins can then be filled in with log segments, or standard dimensional lumber framing.

The crew from Log Knowledge sets purlins on the vertical log gable end, an interior log truss, and a full log gable end.

Purlins with Full Log Gable Ends

If you choose to use full log gable ends, it might take a bit more planning if you allow for settling. While the rafters (and ceiling planks) should be firmly attached to the outside wall (or wall plate), they must be allowed to slide against the purlins and ridge beam as the gable end settles. This can be accomplished by making slots in the planks and rafter straps so the heads of the fasteners are afforded some movement. And, since a shrinking gable end essentially makes the roof shorter from eave to peak, a few inches of extra space should be allowed at the top of the ridge beam to keep the ceiling planks and rafters from buckling as the shrinking progresses.

Benshoof's roof under construction: the purlins are set on the full log gable end (lower left side of photo) and the vertical log gable end (upper right side of photo).

INTERIOR PURLIN SUPPORT

Roof Trusses

Long roofs often need additional support for the purlins and ridge beam, one or two places along the roof's length. Beams are used if there is to be a living area directly below the roof. These are stout logs running directly beneath—and perpendicular to—the purlins, and held together near the top with horizontal log segments, or collar ties.

Trusses, on the other hand, are often used to support the roof beneath high ceilings, where there is no living space below for the truss members (chords) to conflict with. Since a single truss can easily weigh in excess of a ton, they are almost always built on the ground and hoisted into place with a boom truck, or some other suitable conveyance for lifting.

A truss can be held together in several different ways. Most common, perhaps, is the use of gusset plates—either internal, or external—to connect the inner chords to the outer chords. Long bolts, running diagonally through the outside corners, are often used to secure the outer chords to one another.

Trusses can take on many interesting forms, with numerous eye-pleasing variations possible. Any issue of a log home magazine is likely to show pictures of several different truss designs. Coffee-table log home books are another good source for ideas. If you elect to use trusses, they will almost certainly need to be designed (or at least approved) by an engineer in order to meet code requirements.

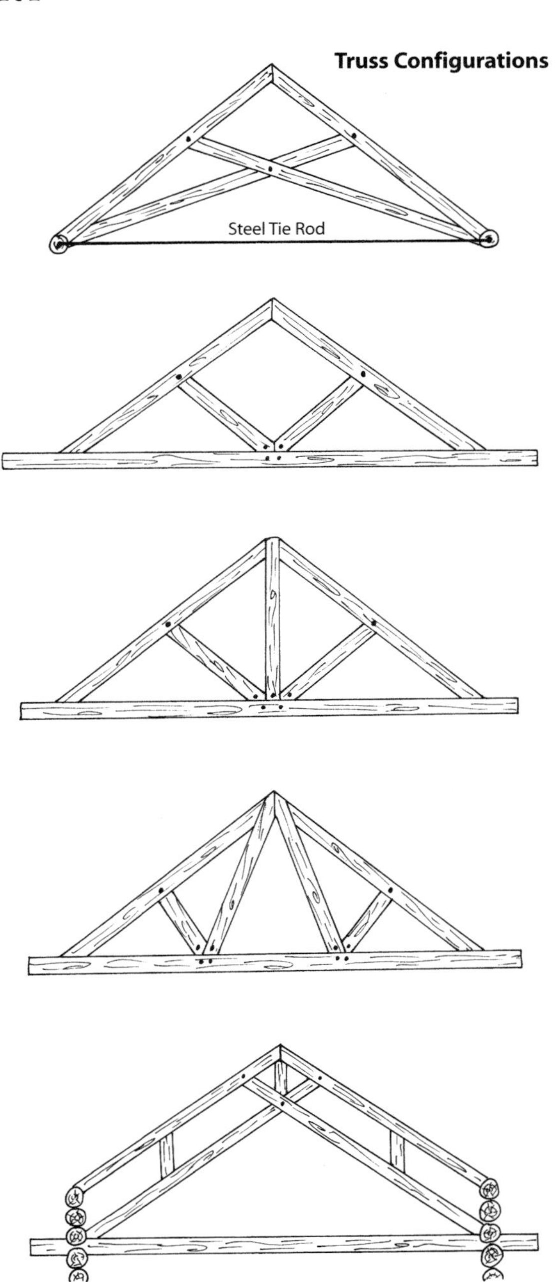

A view of the large log truss at Benshoof's house. Cross-bracing holds it in place until the log purlins are set.

Roof Beams to Support Purlins

Beams are a much simpler matter, as there is nothing particularly vexing about the installation of beams, except that great care and forethought should be used when placing them. In particular, if the ridge beam is of greater diameter than the purlins, then the roof beams will be notched around it. Should you install the ridge beam first, and then the roof beams, or should you erect the opposing roof beams together as a unit, and notch the ridge beam into it? This will depend largely on what technique you're using to raise the logs. The latter method is probably better if you are using a skyline or a boom truck (or a very tall gin pole); the former method would be the more logical choice if you have to roll the logs up on the roof with ramps.

I should point out here that care should be taken when using beams or trusses with full log gable ends, since it is the nature of such structures to be rigid and stationary, and therefore not conducive to roof shrinkage. Unless the logs for the gable end are bone dry and tightly fitted—or some other measures are taken to retard settling—you might end up with a bowed roof.

LOG ACCENTS WITH A SIMPLE ROOF

Of the dozens of people who have toured our home (many of them accomplished builders), no one has yet guessed that our beams and purlins are not the primary system supporting the roof, or that they were installed months after the roof was completed and dry.

You can call it a ruse, if you like, but that would be missing the point. For, although the lion's share of the support is, indeed, carried by the 2 x 10 rafters, our roof is far stronger with the beams and purlins, than without them. So, what the building department calls "decorative logs," I call a "secondary support system."

But enough hair-splitting. It's a method that works well for anyone who needs to cover their structure quickly, since "accent" purlins and beams can be of smaller diameter than structural ones (and can even be erected in sections). It makes them much easier to move into place. Best of all, the roof overhead can serve as an A-frame for lifting.

Inside the house, our roof line is 36 feet long, broken into three sections by two pairs of roof beams that run from the knee walls to the ridge log. Three rows of purlins adorn each side of the steeply-pitched ceiling. The ridge log and purlins were raised in 12-foot sections (so that all the joints are hidden behind roof beams), by running ropes through holes drilled in the dimensional ridge board and rafters. We then countersunk lag bolts into the rafters and filled the holes with dowel sections. To discourage rolling as they were being bolted into place, we lightly milled one side of all the purlins before installing.

So the roof beams would lie flat against the ceiling, we scribed and notched them into the top wall log and the ridge log, and around the purlins, then bolted them to the double rafters running along either side of the dormers.

The middle section of the ridge beam is lifted into place with ropes.

Collar ties were then added, every 4 feet. Ironically, they *are* considered structural, since they prevent the rafters from spreading and pushing out the sides of the wall. For ties between the rafters, we used logs the same size as the purlins. And between each pair of roof beams, we used a horizontal logs the same thickness as the beams.

The final touch came after the soffit was installed: we bolted-up leftover pieces of purlins and ridge beams under the eaves, to make it look as though they extended through the framed gable.

The result of our shortcut method is really quite stunning; even after a year of living beneath our "decorative" log work, LaVonne and I still proudly admire the rustic, hand-hewn view overhead.

Our non-structural roof beam is notched in three places to go around purlins (top photo).

A finished look at the non-structural purlins, beams and collar ties in our loft ceiling (right).

EAVES

There is something about a log house that demands big eaves; they just *look* like they belong. Eaves that would overwhelm a frame house in town seem perfectly natural on a log home in the forest. That's good, because eaves serve the dual purpose of keeping rain off your logs, and summer's harsh sunlight out of your house (and off your logs).

LaVonne, with her unerring sense of proportion, determined that 32 and 24 were the magic numbers for our eaves (32 inches at the bottom, 24 inches on the gable ends). As usual, she was right; they're neither an inch too short, nor an inch too long.

RAIN GUTTERS AND RAFTER TAILS

Should you leave the rafter tails at right angles with the roof, or cut them vertical so you can easily install rain gutters? It depends on the width of your rafters, the pitch of your roof, and your sense of aesthetics. With wide rafters and a steep pitch, a vertical cut on the tails can make for a ridiculously showy fascia board.

On our roof I left the tails perpendicular to the angle of the roof, then used a table saw to rip redwood posts into wedge-shaped strips to rest the rain gutters against. If you need more that a 12-inch fascia board to cover vertically-cut rafter tails, you'd probably be better off to not cut the tails vertical.

MAKING IT DRY

To nail on the plywood sheathing, begin at a bottom corner and follow a chalk-line, across the entire roof. Then start the second row with a partial sheet of plywood. Once the roof sheathing is on, you'll need to apply some kind of underlayment to keep things dry until it's time to install the finished roof. The type of underlayment you use will depend entirely on how long it will be before the roofing commences. If it will be but a matter of days, 15# felt paper should suffice; if two weeks to a month, you can get by with 30# felt. But if it will be an extended period of time, I suggest you dry-in the roof with 90# rolled roofing. All of these products come in

For the winter, plywood sheathing and 90# rolled roofing is nailed on the roof. We cover the walls of the gables and dormers with plywood, and cover the windows with plastic.

36-inch rolls. One roll of 15# felt will cover 400 square feet of roof; the 30# covers 200 square feet, and the 90# covers 100 square feet.

Overlap the seams 2 inches, then use roofing nails to hold it down. Space the nails 2 inches apart on the seams in high-wind areas (less in calmer environs) and make diamond patterns in between the seams. A hammer-tacker stapler can be used to hold paper in place, prior to nailing, and a few rolls of wind strip from the lumber yard can save you some time nailing.

When should you install the finished roof? For starters, all the flashing and fascia should be in place. If you are using composition shingles and know what you're doing, this should be enough, since it is not too difficult to come back later and install the jacks around stove pipes and plumbing vents. If, on the other hand, you plan on a tile roof, or a roof with metal panels, you had better wait for all the pipes to be pushed through the roof before beginning.

Soffits can be installed any time after the roof is dried in.

ROOFING MATERIAL OPTIONS

The roofing material you choose is truly the icing on the cake. From a distance, the roof is as noticeable as your impressive log work. Besides keeping the rain and snow out of your house, the roof will say something about who you are; what your sense of beauty is, and how practical you might be. So what do you use to give that perfect crowning touch to your beautiful home?

Until the middle of the last century, the thought of covering a log house with anything other than sod or wood bordered on blasphemy. These materials are, after all, as much a part of the forest as the logs from which the house was built. And they were right at hand; sod is everywhere trees aren't, and a roof's share of shingles can be split with a broadaxe in a couple of days.

But times change. The engineering required to slide a sod roof past the county building department is formidable, but nothing compared to the labor and material costs incurred in making certain the roof neither leaks, nor collapses under its own weight. And wood shingle roofs—the fact that they come from dwindling, old-growth forests notwithstanding—have a short life expectancy and a fire rating that falls somewhere between old newspaper and gunpowder.

So what's left? I'll briefly cover the three most popular options, though there are certainly more. I will not, however, try to conduct a short course in roofing techniques. I've roofed enough houses in my life to know that it's nothing that can be explained in one or two short chapters, much less in a few paragraphs.

So I won't even try. If you've done some roofing before, or if you know a roofer or two, you may want to go ahead and do it yourself; otherwise, find a reputable roofer—not some scruffy kid in a beat-up Vega, with out-of-state plates and fluffy dice hanging from the rearview mirror.

Metal Roofs

Metal roofs are gaining in popularity by leaps and bounds, and for good reason. They are practically impervious to wind, fire and hail, and they come with warranties of 25 years or better. Snow slides right off a metal roof on the first warm day following a storm, and the new, baked finishes are minimally affected by ultraviolet radiation.

Installation is fairly quick and easy, as most panels simply snap together and are held to the roof deck with hidden clips. And, since metal roofing is lightweight, there are no special structural considerations involved.

There are several manufacturers of metal roofing panels, offering dozens of styles, colors and finishes. You shouldn't have any trouble finding a dealer for any of them, though you should be prepared to pay a pretty penny, since high-quality metal roofing doesn't come cheap.

Concrete Tile Roofs

Concrete tiles are also quite popular, with a mind-dizzying array of styles and colors to accentuate your log work. Though resistant to wind, fire, rain, snow, sunlight and small hailstones, they can crack and break under the force of unusually large hailstones.

Because of the weight of concrete tiles, most building departments will expect to see beefed-up roof specifications, but it shouldn't amount to anything more than changing the size and spacing of your rafters.

Concrete tiles are not nailed directly to the roof, but are elevated by—and nailed to—1 x 2 bats attached to the decking (through the felt paper underlayment). Hips and valleys require a lot of laborious cutting with a concrete saw, so be prepared to spend some time (or money) with this type of roof. If you've got an abundance of both, it's a classy way to go.

UNI-SOLAR® Roofing Products

If you're planning on either a standing-seam metal roof, or an asphalt shingle roof, you may want to consider incorporating *UNI-SOLAR®* roofing products into your design. These innovative products serve as both the roof, itself, and state-of-the-art amorphous silicon solar cells. The standing-seam panels can be blended into most other metal roofing products, and the shingles can be used for as much, or as little, of the roof as desired.

See Chapter 20 for more details.

Asphalt Composition Shingles

This may be a misnomer, since most shingles today contain little asphalt. Instead, they are made from fiberglass, impregnated with either asphalt, rubber, or both. These improvements make for a much better shingle, with superior resistance to fire, water and sunlight.

Considering what you get for the money, composition shingles can't be beat. The shingles we put on our house were manufactured by Malarkey Roofing Company. They are textured shingles that give the roof a rustic (almost mossy) look; something you would expect to see on an old woodcutter's cottage, deep in the enchanted forest.

Our particular shingles boast a 35-year warranty and—best of all—a proven resistance to hail that many insurance companies (ours included) are so impressed with that they are willing to offer a 10 percent discount on homeowner's insurance.

I'm partial to composition shingles for the simple reason they come in small, flexible units. I can put them down quickly with just a handful of tools, and if the roof sustains any damage from wind, raccoons, falling tree limbs or errant micro-meteorites, repairs are simple and easy. Likewise, it's not a major headache to retrofit plumbing or furnace stacks, or to later install lightning rods or satellite dishes.

Besides, they're beautiful.

OPTIONS, OPTIONS, OPTIONS

Without actually taking the time to do the calculations, I feel I can safely say that if every person on the planet built exactly the same style of house, it would be possible for everyone to have a unique roof.

The roof, and roofing systems, I've offered here are the most practical, and the most widely used in North America, but they hardly encompass the totality of what's out there. It would take volumes to do that.

In the end, you'll do what works best for you. And that's the way it should be.

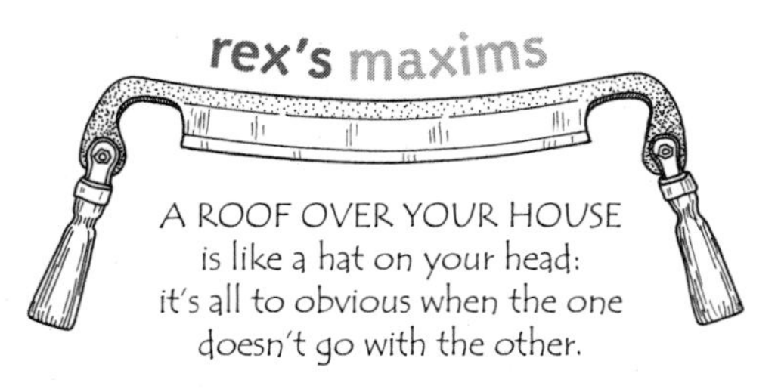

LaVonne's
LOGBOOK 10

April 2000

Spring is here and Rex is ready to abandon the computer for the tool belt. The purlins and roof beams are peeled and ready to be hoisted to the ceiling. Without soffit boards on the eaves, the drafty wind is chilly in the mornings.

First we install the ridge log in 3 sections, pulling each section up with ropes run through holes drilled in the ridge board. Lag bolts firmly hold all the logs to the joists. Next to be raised are the purlins, and then the very tricky roof beams that run diagonally, from the top wall log to the ridge log. We scribe each one to fit over three purlins, so there is no room for big errors. Chinking will hide the small stuff. The log collar ties add the finishing touch, and give dimension to a high ceiling.

21

After asking around, we finally find a crew to do the garage floor flatwork. They level the dirt, getting the slope just right. Rex and I lay down 2" insulation boards so our radiant heat goes up and not down. Then comes wire mesh, so the plumber can tie down the radiant heat tubing [21]. Dick, and crew from Action

22

Plumbing, put the garage area on one thermostat, and the workshop/battery room on a separate thermostat. (The underground plumbing was done last fall.)

The spring snows and rains arrive, just in time to pour concrete. And as luck would have it, the first truck gets stuck about 40 feet from the top. Oh, it is maddening to see the truck, full of concrete, tilted precariously off our road while we wait for the tow truck.

Four hours later the truck is pulled to the top [22] and the contractors start pushing around the mud, which has not set up too much by this point. Soon we will have a another nice flat floor to pile stuff on...

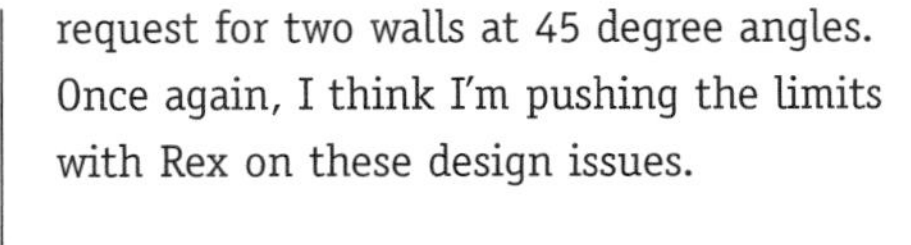

May 2000

While the weather is unsettled, we start framing the interior walls. The main floor walls are easy...everything is square, no funny angled walls or sloping ceilings. We double-plate the bottom of each wall to allow for the gypcrete that will be poured over the radiant heat tubing. (If not, we would have nothing to nail the drywall and mop boards to.)

We allow for settling of the log walls when building the interior frame walls, which really isn't too difficult. Just time-consuming. (But then, what isn't??)

The loft walls are a bit more complicated to frame. It is only a walk-in closet and bathroom [23], but the ceiling, purlins, and roof beams are quite funky, not to mention my request for two walls at 45 degree angles. Once again, I think I'm pushing the limits with Rex on these design issues.

Soffits are a pain to do, and even more so when balancing on very tall ladders in gusty spring winds. We opt for plywood soffits instead of tongue-&-groove pine boards. The seams will be covered with our decorative purlin ends, and the boards will be stained to match the house logs. It's a nice compromise.

The day is finally here when our fort becomes a house....we can start cutting in the doors and windows. The tricky part about windows is the vertical placement. I know exactly where they will fit horizontally, but the up and down placement is unique to each window, except for the walls that have matching windows, side-by-side. We can't cut away too much of the log above or below. Sometimes we get lucky and the window fits between the logs perfectly. Often we need to flatten one or both of the logs.

It is wonderful how much light fills the house now that all the openings are cut in. A dramatic change when standing inside, and when looking at the outside too!

23

CHAPTER 14

WINDOWS, DOORS, LOG ENDS AND WIRING

Letting Light Into A Shrinking House

By now the superstructure is up: your exterior walls are complete and you have a roof (with big eaves) over your head. And all of a sudden your bright, sunny house has become as dark as a cave. This means, of course, that it's time to cut out the door and window openings to let in some light.

If you haven't already taken delivery of your doors and windows, they should at least be on order. Custom windows and doors will have a longer lead-time than their off-the-shelf counterparts, so it's good to order them as soon as you're sure of the dimensions. If nothing else, you should know the exact rough framing dimensions of every door and window going into the house.

The opening for our double-doors is cut into the south wall.

A window opening is cut, and logs are pushed out.

CALCULATING THE OPENINGS

So how big should you cut the openings? The answer to this question is dependent on the answers to two other questions: How thick will the bucks (frames) be? And, how much space should you allow for settling?

Window and Door Bucks

To answer the first question, it's necessary to know just how you intend to trim out the windows and doors. As mentioned in the chapter on wall logs, you should know—*before* spiking down the logs—the thickness of the bucks and the depth of keyways (if any) you plan to cut into the sides of the opening.

Bucks Without a Finishing Trim

Bucks Without Trim

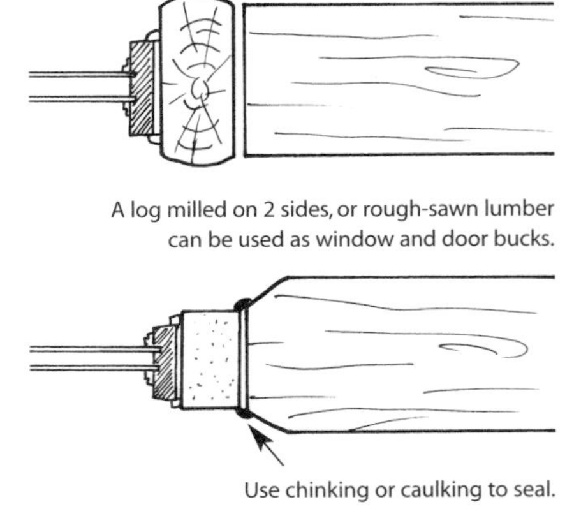

A log milled on 2 sides, or rough-sawn lumber can be used as window and door bucks.

Door and window bucks are often made of logs milled on two sides, with heavy timbers, or simply with rough-cut dimensional lumber, 2 inches or better in thickness. With any of these bucks, a finishing trim board is not needed, since the door or window will already be amply trimmed. The depth of the bucks can range from a little less than the thickness of the logs (in which case the log ends on either side are beveled back to meet the buck), to a little deeper.

If you plan on using bucks without added trim, it is important that your doors and windows *not* have exterior flanges (or worse, brick molding), or you'll have to add an additional frame of dimensional lumber within the log or timber bucks, then cover the flange with a narrow trim board. Obviously, it's important to know if your doors and windows will have flanges *before* cutting the openings.

Bucks With a Finishing Trim

Bucks With Trim

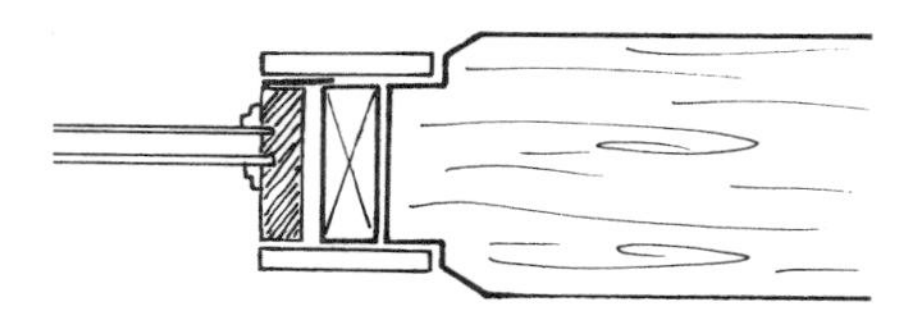

Option 1: Use one 2x buck , and flatten log to same depth; trim boards will overlap the buck and log. Log ends can be beveled for a finished look.

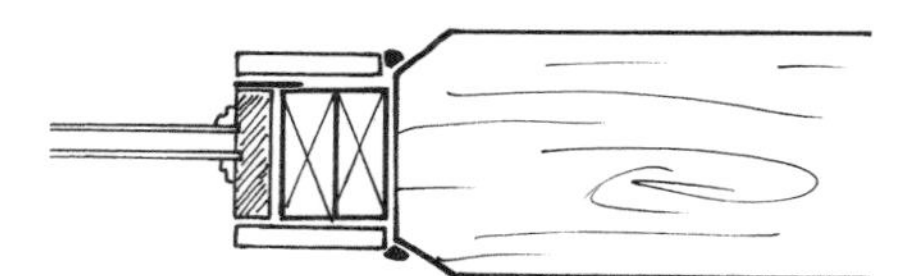

Option 2: Use double 2x bucks , and bevel the logs to match the trim board.

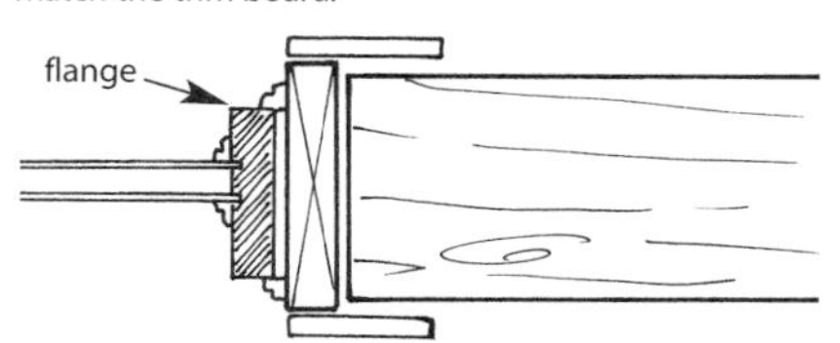

Option 3: Use a buck that is wider than your widest log; trim boards will set on the outside of all logs.

Another option is to use standard dimensional lumber for the bucks, then cut back the logs on all sides to the width of a final trim board, so that the trim boards lie flat against both the bucks and the log wall *(option 1)*. It's a lot of extra work, certainly, but it's a stylish way to finish the windows and doors. And, with insulation stuffed in the spaces between the back of the trim boards and the logs, wind and insects will have a harder time finding a way in while the house is settling (that is, before a final seal can be made with chinking or caulking).

Two variations on this style that minimizes the amount of cutting are also possible. By making the bucks from layered pieces of dimensional lumber, as deep as the window (or door) jamb, and as wide as the trim board, the trim board then fits snugly between the log opening and jamb *(option 2)*. Or the buck is made wider than your thickest log, and the trim boards set on the surface of the logs *(option 3)*.

Flanges work well with either of the the first two options, though brick molding is still a very definite no-no.

Rex bevels back the logs around window and door openings.

Allowing for Log Shrinkage

What about settling? If your roof has been on for a month or two (or better yet, several months), you've probably been taking periodic measurements to determine how much settling has occurred, and if the rate is constant or has been decreasing. On the other hand, if you finished the roof two days ago, you will have no idea how much settling to expect. I would be much less inclined to take chances with the latter scenario, than the former. With a few measurements under your belt, you at least have an idea; with no measurements you know, well...nothing.

As I've stated elsewhere, 3/4-inch per foot is the shrinkage you should expect with green logs, all the way down to 1/8-inch per foot as the lower limit for dry, tight fitting logs. Expect the worst—it's really no extra trouble to cut out an additional inch or two above the top buck, and it may save you a lot of work, later.

But don't go hog-wild, either. Remember: you don't need to take the shrinkage for the entire wall into account, only those logs that lie within the lower and upper latitudes of your opening. In other words, if you have a 4-foot window opening in a 12-foot wall built with green logs, it may very well be that the wall will shrink 9 inches (3/4-inch per foot) by the time it's all said and done, but only 3 inches of that shrinkage will have occurred in the section of wall where the window rests.

Log Knowledge used heavy bucks for all door and window openings, with a settling space above, on Benshoof's home.

Marking and Cutting the Openings

Now that you know how to calculate the size of the openings, all that's left is to mark and cut them out. Hopefully, you have left yourself enough room (between spikes) to position the windows so that you don't cut away more than half of either the top or the bottom log.

Begin by pounding a nail part way into one of the upper corners (preferably a nail with a small head, like a finish nail). Measure down to the bottom of the opening and make a pencil line about where you think the bottom corner should be, then use a level or a plumb bob to find the exact corner location and pound in another nail. Find the other two corners in the same way, take corner to corner measurements to make certain the opening is square, then run a level along the bottom to assure yourself that all is right with the world.

So much for the easy part.

Obviously you will want the opening to be as close to perfect as you can get it, but just how close is up to you. If you plan to use trim boards that will extend over the logs on all sides of the opening, or if you're going to chink the seam between the bucks and the logs, you may be able to get by without using a guide for the chainsaw. Otherwise, I highly recommend that you use one.

If you don't plan to use bona fide saw guide—one that slides along the surface of a 2 x 4—then you can still use a 2 x 4 as a guide for the bar, or you can simply mark a line all around the opening, and cut it freehand. I've tried it both ways; it would seem intuitive that a person could cut straighter using a board for a guide, but it doesn't work for me. I find it much easier to follow a line than trying in vain to stay close to the edge of a board, without cutting into it. I end up watching the board so intently that I don't notice if the saw is cutting perpendicular to the wall, or wandering off at an angle.

To mark a line around the opening for a freehand cut, you can snap a chalk line between nails, then connect the chalk lines in the hollows with a flat-sided carpenter's pencil laid against the edge of a 2 x 4. Another—quite ingenious—method is described by B. Allan Mackie in *The Owner-Built Log Home*. Mackie suggests shining a bright light behind a dry line stretched between the nails, then tracing the line's shadow.

If you've got a brand-new saw chain stashed away somewhere, now is the time to use it, because you don't want to cut the openings with a dull chain (or a worn bar). And while you're

LaVonne's Verities

RULE OF 2: Don't be surprised if it takes two times longer than planned, and costs twice as much.

at it, it won't hurt to pray to the log gods that there are no spikes in the way.

No matter how good you are with a chainsaw, there is a real possibility that the saw will kickback as you begin your cut, so be ready for it. And make sure the chain brake is in good working order.

This may sound like a no-brainer, but it isn't: before you cut, look around the house below the openings, just to be certain the cut logs don't land on anything dear to you as they fall to the ground. Dogs, in particular, like to nap against the sides of houses. (It's one our dogs' favorite pastimes to dig nests in the soft dirt next to the foundation. Curiously, they are not dissuaded by either the noise of a chainsaw, or the steady rain of sawdust.)

INSTALLING THE BUCKS AND WINDOWS

I could tell you that almost everyone who builds a log house takes adequate measures to allow for settling, and those few fools who don't always end up pulling out their doors and windows and re-cutting the holes. But I'd be lying, on both counts.

Many people who build with dry logs simply build window and door bucks with heavy timbers and forget about it. The house will eventually settle around the bucks, with results that run the gamut from not noticeable to comically obvious, but the doors and windows still open.

If you are determined to tempt fate, but want to give yourself a little more cushion, leave a settling space between the header log and the top of the buck. But there is really no point in doing it this way, when it is so simple to build window and door bucks that allow for unimpeded settling.

Settling Options for Windows

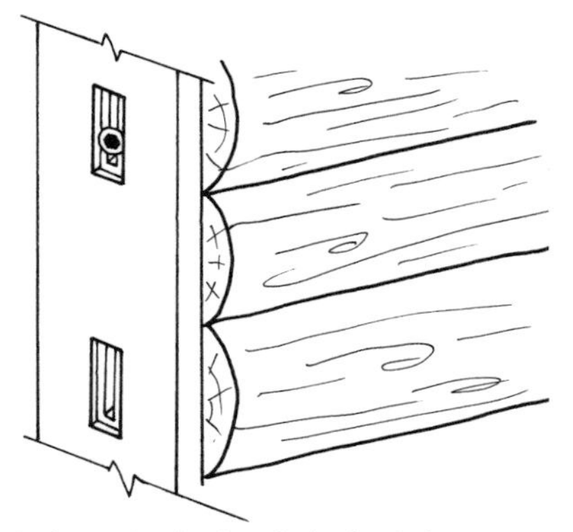

Option 1: Cut slots into the buck so bolts can slide as logs settle.

One easy method involves cutting slots in the bucks for the nails or lags screws (attached through the buck, into the logs) to slide as the house settles *(option 1, at left)*. By using a router to cut a countersink slot for the heads to move without scraping against the window jamb, it's a quick, though inelegant, technique that hardly takes any extra time or effort.

The final two methods (which, I should point out, are the *only* methods accepted by the International Log Builders Association) take a little more work, but are well worth the effort if you want the peace of mind that comes with knowing you've done things "according to

Hoyle." In both techniques, splines (keys) are attached vertically to the sides of the bucks, and keyways are then cut into the exposed log ends to allow for unimpeded movement as the structure slowly settles.

The splines can be made from either angle iron, or wood. If angle iron is used, the edge that lies flat against the buck is recessed into the wood with a dado cut, made with either a table saw or a router, and the angle iron secured with countersunk wood screws *(option 2)*. Most of the keyway in the log ends can be cut with a circular saw, and the corners finished off with a good handsaw, or a drill bit designed to perform router-type cuts.

If you choose wood splines over angle iron *(option 3)*, 2 x 4's set on edge should be used for stability, since part of the reason splines are recommended over other methods is that they eliminate any lateral wall movement in the opening. A strong spline—one that will neither bend nor break—is therefore suggested.

Settling Options for Windows

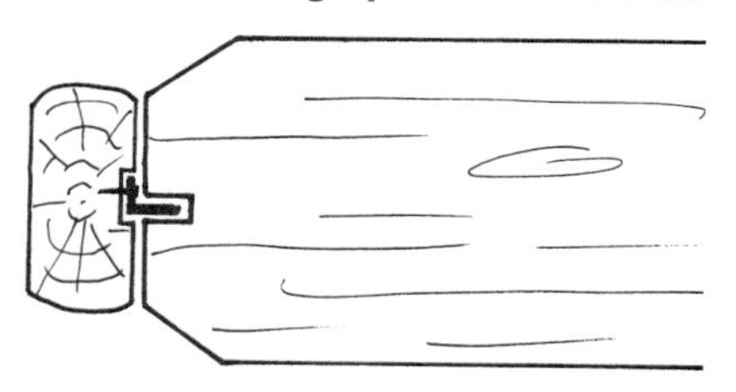

Option 2: Cut a keyway into the log, and attach an angle iron spline to the buck.

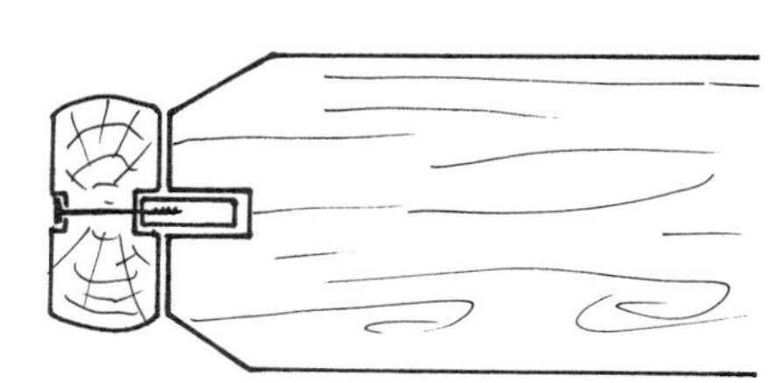

Option 3: Cut a larger keyway into the log, and attach a 2x4 spline to buck.

Keyways are cut into the window openings at the Buckhorn Camp log home.

The keyway for a wood spline is usually cut into the log with a chainsaw, and the corners finished off with a chisel. An alternate—far more tedious—method is to drill a series of holes along either side of the proposed keyway, and removing the wood with a chisel.

Once the bucks are in place and square, measure your openings (height, width and the diagonals) to confirm that your delivered windows will fit properly. If you haven't ordered your windows, now is the time. Keep in mind that you may want extra-deep windows to fit within your thicker-than-average walls. I would suggest beveling the logs (with a chainsaw) around the openings, before installing the windows. Finish off the logs with an orbital sander, and then pop in your windows. Step back and admire the view!

ADDING TRIM BOARDS

Once the bucks and windows are in place, fill the settling space with some type of easily compressible insulation, such as fiberglass. The trim boards can be attached to the header log, or to the buck, depending on the style of bucks you have chosen.

Trim Moves with Top Log

If you attach a trim board to the header log, it will slide down past the buck (and the side trim) as the structure settles. Since the trim board will move with the header log, you can go ahead and install flashing and chinking over the board's top edge to repel water and bugs.

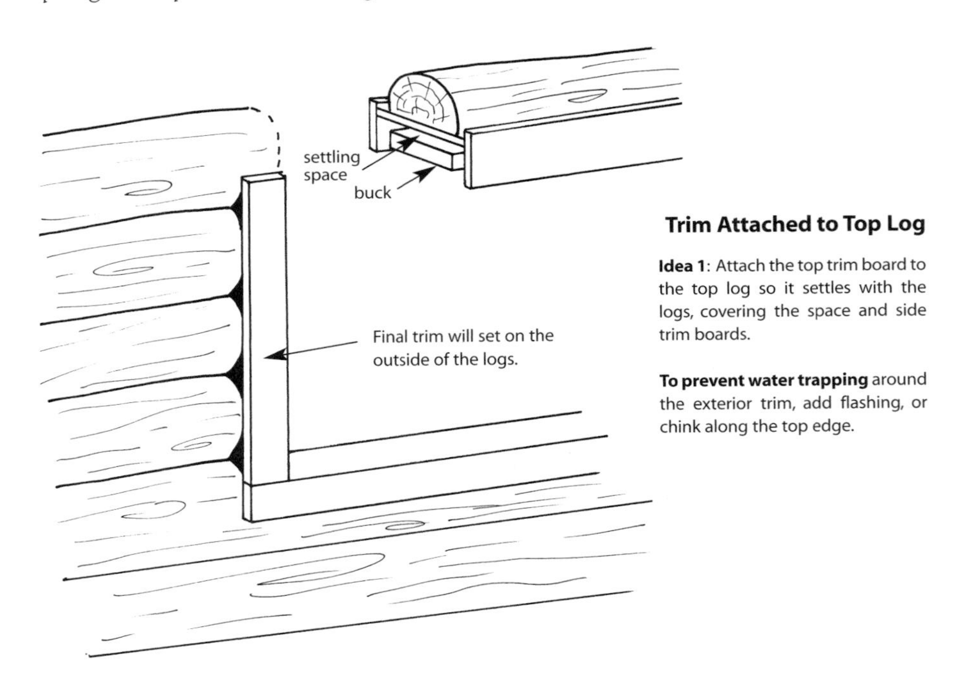

Trim Attached to Top Log

Idea 1: Attach the top trim board to the top log so it settles with the logs, covering the space and side trim boards.

To prevent water trapping around the exterior trim, add flashing, or chink along the top edge.

Trim Fixed to the Bucks

In this case, the top log will settle behind the top trim board which is nailed to the top buck. If you attach trim boards to the bucks, be sure not to also attach them to the log wall, until you are satisfied the house is finished settling.The same goes for caulking and chinking. To stop insects and air drafts from entering the house through your sliding jambs, you can stuff fiberglass insulation into the cracks with a putty knife.

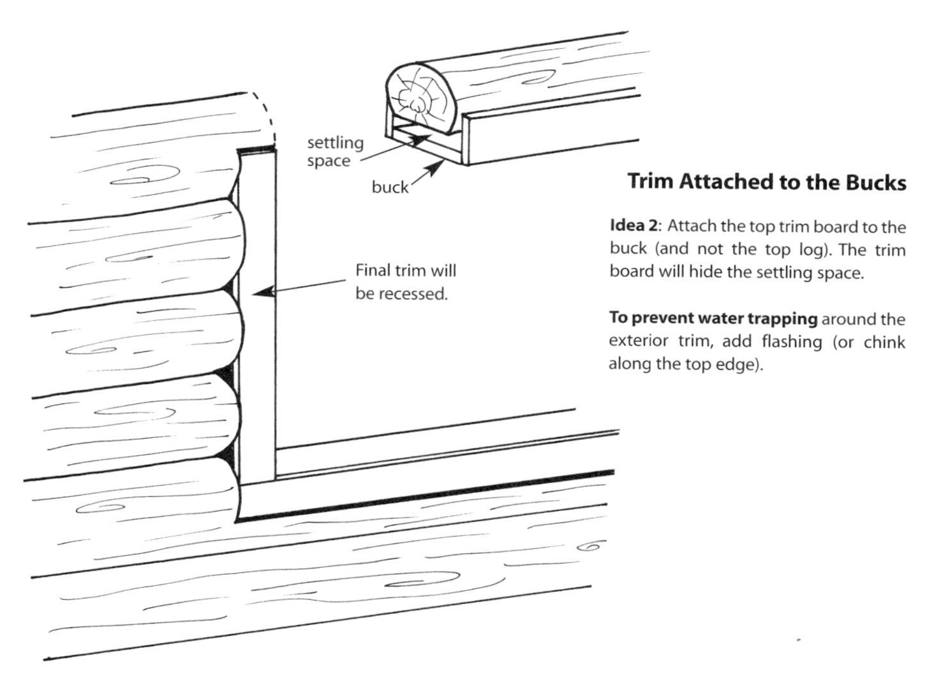

Trim Attached to the Bucks

Idea 2: Attach the top trim board to the buck (and not the top log). The trim board will hide the settling space.

To prevent water trapping around the exterior trim, add flashing (or chink along the top edge).

Admittedly, it's a lot of work to install doors and windows properly, but not nearly as much work as installing them improperly. And once you are finished, you have the satisfaction of knowing that you won't have redo it a year or two down the road.

Staggered Ends

CUTTING THE LOG ENDS

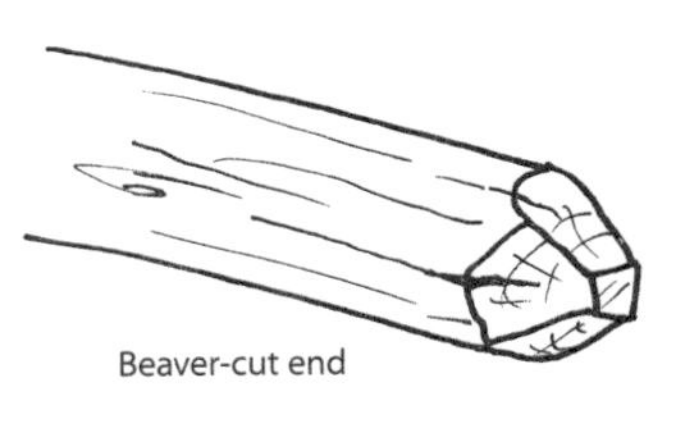
Beaver-cut end

One log wall is pretty much like another, but the log ends don't have to be. What you do with them will set the theme for the rest of the house. Is your home rustic, or refined? Do you prefer randomness over order; straight lines over sweeping curves? It's purely a matter of aesthetics, since no one way is better than any other. There are two rules to follow, however. First, the shortest log end should extend at least 9 inches past the notch and, secondly, all log ends should be protected by overhanging eaves.

Straight cuts can be marked with a chalk line or a straight board used as a guide; curved cuts can be marked (and kept uniform) with a long, template piece of plywood with the desired curve cut out of it. Random cuts depend on one's sense of randomness. I marked each log with a grease pencil per LaVonne's instructions, as she stood back and eyeballed the ends from a distance.

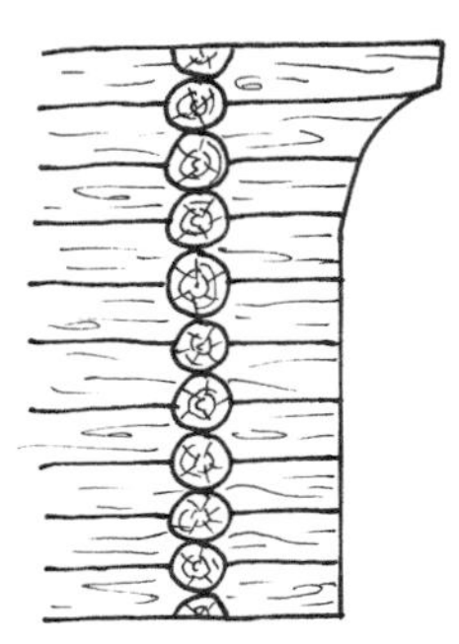
Arched Ends

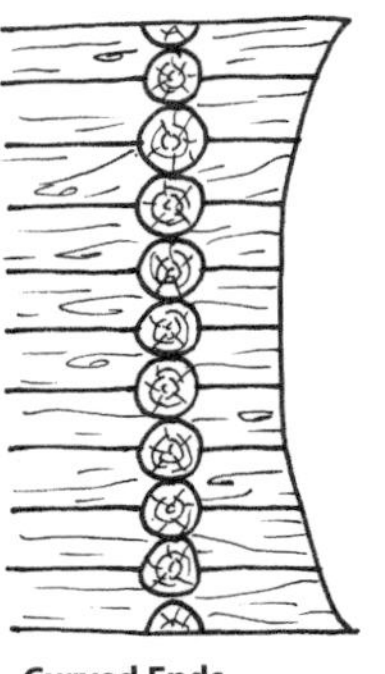
Curved Ends

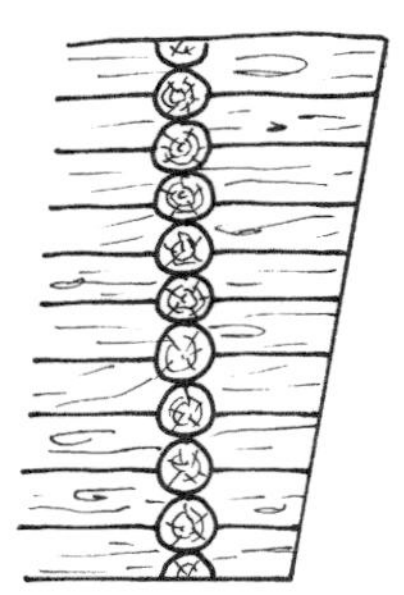
Angled Ends

Using the loader tractor, Rex cuts the log ends in a random stagger, and then beaver-cuts each log end.

FRAME WALLS AND PLUMBING

Your interior frame walls are the ideal place to run plumbing pipes/vents, and electrical wires. Your plumbers will want to have first crack at drilling holes; wiring can be run around pipes a lot easier than pipes around the wires. The next chapter on "Settling" addresses special concerns for frame walls and plumbing.

ELECTRICAL WIRING

There are two ways to run wires in a log home. You can use either method if you are chinking your home, but only one of them is feasible in a chinkless, full-scribe log home. The latter method requires a lot more planning, a little more work, and final result is essentially the same.

As you devise a wiring plan, you should take into account the fact that low voltage wiring—phone lines, stereo speaker wire, cables for satellite television and internet service, computer network cables, etc.—should not be run through the same holes as, or along side of, standard house wiring. It could result in unacceptable interference.

Running Wires Through Predrilled Holes

Before beginning the log work, you will need a diagram showing every wall outlet, smoke detector, ceiling fan, light switch, and light fixture, both inside and outside the house, and their locations should all be marked clearly, and indelibly, on the floor. Then, as the walls go up, you will drill holes—using a long, spurred, spiral bit—through each log to accommodate the wires running to and from each outlet, switch and fixture. Most of the wires are run through the floor joists and up to the height of the electrical boxes. Wires to overhead lights are more easily run through interior framed walls, but can also be run through the logs. Many builders run "fish" wires through the holes in the logs as the structure goes up, making it easier to pull wires later, but if you are careful, and drill large enough holes, this step may not be necessary.

Benshoof's home will have switches and outlets centered in a log. Wires will be pulled through predrilled vertical holes at the back of each box.

Once the structure is complete, the square recesses for the switch and outlet boxes are cut into the log walls, and the surfaces are flattened so the cover plates lie flush. Holes are then drilled through the back of the recesses to meet up with the holes previously drilled to run the wires.

The recesses can be cut with a chisel. You can also use a heavy-duty jig saw, or a reciprocating saw with a short blade, beginning and ending the cuts at holes drilled in opposite corners with a Forstner bit. The wood inside can then be easily removed with a chisel. (The reciprocating saw is a fast way to cut the recesses, but it's a rough ride. Once your eyeballs start rolling around in their sockets, you might want to go back to a chisel.)

The other option is to center the electrical box between two logs (either horizontal for outlets or vertical for switches) and chink up to it.

Running the Wires Between the Logs

It takes far less planning to run the wires between the logs (behind the chinking). With this method, the house wires come up through the floor at the side of a door opening (where they will later be hidden by a trim board), then are stapled into the cracks between the logs, before the chinking is applied. Second story wiring can be run through framed walls, or snaked up along log corners, after the corner notches are opened up with a chainsaw to allow space to hide the wires. (Don't worry—chinking does a great job of hiding the wires, and any unsightly chainsaw work.)

Cutting recesses for boxes is much the same as when running wires through predrilled holes, except that in this case the recesses will be nestled between two logs, rather than entirely into one. Chinking will then hide any part of the box that is exposed.

Low Voltage Wiring

Don't forget the low voltage wiring for your telephone, internet, satellite television, and sound system. Although we don't have phone land lines yet, we wired the house in case the phone company someday decides to run service to our home (for under $18,000). Leroy and Ray from Accent Media Group also ran CAT-5 wires for networking our computers, and satellite TV. And since we enjoy music, we have in-ceiling speakers throughout the house, and outdoor speakers on the deck.

The satellite dish for our Starband internet connection is firmly mounted on our roof.

LaVonne's

LOGBOOK 12

May 2000

We buy a load of 2x6's and frame around each opening. Rex is amazed at how many windows I managed to get by him.

Windows are delivered (all but one that was broken in transit) and in they go [24]...with lots of caulking to seal under the flanges. The house is looking cozier by the day. And I won't miss that rattling plastic that covered the window openings.

June 2000

Rex decides it is time to finish the exterior, and the first project is to cut the wall logs ends in a random stagger [25]. I stand back at a distance and direct Rex with the chainsaw. The beaver cut on the end of each log is a nice finishing touch. Then he bevels each log where it meets the window, inside and out. This is a very tedious job of sawing and chiseling, but the effect is well-worth it. These little things really give a house some character.

25

Our logs are definitely dry enough to finish. Actually, they are rather sunburnt from sitting in the sun for so long. We powerwash the logs, sanding any really obnoxious greyed areas. Then the Penetreat is sprayed, and after drying, we put on the first coat of stain/sealer. To achieve an even coat, it works best for us to roll it on and then brush it. I'm so glad we chose a water-based product; the cleanup is easy and it dries fast (which is good when those afternoon storms threaten).

24

LaVonne's LOGBOOK 13

June 2000

I remember one morning in mid June very clearly. After working on the north side for a couple hours, I poke my head around to the southwest and see a huge cloud of black smoke [26], which can only mean a forest fire. I yell for Rex, and grab the cell phone. Yes, the fire has been reported. Next I call the neighbors and soon we are glued to the radio, which gives precious little information.

The hot, dry, windy conditions are perfect for a raging fire. After two days, the firecrews start using our place as a lookout area. We stand closeby, eavesdropping on their radio conversations. The evacuation order comes just after the firemen told us that we were on our own. They will not defend our properties. We stay, but I pack the truck with the computers, photos and whatever else my scrambled brain can think of. Rex cuts down any bush or tree close to the log house, and the cabin where we are living. Finally, after many endless days of watching the smoke, and sleepless nights of watching the flames, a cold front descends a day early, bringing snow! The middle of June and it snows! Prayers of my nieces for snow have been answered, and we gather together with the neighbors in a state of exhaustion and relief. The Bobcat Gulch fire, from an untended campfire, was extinguished after burning nearly 11,000 acres.

June is not a month to repeat. A week after the fire, I fall off the scaffolding while trying to move a ladder. Three hours later, the HMO doctor finally looked inside my mouth and observed that I needed stitches (tears finally convinced them I wasn't as fine as my face looked!). So off to the oral surgeon I went, but by now, he is out to lunch. Eventually I'm stitched up and Rex takes me home with a 6-pack of Ensure protein drink and homeopathy pain pills.

Before long, I'm back at work on the house, but forbidden to climb ladders and scaffolding (at least for a few weeks).

26

CHAPTER 15

SETTLING ISSUES

When Things That Don't Shrink Meet Things That Do

If you find yourself cringing at the thought of reading this chapter, I assure you there is no need to; by installing the doors and windows, you've already triumphed over the baddest beast in the lair. This is not to say that what remains is a picnic, only that you've been tested under fire, and have emerged with a ton more knowledge and experience that you started with. So let out the breath you've been holding, and read on.

THE BIG PICTURE

Every house built with wood loses height over time. In the case of a frame house, it may only be a fraction of an inch; for kiln-dried milled logs, a little more. In a hand-hewn, round log house the shrinkage is harder to gauge: it may only be an inch or two, but it might be the better part of a foot. A loss in height of even a couple of inches, however, can lead to disastrous consequences if certain allowances are not made in critical areas.

Everyone knows that windows and doors should be installed in a manner that takes wall shrinkage into account, but not everything else is quite so obvious. Sewer pipes, water lines, stove pipes, chimneys, vent stacks and stairs (to name a few) must all be installed in a manner that neither impedes wall shrinkage, nor experiences distortion because of it.

Fortunately, everyone who has ever built a log house with plumbing and heating and second floors has had to deal with the same problems, and some very clever ways to deal with them have been devised.

FRAME WALLS

A slot has been cut in the 2x frame wall stud, and the bolt is partially sunk into Benshoof's log wall.

While you could, conceivably, run all the plumbing pipes through massive holes bored in the log walls, your spouse would probably have you committed after witnessing the temper-tantrum you'd throw, the first time a leak appeared. So, to play it safe, let's say your house will need at least one frame wall through which to run plumbing pipes.

What happens to that frame wall—and all the unyielding pipes going to the second story—when the log walls shrink in height? Nothing, if you go about it right. Let's begin with the wall, and worry about the pipes later.

For all practical purposes, a wall is like a big window you can't see through, and should be treated accordingly. In other words, the sliding bucks you installed in keyways for the doors and windows—and the spaces you left at the top for settling—work equally as well for frame walls. The keyway should be as

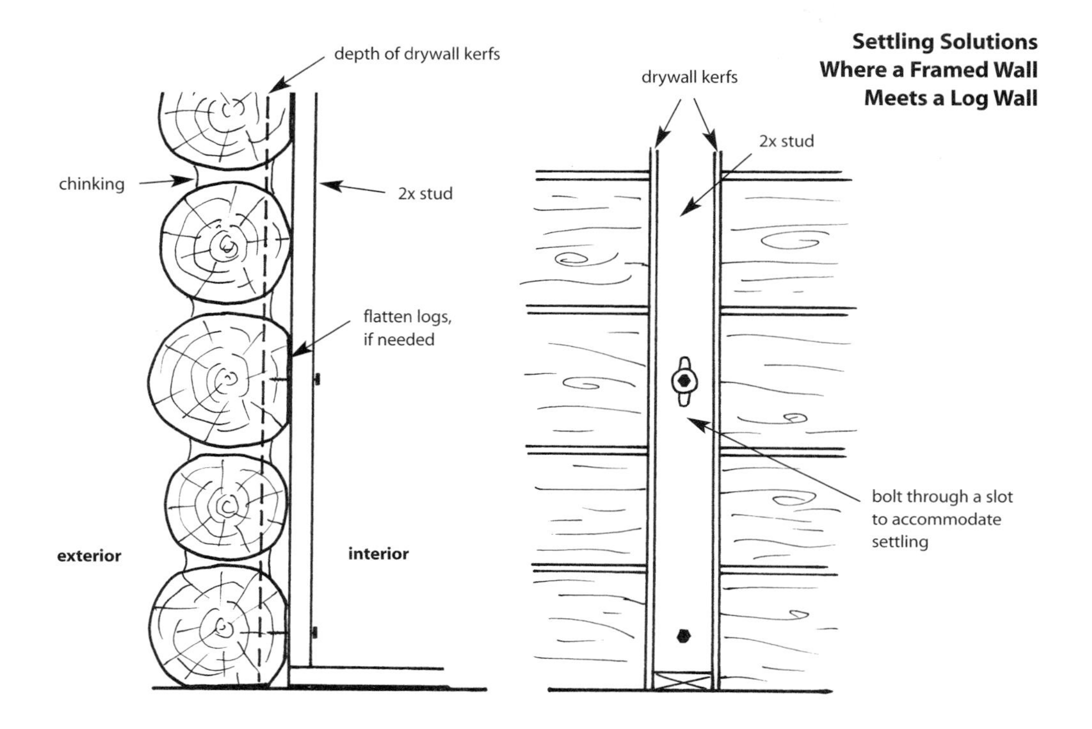

Settling Solutions Where a Framed Wall Meets a Log Wall

shallow as possible, and never more than one half of the log wall's thickness. Though the keyway, alone, will hold the wall in place (provided it's cut properly), you can, if you wish, bolt the frame wall to the log wall by running the lag bolts through slots cut into the end board that will allow for settling.

To cut the keyway, make vertical lines on the wall, using the same method you used to mark the door and window openings. For a crisp, clean cut, a good circular saw can be used to cut the first 2-$^{1}/_{2}$ inches into the log wall. After chiseling out wood between the cuts, a chainsaw can be used to deepen the keyway, if necessary. By directing the saw at a slight angle inward, you will be able to avoid marring your nice beginning cut, while ensuring that you'll have plenty of space for the wall to slide in. It's important that the keyway is perfectly vertical, otherwise the log wall may push against the frame wall as it settles. (**Note**: If you want the frame wall to span the distance between two log walls, you will have to build it in two pieces, then join them after they are erected.)

It is common practice to cut the keyway in the log wall deep enough—and wide enough—to accommodate the wall boards on either side of the frame wall. In this way, the log wall hides the rough ends of the wall board, and will slide past it as the wall settles.

On the other hand, if you are *certain* the house will finish settling by the time you get around to installing the wall board, you can cut the keyway shallow (for the stud wall only), then scribe the wall board around the logs and chink the joints. We were able to do this on our house, with no deleterious effects.

The top plate of the frame wall should be lagged through the settling space to the ceiling joists above (or boards bridging the joists if the wall falls between joists). Install the lag bolts through predrilled holes, so that, as the house settles, the lags do no bind in the plate.

To hide the settling space between the top of the wall plate and the ceiling joists, attach a 1 x nailer—the same width

Settling space is evident above the double plate on this frame wall at Benshoof's home.

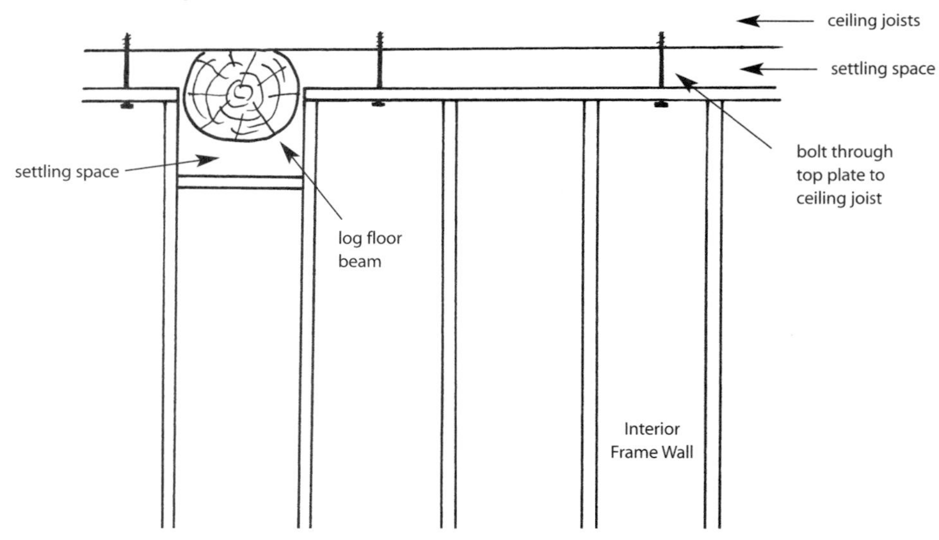

as the wall plate *plus* the finished drywall— to the ceiling directly above the wall. (Be certain to take the thickness of the 1x board into account, when calculating the settling space.) Then, after the drywall is installed and finished, attach a trim board to the 1x nailer. As the ceiling drops, the trim board will slide past the wall board.

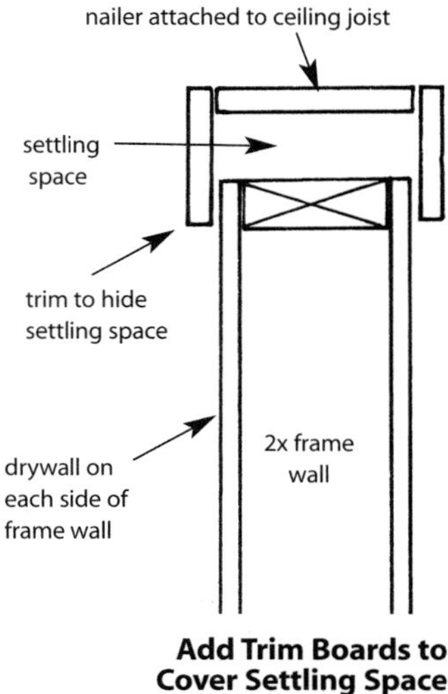

Add Trim Boards to Cover Settling Space

STAIRS

Since stairs are one of the last structural components to be built, there is a good chance that the house will be almost through settling by the time you get around to installing them, especially if the house has been a weekend project. That's good, because stairs are always tricky to build, even when the distance between floors doesn't decrease over time.

A quick and dirty temporary stair, put into service while the house is still settling, is the best answer, though not very satisfying if you anticipate several more years of wall shrinkage.

A straight stair (without a landing) works best in a house that is still settling. Attached (hinged) only to the upper floor, and allowed to slide on the first floor, the stair angle will decrease as the house settles, and the treads will tilt upward. With minimal wall shrinkage these changes in attitude may fall within the parameters of the venerable "slop factor." (For example: with an 8-foot high stair built with 8 inches of rise to 9 inches of run, a 2 inch decrease in wall height would change the stair angle by a little more than a degree, and the stringer would move 1-3/4 inches across the floor.)

By taking an educated guess at how much more the house will settle, you can then place spacers under the bottoms of the stringers and pull them out as needed. To keep from tripping on the first step, I would advise a temporary landing in front of it; one that can be shortened as the spacers are removed. The spacer technique (or a screw jack) can also be used for a spiral stair, with the big difference being that you need to be better at guessing, since you won't have the same slop factor to fall back on.

Stairs with landings, or stairs built into log walls, are better left until all settling has occurred, though if only minimal shrinkage remains—and you are clever enough—you should be able to make it work.

PLUMBING PIPES, AND VENTS FOR FURNACES AND HOT WATER HEATERS

Since they are not pressurized, PVC sewer and vent pipes can be fitted with a series of compression fittings that will allow the pipe sections to become shorter as the building settles. In order to restrict all movement to the compression fittings, solid blocking should be used at all horizontal offsets, and at the top of the uppermost joint and the bottom of the lowest one.

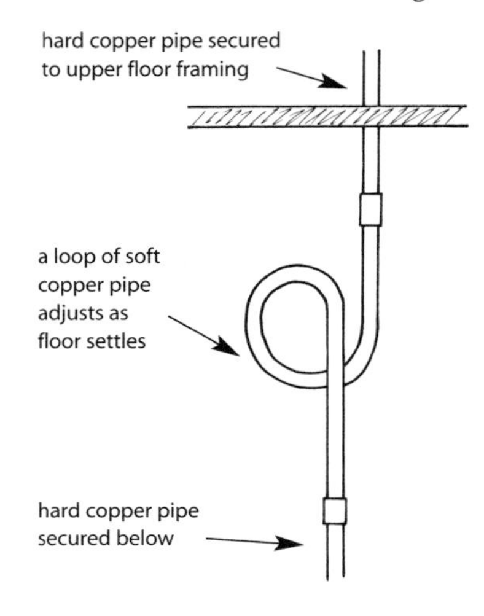

Plumbing in a Settling House

All vertical copper water supply pipes running between floors should be installed with loops of soft copper below the settling space, so that as the top section of pipe pushes down, the loop simply expands. As with sewer and vent pipes, the water supply pipes should be secured above and below the loops.

Any offsets in furnace or water heater vents should be completed far enough below the upper floor that they are not affected by wall settling. Also, the vents should *not* be secured to the roof flashing, or any floor or wall above the first floor, so that they can slide freely through their chases as the house settles.

CHIMNEYS AND STOVE PIPES

Fireplace chimneys should be designed and built as free-standing structures, with no points of attachment to log walls, upper floors, or the roof. (Unless you are inventive enough to figure out some way to do it that takes wall shrinkage into account.) Be sure to make the roof flashing tall enough that it remains covered by the chimney counterflashing, as the chimney increases in height, relative to the roof, due to settling.

In the event that you are installing a wood stove, rather than a fireplace, it just might be that the stove pipe will slide through the roof opening, and roof flashing, unimpeded. If, however, a support box is used to provide necessary clearance for fire prevention, or to make a transition from single- or double-walled pipe, to triple-walled pipe, then a telescoping section of pipe will have to be installed under the support box, and adjusted periodically.

VERTICAL SUPPORT POSTS

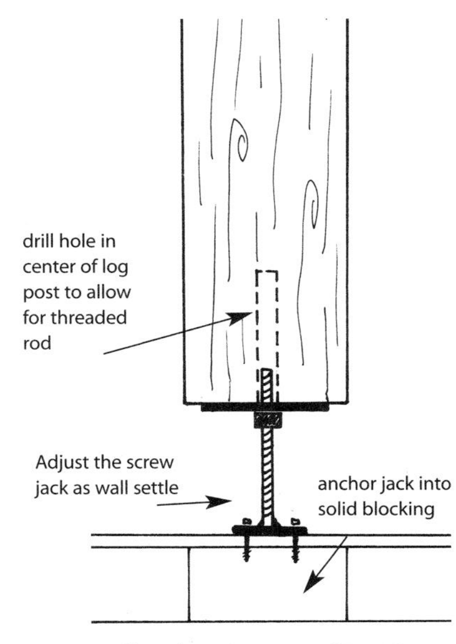

Screw Jack Below Structural Log Posts

Like walls, vertical supports under floor beams or porch roofs must be able to compensate for log wall shrinkage. But, since they are structural components, simply leaving a settling space at the top is unacceptable. Instead, some method should be employed to slowly lower the posts as the walls settle.

Screw jacks are commercially available for just this purpose. Permanently placed under a post, the jack is adjusted incrementally, as needed. It's ugly, of course, and needs to be hidden from view, so you'll have to come up with a box or decorative cylinder that you can slide up the post, or one that has a removable panel, to allow for periodic adjustments to the jack.

We tried another, riskier, method. Fairly certain that our house was not going to settle more than 2 inches, we placed four 1/2-inch spacers under each of our beam supports, then used a hydraulic jack and a post to hold up the floor beams every time we needed to remove a spacer. By the time all the spacer's were out, the house was done settling. If we'd have needed to shorten the post even more, a chainsaw would have obliged us.

It worked for us, but our house was done settling before we got around to installing the hardwood floor, or the lightweight concrete beneath it. If you even *suspect* that your house might still be settling after the finished floor is in place, it would be an expedient gesture of marital goodwill to play it safe and use the jacks.

KITCHEN CABINET CONSIDERATIONS

Cabinet installation on frame walls is easy, but mounting your kitchen cabinets on log walls requires special attention. Not only will the cabinets need to be shimmed to compensate for the uneven nature of the logs, you will need to think about settling. Many experts agree that the majority of settling will occur within the first three years, so if you are like us, settling won't be an issue by the time you get around to hanging the cabinets. If, however, your log walls will settle more than 1/2-inch, you may want to consider mounting your cabinets through small slots (using washers with the screws), or on sliding sleepers notched into the log wall. To avoid the tricky part of mounting on log walls altogether, frame a narrow wall in front of the log wall. Installing back splashes are greatly simplified with this method, but it does take a bit of square footage out of your kitchen. If you have a cabinets that wrap around a log wall to an interior frame wall, this is a good method for keeping all cabinets at the same level over time.

Our best advise is to wait as long as possible.

You'll probably run across other instances where allowances will have to be made for settling; what I've discussed here are merely the most prevalent. As a rule, don't install anything until you've thought it through and concluded that it will not be affected by wall settling. If it will be, don't worry; by now, you're savvy enough to solve the problem.

THE BENEFIT OF EXPERIENCE

Benshoof's house was built in early January by Log Knowledge, then allowed to sit through the winter and early spring before it was re-set on John's site. Naturally, I had a few questions about settling, particularly since the north-south gable was built with full (horizontal) logs at one end, vertical logs at the other, and a log truss in the middle. How did they compensate for settling of the full log gable ends, and the walls the truss was set upon, when it was obvious the vertical logs would not settle at all?

Stanley Johnson, the crew foreman, has built so many log houses that my concern hardly seemed to be an issue for him. He told me he'd cut a few inches off the bottoms of the vertical posts to compensate for settling at the yard, then another inch at John's home site for additional settling, yet to occur. He was confident it would be enough. I believe him.

Since the house was built with dry logs, then allowed a few months to settle in a dry climate, no special precautions were made for settling around doors and windows. Instead, the crew merely spiked heavy-timber bucks to the log ends in the openings, leaving an inch or so above the headers for settling.

After building hundreds of log houses, these guys know what to expect. Had the logs been greener, or had less time to settle, they certainly would have done things differently, but for this particular house, it's all that was required.

CHAPTER 

CHINKING AND FINISHING

Keeping Weather In Its Place

Thirty years ago there were two standard choices for sealing and protecting logs against the ravages of nature: boiled linseed oil; with, or without. Turpentine, that is. The prospects for chinking were even more dismal: mortar, or meticulously cut strips of wood. Both entailed extreme outputs of labor for a woefully temporary solution.

Today, with a log home industry soaring into the billions of dollars, high-tech solutions to the age-old problem of preserving wood, and chinking cracks and seams, abound. This is a good thing for log home owners, since many of these new products really are as good the manufacturers claim they are. But at the same time, it's up to the home owner to sift through the reams of promotional and technical literature to find the best products to protect their hard-won log walls against air infiltration, water, sunlight, bugs and mildew.

Thankfully, the art of chinking does not involve mortar anymore. This old cabin is quite drafty now.

While it is hardly within the scope of this chapter—or the expertise of the simplicity-loving woodsman writing it—to cover the pros and cons of all the various products available, I can, hopefully, offer a general framework upon which you can build your own mountain of knowledge before finally deciding on which products to use.

GOOD DESIGN = GOOD PROTECTION

Wide eaves protect the logs from the harsh elements of sunlight and moisture.

I have touched on these matters in other chapters, I know, but I believe it is prudent to gather them all together here and elucidate them with the same light, at the same time.

The very best thing you can do for your logs is to protect them by designing (and building) a roof with big eaves. Besides keeping rain and snow away from your walls, big eaves also help shield the logs from the glaring rays of the midday summer sun. Log ends are particularly vulnerable to sunlight and moisture, and your eave design should take this into account. Purlin ends should be terminated before the fascia board, and the ends of all wall logs and floor beams should be adequately protected by the eaves.

Below the eaves, all window sills should be canted downward to repel water, as should all bucks and trim boards that stick out past the doors and windows, top and bottom. Metal flashing above doors and windows is also a good idea.

To protect the logs from splash-back from water running off the roof, or from the tons of snow that pile up next to the house in winter, all sill logs should be a bare minimum of 12 inches from the ground. A good metal flashing—again, canted downward—under the sill logs, and sealed against the weather with synthetic chinking, will protect the logs from the buildup of moisture.

In particular, wide, upward-facing horizontal cracks (checks) in wall logs provide places where water can pool, and should be filled with a high-quality caulking material. (For large cracks, relatively cheap foam backer rod can be pushed into the crack first, to save on expensive caulking.)

In general, all log surfaces should be protected from rain and snow, all joints should be designed to shed water, and any places where water can collect should be chinked or caulked.

If all of these measures are taken in due course, your log preservative will only need to work half as hard, and will last twice as long. And your house will enjoy a long, stress-free life.

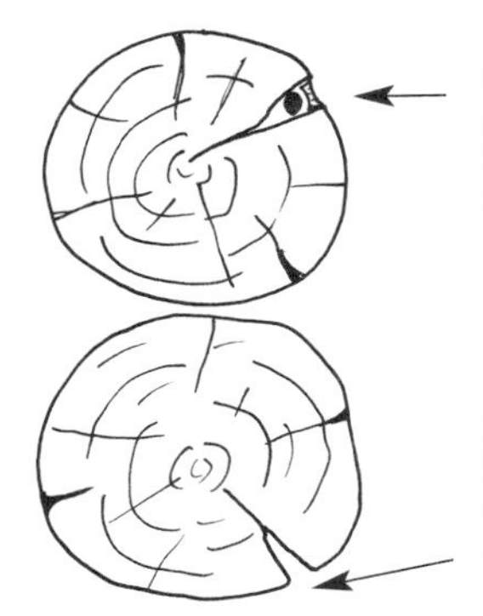

Upward-facing checks should be filled with a backer rod and then caulked.

Large checks (cracks) facing downward do not need to be chinked or caulked.

CLEANING THE LOGS

Logs that have laid peeled in the sun and the rain too long may be stained or discolored. A 5:1 mixture of water and bleach (or any of a dozen commercially prepared solutions), applied with a garden sprayer—followed by a pressure washing—often takes care of the worst of it, though sanding and sandblasting may be needed if the staining is severe. We put four logs in our house that I had peeled months before we began the log work. If I had simply run a drawknife over them a second time, I could have saved myself—and LaVonne—a lot of work, but I didn't realize how tenacious the discoloration was, until we tried to remove it. Bleach and power washing helped, a little, but we still ended up spending several hours with a sander before we were satisfied.

There are products on the market that promise to retard staining and discoloration of peeled logs. Having never tried any of them, I can't make recommendations.

Before applying any type of preservative, your logs should be clean and dry, inside and outside. Cleaning them, of course, means getting them wet. Even if they're still as pretty as the day you peeled them, they will have accumulated layers of dust and dirt that should be removed before applying a finish. A pressure washer is the best tool for the job; nothing fancy—too much pressure makes the logs look fuzzy. Water, alone, should remove all the dirt, though detergent can be used, as long as it is thoroughly rinsed.

The logs are bleached on French's house.

After washing, let the logs dry completely before applying any type of finish.

FINISHES, AND FINISHING

The makers of any type of finish will recommend upper limits for the moisture content of the logs. Most of the products we looked at could not be applied if the moisture level was above 18 or 20 percent. This is roughly considered to be the transition area between green and dry logs. If you have any doubts, you should rent, borrow or buy a moisture meter. It could save you a lot of time and money.

Before sealing and chinking the logs, I highly recommend that you build some kind of scaffolding to work from. You'll still have to use ladders, but at least you will have a firm, level footing on which to place them.

I dug around in our scrap pile for leftover 2 x 4's, secured them to the rim joists, and supported them from the ground with additional 2 x 4's. I then laid 2 x 10's over the top—extra rafters left over the roof, that I had ordered for just this reason—and screwed them in place. A little shaky, and certainly not much to look at, but it worked.

One more thing: are your windows already in place? Do yourself a big favor and tape them off before you accidentally coat them with something that no solvent on the planet will remove without likewise removing the finish on the window frames.

Now, what kind of finish should you use? That depends on what kind of look you want the logs to have, and what sort of environmental challenges the logs will have to face. The very best thing you can do is to talk to someone in your area who has built a few log homes; nothing beats experience. If you don't know anyone, shop around on the internet, then talk to the local sales reps. Or better yet, call a log home supply house that deals in several different brands; they will have knowledgeable people on staff to help you make an informed decision. Be sure to get samples to try on leftover log ends, before putting anything on your house. The sample color charts are not all that accurate.

I used boiled linseed oil on the log house and cabin I built in the 1980's, but I wasn't particularly happy with it. Not only did it darken the logs over time, it also gave them a "dried-out" look.

This time around, we looked at several products before deciding. In the end, we shied away from oils and opted for a water-based stain and sealant. It was a somewhat serendipitous decision, since all the products we used to chink and finish our logs were manufactured by Sashco, and they were all available at our local lumber yard. A young woman who worked there seemed to know the products like they were part of her family, and her easy-going manner, along with her matter-of-fact delivery, convinced LaVonne she knew what she was talking about. And, in fact, she did.

For the outside of the house we used a three-step process, beginning with Penetreat, a borate-based wood preservative that protects against rot and insect infestations. (In an arid climate like Colorado's, where the air is so thin it can't hold much moisture, even when there is any— which is rare—and the insects are all fairly innocuous, it was really a tossup if we needed a wood preservative, or not. In the end, we decided better safe than sorry.)

Since Penetreat goes on wet, we let the logs dry for a few days before applying a single coat of Capture to the logs. This product is an elastic, latex-based stain that protects against UV light and moisture. (Though the directions say it can be applied with a garden sprayer and then brushed-out, we quickly gave up on the sprayer and just used a roller and brush.) There is a small degree of opaqueness to Capture that remains after it dries, but it is not an unpleasing effect.

After the stain dried, we applied a single coat of Cascade, a clear "weather repellent" that is designed to give extra protection against moisture and UV sun rays. Happily, we were able to use the garden sprayer—then a brush—on this operation.

For the interior logs we didn't need (or want) a stain, or a preservative, so we simply applied two coats of a clear finish (Sashco's Symphony) to bring out the grain in the wood.

Two years have passed since we finished the logs, and I have to admit that I'm impressed. The interior logs have remained the rich, honey color they were after they were first sealed, and the exterior logs have neither darkened, nor faded—they still have a fresh, unweathered, appearance. I've never had this kind of luck with any other type of stain or sealant.

CHINKING

Chinking a log house is one of those chores that takes time, no matter how you go about it, so be prepared. On our house—a roomy structure, but certainly not big—I have calculated that, if all of

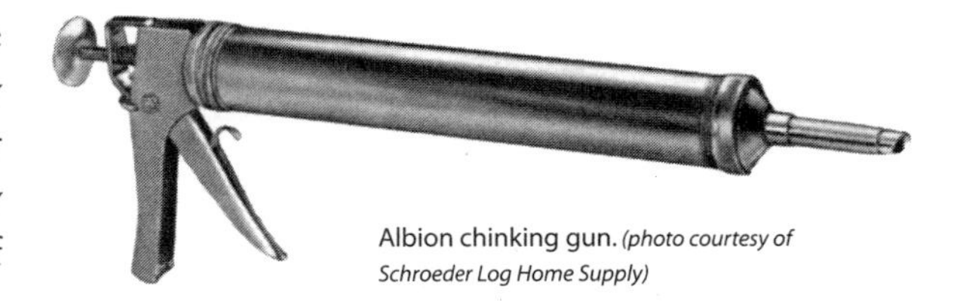

Albion chinking gun. *(photo courtesy of Schroeder Log Home Supply)*

Rex applies the chinking material, and then LaVonne smoothes it, making sure it seals firmly against the logs. A light mist of denatured alcohol and water kept it workable in the dry, hot, windy weather.

the chinking rows were run end to end, there would be a continuous line over a mile long.

Should you chink before, or after, sealing the logs? That depends on what you use to seal them. Many stains can discolor chinking material, so you are much better off waiting until the logs are sealed (also, it's much easier to clean drips and splatters from sealed logs). However, synthetic chinking will not adhere to certain log finishes, especially oils, so check compatibility with the chinking manufacturer before you proceed. We chinked our house after the logs were sealed, inside and out, since we knew the products were compatible; all were from the same manufacturer.

Since the chinking will hide the electric wires run between the cracks in the logs, you will not be able to chink the interior until the wiring is complete. You may need to chink the outside, however, *before* the wires are run—even though you will have to later touchup around outlet and light boxes—since electrical inspectors may expect a house to be completely sealed and dry before it is wired.

Before the chinking is applied to the joint, a foam "backer rod" should be installed. Backer rod serves the dual purpose of minimizing the amount of chinking you use, and works as a substrate against which the chinking can expand or contract, without pulling away from the log surface. It comes in a variety of sizes and shapes, so you shouldn't have any trouble finding what you need to fit between your logs.

Synthetic chinking comes in one quart tubes and five gallon buckets. The tubes cost a bit more and take a very strong hand to apply with a manually operated caulking gun, but they entail a lot less mess. Pneumatic caulking guns, or guns that attach to cordless drills, are well worth the money. If you opt to use the buckets, instead of the tubes, plan to buy a bulk-loading caulking gun or a grout bag, or rent a commercial pump—designed especially for chinking—to make it easier. Either way, leave yourself plenty of time clean up at the end of the day.

You may feel like a fish out of water when you first try your hand at chinking, but you'll soon get the feel of it. I'd shoot chinking along an 8- to 10-foot section, then LaVonne would tool it. Her favorite tool was a small putty knife with rounded corners (I did the rounding with a file), but she also used foam brushes and, occasionally, a cheap little cheese knife with a bent blade. And, of course, a wet rag to wipe up spills. A spray bottle filled with water and a little denatured alcohol was used to keep the material lubricated as she tooled it, and was especially helpful to keep the chinking from drying out, when she worked in the sun and wind.

Though it hardly took LaVonne any time at all to achieve a laudable degree of proficiency at chinking, I'd be lying if I said she ever actually warmed up to the task. But she sure was proud of her work when it was all done.

By the time you finish sealing and chinking your logs, you will have covered every square inch of your walls several times. You may never want to set eyes on a paint brush or a caulking gun again. Probably you will have a hard time believing that an interminable task has really come to an end. But it has, so go to town and kick up your heels; you deserve it.

LaVonne's
LOGBOOK 14

July 2000

Outside work continues with staining and more finishing. While Rex works on the house, finishing the log staining, I work from the ground, staining and sealing the trim boards for the eaves, windows and doors. I choose a lighter color of stain for contrast. When you have lots of windows, you have LOTS of trim boards. Rex puts on the trim boards as soon as I'm done with them (those fascia boards require some tall ladders! [27]) The rough-sawn trim boards are a nice contrast to the round, smooth logs.

27

I wash the interior log walls by hand, scrubbing with a brush to get off the dirt and grime. Then I brush on the clear satin finish, which really enhances the character of the logs. No more procrastinating. We buy a few 5-gallon buckets of chinking, a dispensing gun and try our hand at chinking. Rex fills the gun and applies the chinking between the logs; I follow soon after with the putty knife, foam paintbrush, spray bottle and rag. The first few rows are maddening, but after awhile, we get the hang of it. You really need to be in the right frame of mind. I keep threatening to write about "Zen and the art of chinking."

August 2000

Our moderate-size house is getting larger by the day. Chinking goes on forever. Every time we go to town, we buy more buckets of LogJam (a sizeable investment). I've determined that chinking is "the great equalizer;" it visually evens-out any disparity in gaps between the logs.

While we chink, the stucco man and his son start the many-day process of stucco-ing our gable ends, around the garage doors, and below the unbuilt deck. We also schedule the radiant heat to be installed on the main floor. The plumbers lay the tubing and pressure test for leaks.

It is a crowded job site that morning when the 6-man gypcrete crew from Denver shows up, along with the stucco team. The gypcrete is very runny mortar-looking stuff that sets up in a few hours. I am very happy with how careful the guys were; very few splatters to clean off the log walls (and that will be easy since I sealed the logs first).

LaVonne's
LOGBOOK 15

August 2000

Early August and Rex decides it is time to assemble the wind tower base. He welds together pipe for a base that will attach to the lattice tower; this base will be sunk in a huge concrete filled pit, which is also reinforced with rebar. I'm confident that Rex's tower will withstand the worst of winds.

The well was drilled over a year ago, but now we dig a trench for the water line to the house. The wizard of pumps, Demetri, who installed the pump last year, connects everything to the pressure tank in the house, while the plumbers install the boiler and indirect water heater. It pays to have knowledgeable people doing these jobs, and we were lucky to get the best.

Chinking continues to the corners [28]. If I had a dime for every time I climbed up and down a ladder, I'd be rich.

For a change of pace, Rex suggests we dig a trench. (Dirt work and concrete are my two least favorite things.) Under the 'watchful' eye of our dog, Micky, we start the arduous task of hand-digging a trench from the wind tower to the house (110 feet), and from the solar array (only 40 feet) to the house [29]. Rocks, rocks and more ROCK. A day with a jack hammer leaves Rex numb. Why didn't we hire this out? Because it is impossible to find people to work in the mountains, I keep telling myself.

Power with Nature

CHAPTER 17

A NEW PHILOSOPHY OF FREEDOM

Notes on Developing an Off-the-Grid Mentality

STARTING WITH NOTHING

When LaVonne and I turned our backs on our old farm for the last time, we were facing a sudden and irrevocable change in lifestyle. The fact that we had just sold a 2000 square foot house, so we could live in an amenity-free cabin with a footprint smaller than a one-car garage, was the least of it. The real challenge was learning to deal with the sum of all the other changes.

Where before we had a well that pumped water at the rate of 30 gallons per minute, we now had to drive 20 miles to town once a week to fill a 200-gallon tank, roped into the back of a pickup. Our toilet was an outhouse, our bathtub a creek. A large cooler had replaced our spacious refrigerator (sorry, no more ice maker). We now used a wood stove for heat, a gasoline camp stove for cooking, and kerosene lanterns for light.

And when we simply *had* to have electricity, I would go solemnly into battle with a war-hardened, 4,000-watt Coleman generator. If I prevailed over the surly beast, then we could run a saw, or a vacuum. If I was bested, then we just had to wait until I could sneak up on the ornery brute in its sleep and yank its cord, before it had a chance to suck in a carburetor-full of gas, belch flames, and flood itself.

One would think that such an abrupt "lowering" of living standards would manifest itself as individual stress, or even marital strife, but nothing of the sort occurred. Quite the opposite, in fact; more than anything, LaVonne and I embraced our new life with all the energy and ambition of a couple of kids on an extended camping trip. Having purged our lives of the leaden inertia that crystallizes in the consciousness of anyone in the habit of having an instant remedy for any earthly desire, we quickly came to appreciate every drop of water, every morsel of food; every ray of light in the midst of darkness.

THE FIRST PRECIOUS AMENITIES

We were, quite literally, starting over from scratch. Any comforts or conveniences we hoped to enjoy would have to come as a direct result of hard work and mutual cooperation, not from wringing our hands over the nature of our plight.

Living just a notch or two above primitive, we quickly prioritized our desires. (I say "desires" because we actually didn't *need* anything more than we had.) First on our wish list was hot water. And not the kind you heat on the stove in a brass pot for a cup of tea, either; we wanted hot water that flowed copiously from a showerhead, inside a closed shower stall, within a warm room, walled off from the clouds and the wind.

Toward that end, we built a small (6-foot x 16-foot) addition on the back of cabin, just big enough to hold a tiny shower stall, a used 35-gallon propane hot water heater, a propane refrigerator (which, as it turned out, wouldn't arrive for several months, thanks to Y2K), three water barrels, and everything we needed for a simple solar-electric system.

We pressurized the fresh water system with a small 12-volt RV pump, which was powered with a pair of 12-volt deep-cycle batteries; one to power the pump, the other hooked to a small solar module, for charging. When the battery in use ran down, we switched them out. (Since the DC side of the PV (photovoltaic) system we had yet to install was 24 volts, it was cheaper to use batteries we already had, than to buy an expensive converter to step down from 24 volts to 12 volts, just to run the pump.)

The electrical system followed the plumbing and gas piping. Using the solar modules and power inverter we'd purchased for the log house—which, at this point, was no more than a muddy hole in the ground—we had more power than we could have ever used in that small cabin, even during a run of cloudy days of biblical proportions.

Considering that, until then, my most meritorious achievement as an electrician was running AC power to a few stock tank heaters for the horses, the complexity of that first, bare-bones PV system seemed daunting. I read every manual, front to back, one, two, three times. I put every component of the system into place, and then slowly, meticulously, hooked-up my wires, using a multimeter to check—and double check—every step along the way.

I will never forget the day when that first PV system came online. I had tested every connection ten times over, before I finally flipped the switch to the DC disconnect and turned on the inverter. No sparks, no explosions. Just a steady hum and the soft, green glow of back-lit LCD's. After testing the AC side of the system—to see if my multimeter was as convinced as I was that we actually *were*

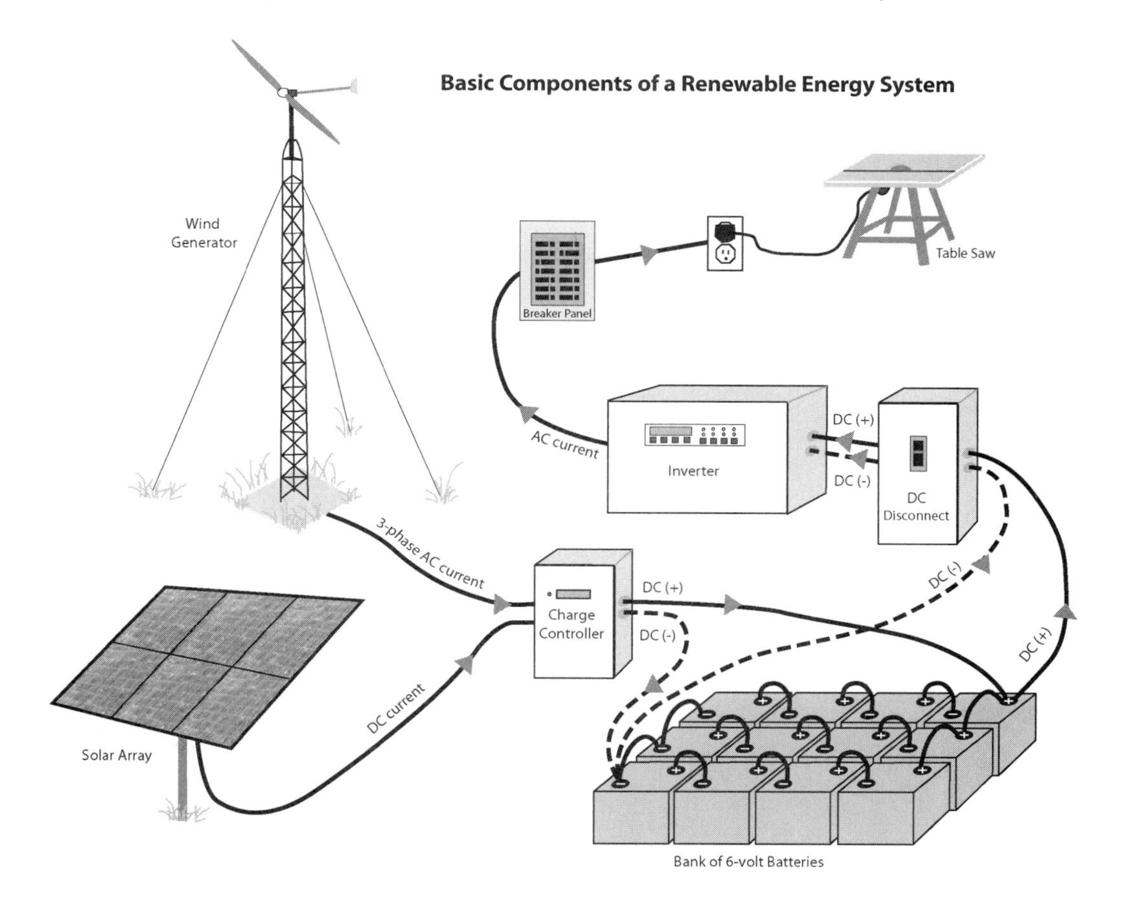

producing usable power from the sun—I began trying different loads. First a small light, then an electric drill.

Impressed, but still not convinced, I opted for the ultimate test: a voracious 15-amp table saw. It was the single piece of equipment that could make the burly old Coleman generator convulse with fear (of a herniated head gasket, I would imagine). I plugged it in, hit the switch (after a fleeting, jumbled moment of pensive hesitation) and watched with consummate awe as the blade spun quickly and effortlessly into motion.

Though my left brain knew the whirring saw blade was merely the logical outcome of applied technology, my right brain insisted that I had just witnessed a miracle.

Regardless of which interpretation one chooses to embrace, it was in that instant, when the table saw came to life, that the idea of sustainable, free power from the sun was transported from the theoretical realm to the practical.

MOVING UP

By the time we were far enough along on the new log house to run wires and install the PV/wind system, I thought I knew practically everything there was to know about solar energy. It was a thoroughly absurd notion, of course; kinda like the teenager whose first, distant glimpses of adulthood lead him to overlook life's myriad subtleties and draw the erroneous conclusion that life is a simple subject. (And any grownup who doesn't agree is an idiot.)

The first cracks in my thin, hard shell of ignorance came when our electrician—after not showing up for several weeks—made the grievous mistake of mouthing-off to LaVonne.

He'd have been better off poking a wildcat with a sharp stick.

With the building-boom in town, there was zero chance of finding another electrician that would be willing to drive up into the hills, anytime soon. And we couldn't wait. So, (very) reluctantly, I told my wife that, given enough time—and enough books on the subject—I could finish wiring the house, and install the solar and wind systems. And (I nearly choked on this part) do it all to code. I didn't have much idea about what the National Electric Code was, of course, but I was pretty sure I was about to find out.

On my first inspection after countless hours of work, the kindly inspector wrote me up for eighteen violations. He later called back and admitted he was wrong about two of them, leaving me with a mere sixteen violations to deal with.

In an attempt to ensure that my next inspection wasn't an encore performance, I must have ended up talking to every high-level electrical inspector in the state, at one time or another. No one remembered my name, but they all knew "the guy with the wind tower," since it was one of the sticking points in our negotiations. (Code requires all sources of electrical power to have a manual disconnect, while design requires a wind generator to be connected to a load at all times. In the end, design won out over code.)

Happily, my wiring passed the next inspection without a hitch; for the first time in two years, we were living in an electrically-correct house.

It was only then that my real education began.

LEARNING THE SYSTEM

Once we moved into the new house, we realized that—even by more than doubling our generating and storage capacities—we now possessed the means to use up energy faster than we could produce it. The well pump was the main culprit, followed by the dishwasher and the hot water circulating pumps for the propane-fired radiant heat boiler. (The usual suspects, namely the refrigerator, range and clothes dryer, are all powered by propane.)

It quickly became clear that a means to monitor our energy usage was necessary—for peace of mind, if nothing else. We checked around to see what was available, then bought a TriMetric Meter from Bogart Engineering. It was a little tricky to install and calibrate, but well worth the trouble. Not only can we use it to see how much wattage each of our appliances is consuming, it also keeps track of amp hours going into the batteries, versus amp hours going out, providing a digital fuel gauge for the system. (The TriMetric performs lot of other useful functions, as well. It's worth it's weight in gold, though it didn't cost *quite* that much.)

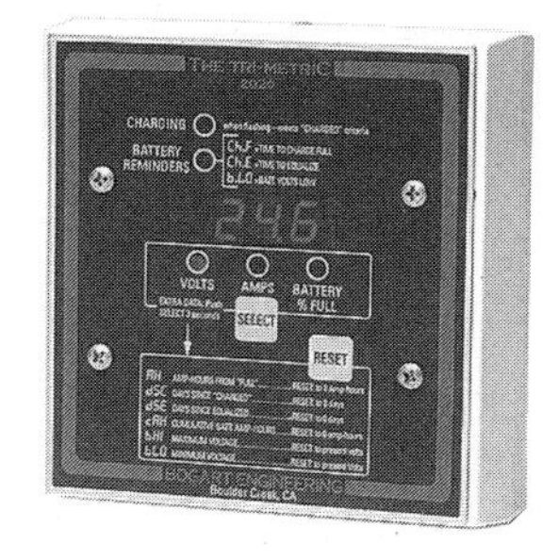

TriMetric Meter
(photo courtesy of Bogart Engineering)

Once the batteries are full, the charge controllers for both the wind and solar systems back off the power delivered to the batteries. It is, therefore, most efficient to use all the energy you can, while it's there for the taking. Make hay (wash clothes, run the dishwasher) while the sun shines, as the expression goes. Ideally, you don't want the batteries to become fully charged until the end of the day.

Seeing how the wind plugs into our energy equation has been as fascinating as it has been instructive. While the solar array is the real workhorse of the system, the wind is like a whimsical sprite that always seems to show up, just when we need it most. More than one of our neighbors has remarked that extra solar modules would have been cheaper—watt for watt—than our wind generator and tower. And they're right. But they also completely miss the point, since the wind most often provides power at night and during stretches of cloudy weather, when the solar array is idle, or nearly so. This means that we can get by with less storage capacity than any of our solar-only neighbors, since we're charging our batteries while they're depleting theirs—a fact that is particularly gratifying after three days of cloudy, windy weather.

Daily I feel more respect for our wind and solar system, and its remarkable ability to rejuvenate itself. I have seen our bank of 20 batteries go from 65% charge to 100% in a single day, after a three-day stretch of calm, gloomy weather. And that's while running two computers and a stereo all day long.

Consequently, my attitude toward energy usage has become much more relaxed, since I know that we'll gain it all back, in due course. LaVonne, too, has taken notice of my moderated vigilance over the wattage reserves. She hardly ever calls me an "Energy Nazi" anymore.

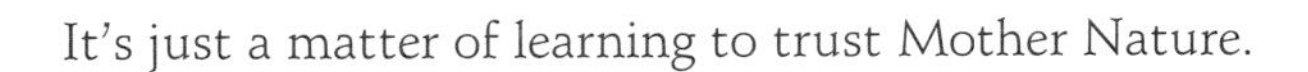
It's just a matter of learning to trust Mother Nature.

CHANGING WITH THE WEATHER

a metaphor

Imagine that all of your fresh water comes from a small, clear spring. You know, instinctively, that if you use the water wisely, there will always be enough. Right away, you notice that when the sun shines, and the wind blows, the water flows. Sometimes it gushes; other times it merely trickles. On calm nights, or when the clouds roll in so thick the wind can't blow, the flow of water stops, altogether.

All day long, every day, you fill vessels from the spring. When they overflow with water you bathe and wash and clean and drink deeply. But when darkness comes, and the skies grow still, you take only what you absolutely need.

At first, it seems a capricious existence. After all, you used to live next to a bottomless river; no matter how much water you removed, the river seemed just as full. But life is vastly different, now, and you can't go back to the way it was before.

You have always thought that weather was a fickle, random thing, but soon you begin to discover certain underlying patterns you have never noticed before. You see that the breeze blows one way during the day, a different way at night, and storms are almost always heralded by winds. The brightest, clearest days are those right after a storm system passes. An abrupt change in temperature means an increase in the strength of the wind. Each season, you discover, comes with a different breed of clouds, and its own special wind.

Every morning you watch where the sun rises, and where it sets in the evening. You watch to see how high it climbs at midday. You come to know how much water will flow at each hour of the day, in every kind of wind, in every degree of cloudiness.

Each day that you learn something new, your fear of running out of water grows less acute, for you have come to know—almost as a matter of instinct—when your vessels will overflow, and when they will run nearly dry.

After a time, as you begin to learn the rhythms of nature, your initial annoyance at being occasionally inconvenienced evolves into a feeling that approaches reverence for the ever-changing skies. The heartbeat of nature becomes the heartbeat of your house, and of your life. You become attuned to your surroundings in a way you never thought possible, before. Though the weather is still unpredictable, for the first time in your life you begin to trust in constant change, for you know that the water you were denied one day will be replenished the next. And, even though you are using far less water than ever before, somehow you don't miss the excess.

Finally, on the day when you truly understand that whatever nature gives you is exactly what you need, a new, unfamiliar feeling will wash over you. Don't worry—it's called Freedom.

September 2000

The stucco work is finally finished [30] and we take down the ladders, roof jacks and planks, and scaffolding. The house looks really beautiful now. I'm getting anxious to move in, but I think we are a few months off.

30

Mid-September is fine weather for assembling a wind tower. Rex rounds up cousin Bob and neighbor Lane to help. I went to town, but I did climb the tower later; the view from 45 feet off the ground, on top of a mountain, is truly spectacular.

The electrician shows up (amazingly) to pull wire through the wind tower conduit, and to connect the wires to the wind generator. He said he didn't mind heights, but he never showed up again.

September 24 and it snows about a foot. A great day for sledding [31] before working on the ceiling inside. We find that cold weather is not bad at all for hanging insulation... we don't mind being bundled up, head to toe, to keep the fiberglass off.

31

I seal the ceiling logs while Rex does the insulation [32]. (Yes, I'm allowed to climb scaffolding again.)

32

CHAPTER 18

THE EVOLVING SYSTEM

An Unlikely Tale of a Pond Pump

It is the purpose of any photovoltaic (PV) and wind system to convert sunlight and wind into usable electricity. That much is obvious. But, as much as we'd all like to, we can't just plug our house directly into the wind generator and the solar array; certain, essential components must be installed along the way to ensure that the power going to our lights and microwave oven is the kind of power these things need to work properly.

There are two distinct sides to a PV/wind system: The low-voltage side (primarily, but not entirely, DC, or direct current), and the high-voltage, AC (alternating current) side. The low-voltage side begins with the generating source (solar array, or wind generator) and ends at the DC side of the power inverter. The high-voltage side begins with the AC side of the power inverter, and ends at the loads (the above-mentioned lights and microwave oven).

In later chapters, I'll go into more detailed discussions of the individual components of a basic PV/wind electrical generating system. Now, however, it's time to build an imaginary system, adding each component as it becomes necessary.

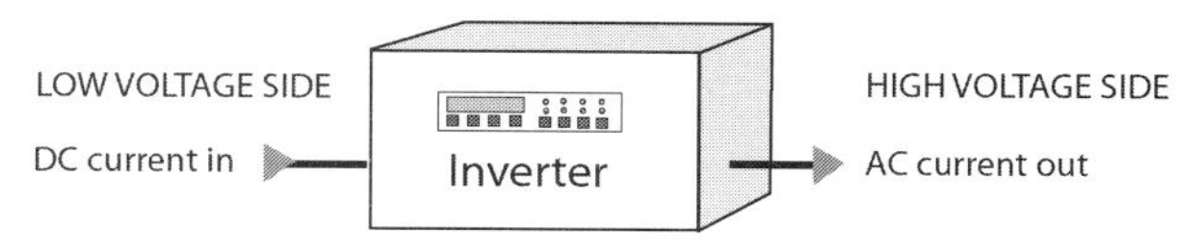

THE LOW VOLTAGE SIDE

~ a modest pond pump ~

One day, while paging through an environmentally-conscious mail-order catalog, you see a cute little 12-volt pond pump for sale. The pump is wired directly to a small solar module. As long as the sun shines, the pump circulates a modest amount of water, keeping the pond aerated. Thinking this is a great idea, you order the pump and solar module, and set about digging yourself a pond. When your order arrives, you hook it all up, and are quite pleased with this novel use of solar electric power.

After awhile, though, you decide you want the pump to run at night, hoping that the sound of running water will attract wildlife to your pond. This is easy enough; all you need to do is install a 12-volt battery between the pump and a second solar module, and make sure that the combined modules are of sufficient wattage to charge the battery for nighttime use while still running the pump during the day. As long as the sun shines every day, this simple little system works great.

Finally you're happy. At least until, after a long stretch of cloudy weather, you notice that the pump is sitting idle, and the wildlife have disappeared. You get out your 30X spotting scope and train it across the valley, on your neighbor's place. There you spy *your* deer (or wildebeests, depending on where you live) frolicking around *his* pond, the one run by the big pump that's hooked into the grid. Obviously, one battery is not enough, so you buy another one, and wire the two in parallel (to increase the storage capacity, without changing the voltage). And, of course, you have to buy another solar module.

Now the pump runs all the time and you've managed to lure the deer back to your side of the mountain, but after several days of sunny weather, you notice that the batteries sizzle and bubble, and you have to continuously add water. By beefing up the solar output to run the pond pump through all kinds of weather, you've opened up another can of worms, since you are now over-charging the batteries during extended periods of sunshine.

You don't worry, however: you just install a charge controller between the solar array and the batteries. The charge controller senses the state of charge of the batteries, and adjusts the amount of solar output that reaches them.

At last, your system is perfect. Until a change of seasons, that is. Fall brings extended periods of cloudy, windy weather, and after a few days your batteries are depleted, the pump has stopped running, and the deer are back at your neighbor's pond. You don't want to invest in the extra solar modules and batteries to keep the pump running day and night on such sparse sunlight. Instead, you decide to add a wind generator to the system to supply the pump with power when the sun goes into hiding.

It's a fairly large wind generator, and it sends AC current through the wires, rather than DC. Luckily, it comes with its own charge controller—one with rectifiers that convert the AC to DC before sending the current to the batteries. It also has inputs for both wind and solar, so you wire your solar array into the new charge controller, and put the old one in storage.

Finally, you are completely satisfied. Not only do you now have a pond pump that works under any meteorological conditions, you have safeguards in your system to ensure that the pump will always receive a near-constant voltage, and your batteries are no longer overcharging.

And, though you don't realize it yet, you have put together all the essentials of the low-voltage side of a working PV/wind system.

THE HIGH VOLTAGE SIDE

bigger and better pond pumps

You are growing restless. After two years of watching a feeble column of water dribble out the mouth of a ceramic carp, you decide that your little 12-volt pump just doesn't provide enough action. You check around to see what's available and after a little research you find just the pump you want. But to your dismay, this pump runs on 120-volt AC current, and a lot of it.

It doesn't matter—this is *the* pump, so you upgrade to a bigger wind generator and buy more solar modules. And, of course, you add more batteries. This gives you the generating and storage capacities you need to run the new pump, but not the right kind of current.

One more component should do the trick. You add a power inverter between the batteries and the pump. This gives you the steady, clean, AC power you need to force a powerful spray of water out the breathing hole of a three-foot-high whale with a mermaid sitting on its back.

At last, you are profoundly satisfied with your pond. So popular is your pond that an entire wildlife ecosystem has blossomed around it. You only have to look out the window to feel like you are on safari.

Then your luck gets even better, for as fate would have it, you chance to meet the perfect woman. Matrimony follows a whirlwind courtship. All is right with the world. But then your new bride delivers a crushing observation: she has always thought that your anatomically-correct bronze mermaid—sitting on the back of a smiling whale—is obscene. Wouldn't it be better, she innocently asks, if you enlarged the pond—an acre would be about right, she thinks—then built a 20-foot high rock and mortar mountain in the middle, from which would gush a scaled-down Niagara of bubbling water?

She's right, of course (you said yourself she was perfect). So, while the excavating crew enlarges the pond to the size of a small lake, and the stone masons build a re-creation of the Matterhorn in the middle of it, you buy a bigger wind generator, a vast solar array, and several more batteries, because you know the old pump for the mermaid and the whale just isn't going to cut it, anymore.

The new pump, of course, runs on 240-volt AC current, and your inverter only produces

120-volt AC. Should you buy a new inverter, you wonder, and wire it in series to the old one to get the required voltage, or is there another way? You do a few calculations and discover that the original inverter produces enough wattage to drive the new pump, so you take the much cheaper route of installing a 240-volt transformer between the pump, and the inverter.

The transformer works perfectly, and your waterfall gurgles to life. It is truly a sight to behold. At least until darkness sets in, and you have to view it with a flashlight. So, with a gleam in her eye, your new bride asks if it would be too much trouble to put in a few teensy-weensy lights around the waterfall, maybe 20, or so? Sure, no problem, you say. But the lights, you quickly realize, don't run on 240 volts. To remedy the problem, you simply install a 120-volt breaker panel between the inverter and the transformer, to provide a few 120-volt circuits before the current changes to 240 volts to power the waterfall.

At last: your wife is elated, your waterfall is the eighth wonder of the world, your lake is brimming with fish and exotic waterfowl, and you are eminently proud of yourself for putting together an unassailable PV/wind system.

BACK TO REALITY

The above example does, of course, bend the edges of credulity. Though it's certainly possible to build the gargantuan system it would take to run such a large pump, day and night, it would more than likely cost more than your house. And depending on the size of the pump and the lights, it would probably take more than one inverter. (As far as the wife part goes, isn't it hard to believe that she would do such an about-face, so soon after marriage?)

On the other hand, the pond pump system contains all the essential components you will need to power your house with solar and wind energy—minus certain safeguards (such as fuses, disconnects, and breakers) you will want to install along the way.

This, then, is the bare-bones of a functional PV/wind system. The next few chapters will flesh it out.

CHAPTER 19

SIZING THE SYSTEM

A Short, No-Tooth-Pulling Course on Practical Electricity

BEYOND OHM'S LAW

The more you delve into the electrical particulars of renewable energy, the more you will hear the term "Ohm's Law" bandied about. This is curious, because electricians—not to be confused with electrical engineers, who actually do use Ohm's Law—hardly ever have occasion to refer to George Simon Ohm's most notable accomplishment; at least not in its basic form.

Ohm's Law (*resistance* = *volts* divided by *amperes*) is very handy for determining volts, amperes, and ohms (units of electrical resistance) when two of the three variables are known. If, for instance, you want to know the amperage of a circuit, you can measure the change in voltage across a conductor of known resistance. Likewise, you can use it to determine resistance and voltage.

But you won't. You are not concerned with the "R" part of the equation. That's the reason you have "wire size/line loss tables" in every book ever written on the subject (including this one). Thanks to Ohm's Law, and a zillion or so formulas based on it, the phenomenon of resistance has been standardized in the electrical industry to point that it is there without you even knowing it.

Let's put it in human terms: You want to brew a few cups of coffee in the morning. If the people who designed and built the coffee maker were ignorant of

Ohm's Law, it would be a real hit-or-miss affair. But they knew all about it, so you don't have to. All you really want to know is how many minutes of direct sunlight it will take fill your cup with aromatic black liquid. In other words, how are the volts (V) and the amps (I) required by the coffee maker related to the power your solar and wind system is capable of? Resistance doesn't do you any good here—you're interested in watts (P). That is, after all, the units used to rate wind generators and solar modules. Fortunately for those us who enjoy mental math, the formula is every bit as easy as Ohm's Law: **P = VI, or: watts = volts x amps.**

The above mentioned coffee maker runs on 120 volts, and draws 7 amps, so it will take 120 x 7 = 840 watts to run it. That's simple enough. So how much energy did it use? Well, if it takes 6 minutes to make coffee (and you don't leave the warming plate on after it's done brewing), then that's 1/10th of an hour (.10 hours, for those of you with calculators). So, taking 840 times .10, you require 84 watt hours to scald the sleep out of your brain in the morning.

How much energy will it use over the course of a year? If you divide 84 by 1000, you will see that your coffee maker requires .084 kilowatt hours per day. Multiply that by 365 (days in a year) and you arrive at 30.66 kWh/year. This is about two sunny days' output on a 1200 watt PV system, meaning that two days of each year are dedicated to making your coffee in the morning.

Do it. It's worth it in spades.

There are two other expressions of this equation: I = P/V is the most useful, since you will refer to it to determine wire size from the charge controller to the solar array and the wind generator (among many other places).

On the other hand, since voltage is almost always a known variable, the final expression, V = P/I, will probably be of little use to you, or anyone else. You may find it ironic, then, that voltage will be the one immutable factor in the final configuration of your system.

watts = volts x amps

amps = watts / volts

The Appendix discusses in detail the formula for calculating exact line loss, plus examples on how to use the three Wire Size/Line Loss tables, also found in the Appendix.

12, 24, 48 VOLTS, OR MORE?

Almost all residential solar modules are rated for 12 volts. More than likely, the batteries you buy will be 6 volts. Either of these components can easily be wired in series to increase the system voltage. If you buy a good charge controller, you can change the voltage from 12 to 24, to 48 volts, by changing a single jumper on the circuit board.

After that, you run into a low (or high) voltage wall. The wind generator you buy may or may not be adjustable to different voltages. And here's the kicker: the inverter—the first or second most expensive component in your system—will definitely *not* be adjustable.

It's decision time.

By running the formulas in the Appendix (or taking the easy way out, and referring to the line loss tables) you will see that by doubling the system voltage (and thereby halving the amperage) you can drive the same wattage four times the distance through the same wire! It would seem, then, that a high system voltage would be the answer. And it is; but how high?

If you are looking for a catch, it isn't the price of the components. There is no difference in price between a 12-volt inverter, and a 48-volt inverter. The same holds true for everything else. If you want to include a few 12-volt DC circuits in your house, you'll have to buy a step-down converter to pull the lower voltage out of the system, but the money you save on wire will pay for that minor piece of equipment several times over.

The only real downside in systems over 12 volts is in the multiples of solar modules and batteries you will have to buy (initially, and if you need to add on later). In 24-volts systems, the solar modules are wired in pairs, and the 6-volt batteries wired 4 in a series. Double these numbers for a 48-volt system. So, if you have 12 solar modules charging a bank of 16 batteries in a 48-volt system, and you want to increase the system size, at a bare minimum you'll have to up the modules to 16, and the batteries to 24. It could get expensive, especially if you are using the big 390-amp hour, L-16 batteries. (It is possible, however, to run a 24-volt system with a 48-volt array. *See Chapter 22, Charge Controllers.*)

A 24-volt setup is a good compromise, if you don't have the physical space or the financial resources to enlarge your system in such large chunks. You can add onto it without breaking the bank, and still get 4 times the current-carrying capacity from your wires, over a 12-volt system.

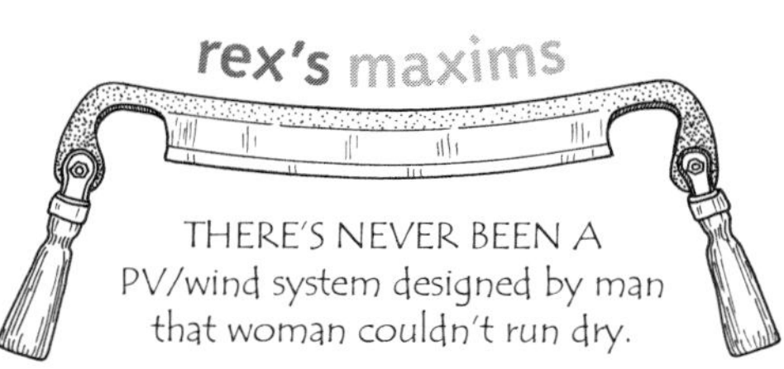

Is it possible to design a system over 48 volts? Sure, but it's hardly a practical solution for a private residence. Such systems are expensive, inflexible, and far more difficult to build within the constraints of the National Electric Code (NEC).

We opted for a 24-volt system years ago, when we knew a lot less about this business than we do now. Nonetheless, it was a good decision, and we'd do it again if we were starting over. It allows us to run enough wire of a manageable size that we don't need to have the array crowded right next to the house, and we can increase the size of our system without having to sell our pickup to pay for it.

HOW MANY BATTERIES?

Note: *A Battery Sizing Worksheet is provided on page 291.*

While one of the most common problem with off-the-grid PV/wind systems is too few batteries, it is also possible to have too many. Why? Because it's not nearly enough just to keep the batteries in a so-so state of charge. The batteries really should be brought to a full charge regularly, especially if you are using a meter to monitor the batteries' state of charge, since most meters begin to lose their calibration after a few days without the batteries reaching a full-charge state. More than that, however, the batteries need to be equalized (over-charged, under controlled conditions) every so often to ensure that the plates remain free of sulfates.

As battery voltage increases, it likewise become increasingly difficult to push the voltage to a full state of charge. Often, in the late afternoon, our batteries will be over 95 percent charged, but if the wind isn't blowing, there isn't enough sunlight to take them any higher, even though the solar array is putting out more amperage than we are using.

With the sun and wind, we average about 1300 watts during peak hours. With twenty 220-amp/hour batteries wired 4 per series, our battery bank is rated at 1100 amp hours, or a little less than 1 amp/hour per watt. I would estimate that our batteries are brought to a full state of charge 250 days of the year. I like to equalize every 2 to 3 months, depending on how deeply they've been discharged in the interim.

There are days when the batteries are topped-off at 10:00 a.m., and I wish I had more batteries to charge, but that's more the exception that the rule. Unless we add more appliances (and therefore more solar modules), I'll probably keep things just the way they are.

With so many variables to consider, if you size your system perfectly, the first time out of the gate, then your success is attributable as much to luck, as to math. The key to sizing your system, then, is to leave yourself room to add on later. This means starting with the right inverter. It means running heavy enough wire to the array that you can later add more modules, without sacrificing too much voltage. And it means leaving yourself space in the electrical room—and the battery box—to add more batteries, if need be.

CHAPTER 20

SOLAR PHOTOVOLTAIC MODULES

How to Capture Ray of Sunshine

The first time I ever saw a polycrystalline solar module from 2 feet away, I had the feeling I was looking at something magical. Deep inside, it looked like thin slices of the finest Persian lapis, overlaid with semi-transparent crystalline mirrors, tinted in a hundred hues between blue and purple. It might have been a master jeweler's creation, it was so awe-inspiring, except that closer to the surface lay a thin grid of aluminum channels; pathways for the energy with which this strange creation resonated. Were such a rectangular jewel of modern alchemy to travel back through time, I mused—to ancient Sumer or Babylon, perhaps—it might have changed the history of early civilization. Certainly it holds the power to change the history of *this* civilization, if only we, desensitized as we are to the finer facets of technology, could feel the pure wonder of what these sparkling blue panels are capable of.

Polycrystalline solar modules.

Until then, a minority of us will continue to eschew fossil fuels, in favor of sunshine—one bright ray at a time.

No one ever intended solar modules to be so beautiful, of course; they just turned out that way, as a direct result of their design. Made from the basest of materials—nothing more special than thin layers of silicon (the stuff beaches are made of), coated (doped) on either side with oppositely charged ions—they take on their other-worldly appearance and their special properties through a laborious and painstakingly precise manufacturing process. The end result is a multilayered substrate through which electrons are set in motion, after being jostled by sunlight.

The phenomenon of converting sunlight into electrical energy was first observed more than two decades before the outbreak of the Civil War, but it wasn't until the 1960's and the Cold War that the first efficient solar cells were produced for use in the space industry. Though exceedingly expensive, by 1970 more solar modules were produced for use on Terra Firma than in space. Since then, the use of solar modules has steadily increased, while the price has been driven down, from Buck Rogers' price of over $1000 per watt, to less than $5 per watt for contemporary earthlings. Still a little pricey, true, but no longer out of reach for most people. For many of us (LaVonne and I included) the cost of a more-than-adequate PV (and wind) system is less than what we'd have to pay the power company to run a string of ugly utility poles across our property.

TYPES OF SOLAR MODULES

The primary energy producing unit of any photovoltaic system is the cell. Crystalline, or polycrystalline, silicon cells each produce about .45 volts (a little less for amorphous silicon, which will described in more detail below), regardless of how large or small they may be. (Bigger cells produce more amperage, but the volts remain the same.)

To increase the voltage to the point where it can be used to charge a battery, several cells are connected in series, and arranged together within a module. Also commonly known as a "solar panel," a module is one of the glass-covered, aluminum-framed units you buy from the dealer and install on or near your house.

Most residential modules on the market today range from 16.5 to 18 volts. This may seem high for a 12-volt system, but it's necessary to keep the current flowing from the module to the battery, rather than the other way around. Solar cells experience a drop in voltage with increased temperature (during the middle of summer), and batteries, while equalizing, often reach 15.5 volts or more. If the module voltage were any less, there wouldn't be enough electrical "pressure" to bring the batteries to a full state of charge.

Modules are rated in the number of watts they produce under optimal conditions—direct midday sunlight, at a cell temperature of 25 degrees Celsius (77 degrees Fahrenheit). Performance drops off with a change of sun angle, a rise in temperature, or, of course, the appearance of clouds. Common sizes for modules in residential arrays range from 40 to 120 watts. While it would seem that you would be able to get more watts per dollar by buying bigger modules, it's not always true. Prices fluctuate from dealer to dealer, week to week. If you're not too picky about size, you can usually find some good deals. (If you do buy smaller modules, however, you need to realize that they will entail more wiring per kilowatt, as well as more work and material for the mounting frame.)

A Note on Terminology

Technically, a solar panel is a collection of solar modules within a frame, and an array is a collection of panels. There are some problems with these distinctions, however. Sometimes two modules are factory mounted as a single unit. Is it still a module, or has it become a panel? Or, if you make one massive frame to hold 10 modules, have you created an array, or simply a big panel? Nor is the correct terminology universally used, even within the industry. Some solar supply houses routinely refer to their modules as panels. Unless you are writing a book, it's really pretty easy: a module is a "panel," a panel is a "few panels," and an array is "a bunch of panels."

Most solar modules in use today are made from crystalline, or polycrystalline silicon, protected by a layer of tempered glass. They work well for most people in most applications, but they are not without certain shortcomings. As I mentioned above, the voltage begins to dwindle as the cells heat up. In addition, performance drops off considerably under conditions of partial shading, as often happens when snow slides off one half of a module, but not the other. In this case, the clear side tries to run current through the shaded side, to no avail. Since the module voltage is the sum of all the individual cell voltages, a partially shaded module may not have sufficient voltage to charge a battery. The same thing occurs when one of two modules wired in series is shaded. In systems over 24 volts, damage can occur to the shaded module when the unshaded module tries to drive it. For this reason, module manufacturers suggest the installation of bypass diodes to avoid damage when operating at higher voltages.

UNI-SOLAR® products include flexible and portable modules, framed solar panels, as well as solar shingles that can replace traditional roofing materials. *(photo courtesy of Bekaert ECD Solar Systems LLC)*

All of these problems have been

overcome with the recent introduction of thin film, or amorphous, silicon modules. Utilizing the same technology as the solar cells on pocket calculators, these modules operate better than crystalline silicon in high heat, low light, and partial shading conditions. The only drawback—besides being less fascinating to the eye—is that they are less efficient, meaning that each thin film module needs about 85 percent more surface area to produce the same wattage as an equally rated crystalline silicon module. Unless you are cramped for space, the extra size shouldn't be a problem. (You can figure, roughly, that a thin film module will produce 5.85 watts per square foot, compared to 10.85 watts per square foot for crystalline silicon modules. A 1200-watt array of thin film modules, then, would take up over 200 square feet of space, while a similar array with standard modules would require only a little more than 110 square feet. In terms of dollars per watt, the two types of panels are practically the same.)

An added advantage of thin film silicon is it's inherent flexibility, making it ideal for certain roofing applications. Bekaert ECD Solar Systems, in particular, has a developed a full line of thin film photovoltaic products (*UNI-SOLAR®*) that can be used either in conjunction with standard roofing, or in place of it. (You should be aware, however, that amorphous silicon modules may have shorter warranties than their polycrystalline counterparts.)

FINDING A PLACE FOR THE ARRAY

While it would seem logical that the roof would be the best place to locate your array, there are some (three, to be exact) drawbacks to rooftop mounts that you should consider. First, it's difficult to sweep off the snow. In the winter, when the mercury hovers around zero the day after a snowstorm, the snow may cling to the array all day, even if it's bright and sunny. You could be charging at full power, but you won't get any power at all if your modules are buried under 6 inches of snow. Even on days when it's foggy following a storm, there's lots of power to be had, as long as you can remove the snow.

Cleaning snow off the ground-mounted solar array is easy.

Second, rooftop-mounted modules are hard to clean in the summer, after a little sprinkle leaves a hundred dust particles, for every drop of rain. And third, it's a lot more work to adjust the array for seasonal variations in the sun's angle.

Curt and Kelly's roof-mounted array.

Of all the people we know with solar arrays, only one uses a roof mount; the rest either mount their panels on a south-facing deck, or on the ground near the house.

Whether on the roof or on the ground, the array needs to be as close to the house as possible, in a location where it can receive full, unimpeded sunlight for the 3 hours on either side of noon. Bushes or trees that cast a shadow against any part of the array can greatly reduce the energy output, even in winter when the branches are bare. You should either remove the foliage, or find a more suitable spot to place the array, even if that means the roof.

Ed and Val's deck-mounted solar array.

Arrays should always point due south, as long as there are no peripheral obstructions. *(To find due south, refer to "Where is North?" in Chapter 6.)* Trees or hills to one side of the array may make it more advantageous to position the array at an angle that makes the most use of what sunlight there is.

If the best spot to locate the array is farther from the house than 50 feet, you might consider designing your system to operate at 48 volts, since this will greatly decrease the diameter of the wire needed to carry current to the house with a minimum loss of current through the line.

TILT ANGLE OF THE ARRAY

The sun passes through 47 degrees of arc on it's yearly trek from the Tropic of Capricorn to the Tropic of Cancer, and back again. At 40 degrees north latitude (as we are here, in northern Colorado) the sun moves from 26.5 degrees above the horizon at noon on the winter solstice (December 21st), to 73.5 degrees at noon on the summer solstice (June 21st). Obviously, a solar array that is perfectly perpendicular to the sun will produce the most power. If you diligently adjusted your array every few days, you would want to set it at 90 (degrees) minus the sun's angle. The array on the first day of winter would be set at 63.5 degrees (90 - 26.5 degrees), and gradually adjusted to the first day of summer at 16.5 degrees (90 - 73.5 degrees).

But you won't adjust the array angle every few days, of course; no one would (at least, no one I know). So what's the best compromise?

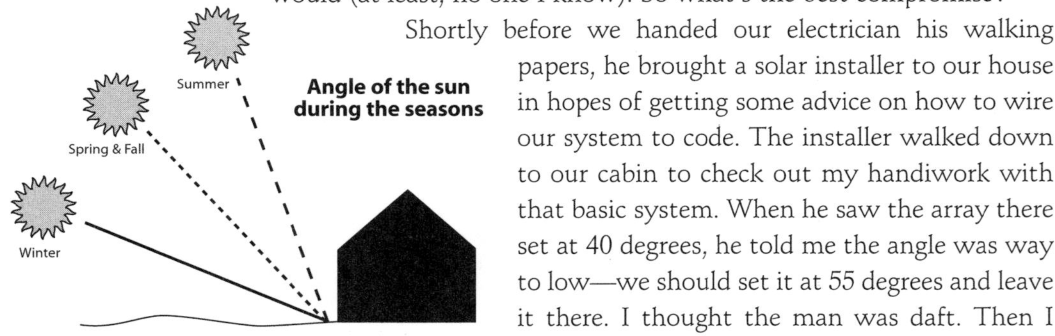

Shortly before we handed our electrician his walking papers, he brought a solar installer to our house in hopes of getting some advice on how to wire our system to code. The installer walked down to our cabin to check out my handiwork with that basic system. When he saw the array there set at 40 degrees, he told me the angle was way to low—we should set it at 55 degrees and leave it there. I thought the man was daft. Then I realized that his logic was shared by almost everyone around here. This is how it goes: if you set your array to capture the most light during the coldest, darkest time of the year, then whatever percentage of energy you lose in warmer months will be more than compensated for by the extra hours of sunlight.

This line of reasoning is based on the assumption that cloud patterns are essentially the same throughout the year, but they're not. In Colorado, the sky is clearer in winter. In summer, though it doesn't often rain, the clouds roll in over the western mountains practically every afternoon, greatly diminishing the amount of

Should you tilt your array for the seasons?

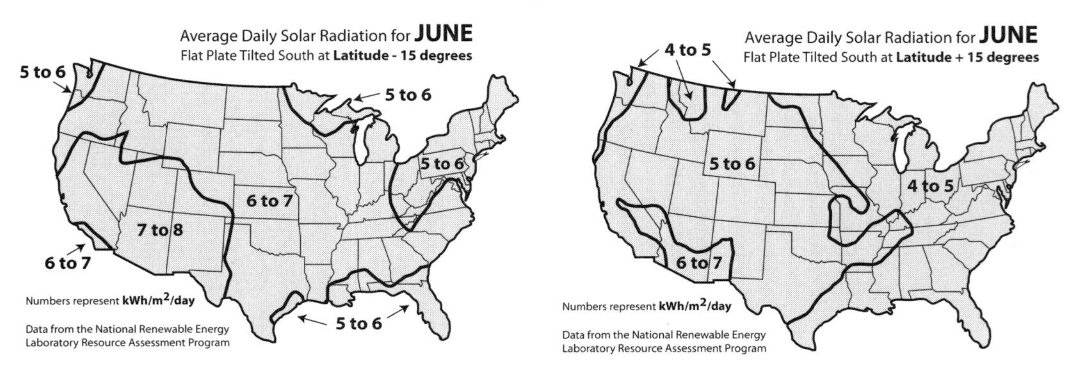

These maps show the difference in sun hours in June, if you tilt for the optimum sun angle of **latitude - 15 degrees** (left), or leave it at a winter setting of latitude + 15 degrees (right).

light that falls on the solar array. Couple this with the fact that sun rises and sets so far north in the summer that the modules need a low angle to capture any early and late day sun, and the argument for a steep, stationary angle falls apart.

That being said, I have to admit that every one of the dozen or so people we know who live entirely off the grid have their array set at a steep angle, and never bother to adjust it for the seasons. It's probably the reason why LaVonne and I are often treated to a chorus of generators running in the cool, night air, while our generator is resting comfortably in the garage.

Reckoning Where The Sun's Going To Be

If you choose to adjust your array (and you should), it's very simple to measure the sun's angle; all you need is something that casts a shadow (like a deck railing, a fence post, or even the backside of your solar array), a long, straight board, and a floating-pointer angle finder that you can buy at any lumber yard or hardware store. At midday, when the sun casts a shadow directly north, place one end of the board on top of the post (or railing), with the other end resting at the end of the post's shadow (on flat ground, of course). Place the angle finder flat on the top edge of the board, and it will show you the sun's angle; turn it 90 degrees on its side, and it will show you the optimum angle for your array.

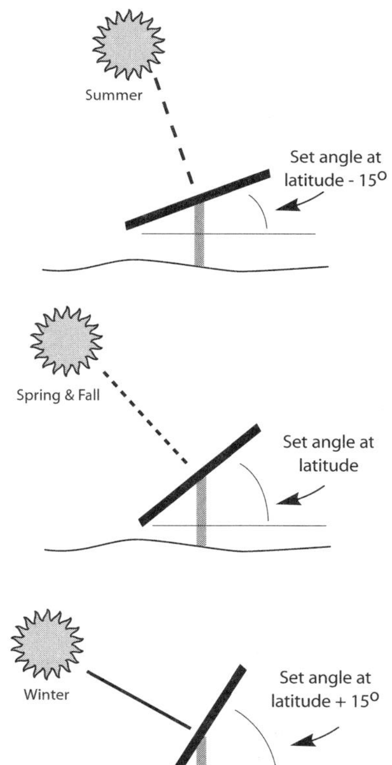

Seasonal tilt of the solar array

Interestingly, if you take a measurement at midday on the spring or fall equinox, you will find the sun's angle to be 90 degrees, minus latitude. At 40 degrees north latitude, for instance, the sun will be at 50 degrees on the equinoxes, and will change 23.5 degrees up or down as the seasons change.

Place the angle finder along a board at high noon to find the sun's angle.

Using this information, we adjust our array four times a year, going from latitude + 15 degrees in winter; to latitude in spring; to latitude – 15 degrees in summer; and back to latitude in the fall. These seasonal adjustments give us optimal sunlight for each 3-month period.

You can use the angle finder method to track the sun's progress through the seasons, and determine on which days of the year you should adjust the array, providing that you made sure to mount your modules in adjustable frames.

MOUNTING THE MODULES

Dave's custom-made rack holds six modules.

We began our solar venture with six 110-watt Solarex modules. Lacking the keen edge of experience, I built a massive frame to hold the 72 square feet of modules. The exterior frame, as well as all the inside rails, were made with 2 x $^3/_{16}$-inch angle iron. It weighed about as much as a (big) full-grown man, and it took four men to carry it down the steep, rocky slope in front of the cabin to mount it on the concrete piers we had poured a week before. (As unpleasant as that may have been, it was a picnic compared to the chore of carrying the frame back up the hill, when it came time to move it to the log house.)

Being several degrees wiser when it came time to mount the four 120 watt Kyocera modules we later added to the array, I used 1-$^1/_2$ x $^1/_8$-inch angle iron for the outside frame, and 1-$^1/_2$ x $^1/_8$-inch strap iron for the inside rails. The finished frame weighed—and cost—about a third what the first frame did. It was easy to mount, and affords all the support the modules will ever need.

While commercially manufactured, pole-mounted aluminum frames are available, you may be better off building, or having them built, yourself. That way, you can engineer them to fit the terrain, and to adjust in the way you would like them to. The bottom sides of our frames pivot on heavy iron supports set in concrete. For adjustment, we have three sets of legs for the top sides (one set for winter, one for summer, and another for spring and fall). The only problem with this arrangement is that panels and their frames can get heavy, making seasonal adjustments a two- or three-person operation.

To minimize heavy lifting when changing the array angle, you can design a mount where the frames pivot in the middle. Centering the frames on one or two heavy steel pipe posts is an ideal solution, providing you can set the posts deep enough in the ground—and with a broad enough concrete base—to prevent the whole array from toppling over in high winds. (Since bedrock is less than a foot down where we set our array, we'd have been tempting fate by mounting the frames on a pair of central posts.)

Commercial mounts called trackers are available for anyone who wants to maximize the potential of their solar array. Trackers move the array in step with the sun as it travels from east to west across the horizon. Conventional wisdom holds that trackers are a good investment in the sun belt, but not in higher latitudes where the sun—during the winter months—rises and sets so far south that the small amount of extra sunlight wouldn't be worth the extra expense, or the hassle of having an added component that might occasionally require service or repair. Although we've never felt the urge to try one, I know that many people use them successfully.

Basics of Wiring Photovoltaic Modules

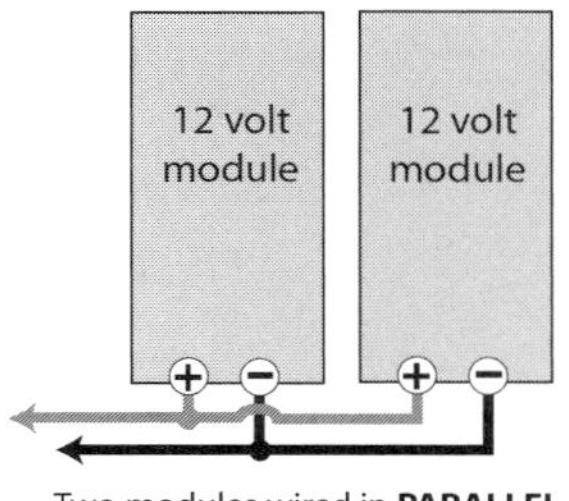

Two modules wired in **PARALLEL for 12 volts**

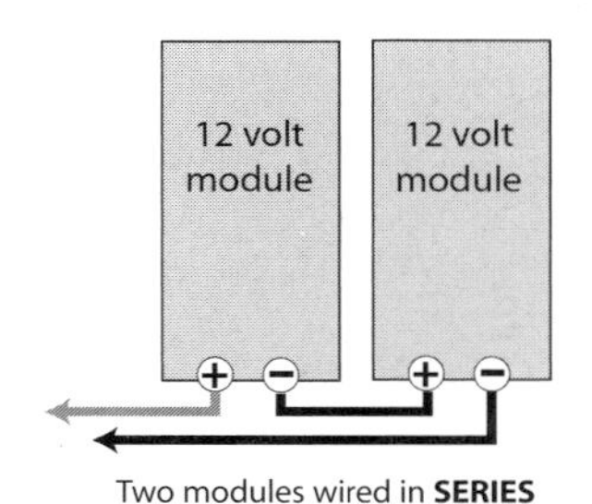

Two modules wired in **SERIES for 24 volts**

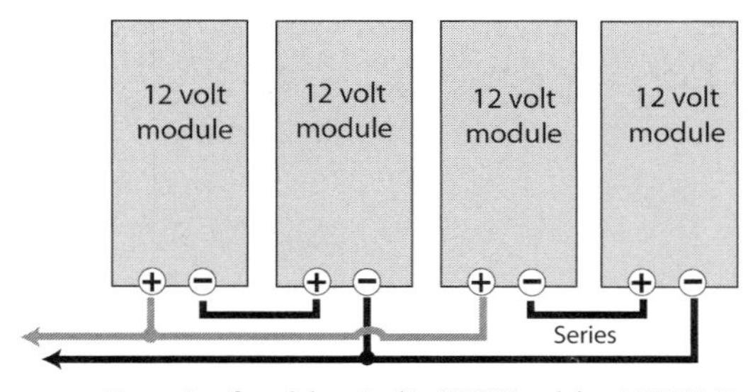

Two pairs of modules wired in **SERIES** and then **PARALLEL for 24 volts**

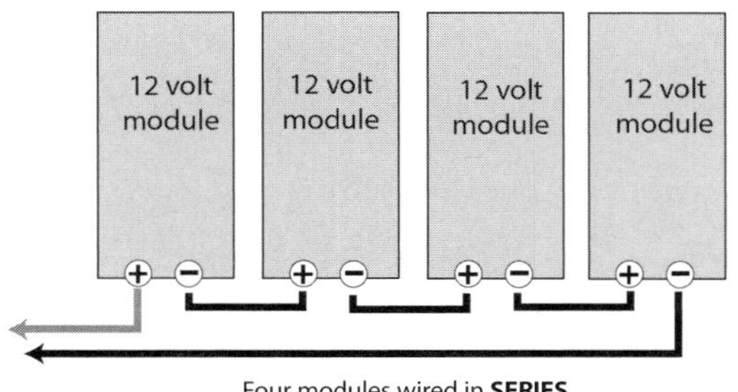

Four modules wired in **SERIES for 48 volts**

WIRING THE ARRAY

All the modules you buy will come with diagrams detailing how to wire them in parallel and in series. Since every brand of module is set up a little differently, there's no point diving into specifics here. A run through the basics, however, would be helpful before you order the modules.

In a 12-volt system, all the modules are wired in parallel—positive to positive, negative to negative. Thus, the amperage of each individual module adds to the total amperage of the array, without increasing the voltage.

In a 24-volt system, each pair of modules is wired in series—positive to negative, and vice versa—doubling the voltage (from 12 to 24). Then each series string is wired in parallel to increase the amperage. (Likewise, in 48-volt systems, every 4 modules are wired in series.)

The important point to remember is this: only modules of identical wattage should be wired in a series string, since the amperage of the string will be equal to the amperage of the weakest module.

Fuses and Breakers

Beginning with the fragile aluminum channels on the surface of the individual solar cells, and ending with the heavy copper leads going to the charge controller, the wiring of a solar array is like a complex watershed. Hundreds of tiny tributaries flow into dozens of larger ones, which in turn dump their current into a few, even bigger channels, before emptying into the great river that ends at the load. (It doesn't exactly end at the load, since there is a pathway back to the source, but that's another story.)

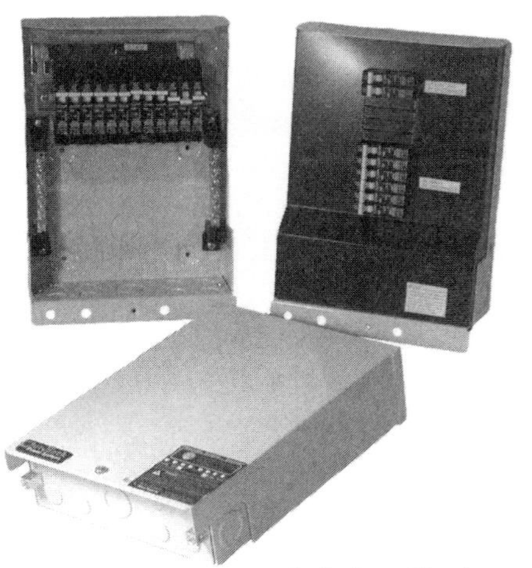

OutBack combiner boxes.
(photo courtesy of OutBack Power Systems)

As long as the integrity of the system is intact, the flow of current is orderly. But when a short circuit occurs somewhere along the line, large amounts of current can be sent back in a reverse flow, with potentially disastrous results. It's like what would happen if a cataclysmic seismic event sent the waters of the Gulf of Mexico raging back up the Mississippi River into each of it's progressively narrower tributaries: the small streams would certainly burst their banks.

To keep a similar occurrence from taking place within the confines of your array wiring, it's important to install fuses and/or circuit breakers wherever amperages are combined. Usually, the leads from each series of modules terminate into a combiner box, where the individual positive leads are directed through fuses or breakers of appropriate size. To reduce the risk of a costly mishap while working on the array wiring (and to satisfy the electrical inspector), the main lead coming from the combiner box is then run through a circuit breaker before going to the charge controller.

Grounding

You should pound in a ground rod next to the array, and then run a heavy copper wire from it to the common house ground. Also, you will have to be sure that each frame, and each module within the frame, has a path to ground. To be certain, you can use a multimeter to run a continuity test from the ground wire to the frame of every module.

LEAVING ROOM TO GROW

Even with the most assiduous planning, there is always a certain degree of guesswork involved in determining how many watts of solar power you will need. You don't want to be running the generator every time you wash a load of clothes, but you also don't want to ravage your kids' college fund to buy modules you don't need.

The best answer is to start with what you *know* you'll need, and then add more modules after you've had a taste of what the system is capable of. This is especially true if you are including a wind generator in the equation. Aside from ensuring that you have adequate space (on the ground, on the roof, or in front of the deck) all you will really need to do when you set up the initial system is to run heavy enough wire to handle the amperage of any system you might conceivably build. It will save a lot of digging, later. Then, when you look at your array, rather than thinking of work, you can admire its inherent beauty.

Benshoof's pole-mounted solar array with 4 modules, and room for 4 more.

LaVonne's
LOGBOOK 17

October 2000

Two ominous piles of drywall fill the garage. I can't believe we are going to hang 218 sheets of that heavy stuff! We rent a lift for the week to do the ceilings [33]. What a back-saver this is! We soon find a system for measuring and cutting, screwing and nailing.

33

The garage needs to be totally encased in drywall, since the living space is above it. That was the easy part. The main floor ceiling wasn't bad, but the loft ceiling is maddening. If the purlins were not there, it would be a snap, but each piece of drywall must be scribed and cut to fit the taper of the logs. And if the ceiling wasn't bad enough, the funky closet and bathroom walls make us pull out our hair!

We take a break to buy a wood stove and install it. Nights and mornings are getting pretty cold.

November 2000

We are still hanging drywall. Will it ever end??

The gutter company puts on the gutters and downspouts, and the cabinet manufacturer delivers the pine cabinets for the kitchen and bath. We'll store them in the basement until the walls are completely finished and painted.

Since we are thoroughly sick of drywall, we hire our neighbor Dave to do the taping [34]. I can handle filling the nail and screw divets.

Time to finish out the ugly stairwell to the basement, which means putting on furring strips so we can nail on the tongue-&-groove pine boards. What an improvement!

34

December 2000

Rex relocates the solar system to the house from the cabin, and proceeds to learn all about wiring houses, and how the electrician ran the wires in *this* house before bailing out on us. I don't think Rex is happy about this.

WIND GENERATORS

Making Good Use of the Stuff of Clouds

It's early April, as I write these words. The mercury hangs just above freezing and the skies are thickly overcast. Beyond my office door, a wind chime rings melodically. If I walk outside, I can see our 1000-watt wind generator working, just beyond a copse of juniper trees. Though I can only feel a light a breeze from where I stand, 50 feet above me the propeller blades are spinning furiously. I judge it to be about a 6- or 7-amp wind. The gentle whirring of the blades is a comforting sound. It's the sound of nature's energy being refined and transformed.

To me, it's music.

For months now, the wind has sorely tested your sanity. Every time you try to drop a plumb bob, the wind comes out of nowhere and deflects it. Throw a sheet of plywood over your shoulder on a perfectly calm day, and you instantly feel a playful breeze, trying to wrest the sheet from your grasp. Walk up a ladder with it, and the breeze grows stiffer with every rung. Move the ladder to the other side of the house, and the wind changes direction and follows you.

By now you've probably become convinced that you can control the speed and direction of the wind, just by how you select your activities. And who's to say that you can't? Not me; I'm a believer.

But, even if you can—by using plumb bobs and plywood—make the wind do a few parlor tricks, it's a fact of nature that you will never be able to outsmart it. Yelling at the wind, or trying to ignore it, just encourages it. Pleading with it will elicit no sympathy, whatsoever. So you might as well face the facts: you'll never get along with the wind until you change the nature of your relationship.

Our Whisper 1000 turbine and double blade propellers.

Having put up with the wind through the entire construction of our house, I couldn't wait to hook up the wind generator and watch the wind do some good, for a change. After we laboriously erected our tower, and installed and wired the generator, we had the pleasure of watching the propeller spin in the light breeze for about five minutes, before stopping, altogether.

For two full days, the blades didn't make a single revolution. By the end of the second day, I began thinking that buying a wind generator was the stupidest thing I ever did. What was I thinking? I could have bought 500 watts of easy-to-install solar modules for what I paid for one obstinate machine, sneering at me from 50 feet up.

It was almost as if the wind wanted to know it would be appreciated, before it was willing to do any work. And appreciate it, I did, when it finally began to blow again, after two day's absence. I believe it was the first time in my life I was actually happy to feel the wind. Obligingly, it blew more or less steady for the next several days, before settling back into its old, unfathomable non-patterns.

Since that rocky start two years ago, when I wasn't at all certain if we'd made a good investment, I've begun to learn just how important the wind factor is in our energy equation. Though predicting the strength and duration of the wind at any given moment will never be more than a guess, over time, the wind always comes through for us.

Would I now trade our 1000-watt wind generator for 500 watts of solar panels? Not a chance; nor 1000, or even 1500 watts. And the reason is simple: the wind provides us with power when the sun can't, which means that we can get by with fewer batteries (and a lot less worry). Our wind generator may not supply *all* the power we use during a stretch of cloudy weather, but it usually provides enough. Then, when the sun finally does show itself—escorted by a breezy change in atmospheric pressure—the batteries recharge all that much faster.

LaVonne's Verities

IF YOU'RE LOW ON ENERGY and need the wind to blow, serve a meal on the deck. For a gale, hang out the laundry.

HOW MUCH WIND IS ENOUGH?

At the beginning of the book, I suggested that you probably have enough wind at your building site if it blows hard enough, and often enough, to annoy you. I'll stand by that assessment, unscientific though it may be. However, since no two people have exactly the same tolerance for wind—or pain, or screaming children—it might be helpful to have a more objective set of criteria to work with.

With a commendable use of our tax dollars—actually, our grandparents' tax dollars, considering how old the data is—the Department of Energy has painstakingly put together wind velocity tables for hundreds of sites around the United States. They give the average wind speed for each season of the year, as well as a yearly average for each site. *(See page 297 for the Wind Energy Maps/Tables website.)*

Wind Speed Conversion
meters per second (M/S) x 2.23 = miles per hour (mph)

It's highly doubtful that you will build very close to where actual wind measurements have been taken, but you should at least have spent enough time near one or more of these sites to know if the wind blows more there, or less, than it does at your building site.

The closest DOE site to us is Denver's (now defunct) Stapleton International Airport. It's 60 miles away, as the crow flies, and 1800 feet lower in altitude. According to the DOE tables, the average wind speed there is 4.2 meters per second (9.4 mph). I've spent enough time in and around Denver (unwillingly, I assure you), to know that the wind blows more here, than there. And, being so close, I also know that we are subject to the same seasonal variations as Denver: the wind blows more in the winter (low sun) months, than in the summer (high sun) months, a fact that adds greatly to the appeal of a wind generator.

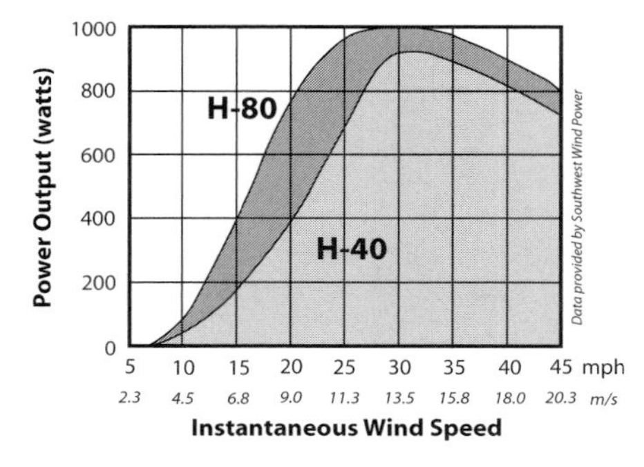

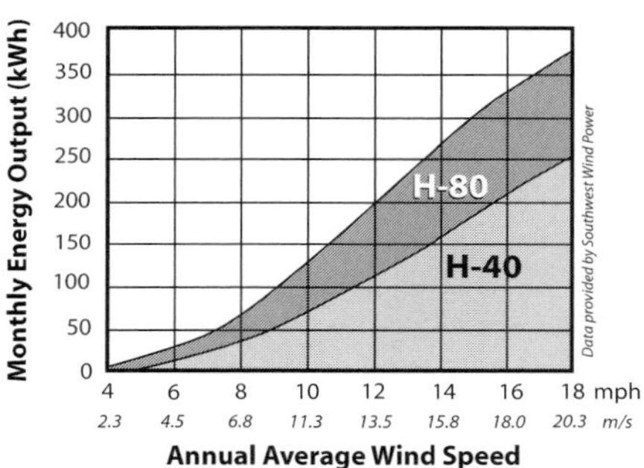

Two power curve charts compare the Whisper H-40 and Whisper H-80 models by Southwest Windpower.

LaVonne and I never bothered to look at the DOE tables *before* buying a wind generator; we simply made a judgement based on the annoyance factor, and it paid off. You'll have to decide which criteria will work best for you, but there are a couple of considerations that may be helpful:

Does the wind blow fairly steady where you plan to build, or does it vary considerably? Most modern wind generators begin producing small amounts of power at around 7 mph, and the output rises dramatically with increased wind speed. Ideally—for a PV/wind system—the best situation would be if the wind is fairly calm during nice (sunny) weather, and appreciatively more intense when the clouds roll in.

Mountainous regions, with large fluctuations in altitude, are cauldrons of atmospheric change. Even without significant variations in atmospheric pressure (fronts), air will rise from the valleys during the day, and flow back into them at night, providing usable power while the sun is absent. If you are fortunate enough to have a building site above a valley, but below a distant ridge, you should have all the wind you'll ever need.

You will see a lot of different numbers thrown around for how much wind you will need to make a wind generator economically viable. The usual range is from 8 to 10 mph. Again, it depends on the nature of the wind. If it blows fairly steady all the time, then I would agree with the higher estimate. But if most of the wind comes at night, or in concert with storm fronts, I would feel safe with the lower number.

It is also important to know that not all wind generators are created equal. Some are designed with a broad sweep area for light to moderate wind; others are more compact, for heavier winds. Southwest Windpower, for instance, has two closely rated models: the H40, rated at 900 watts; and the H80, rated at 1000 watts. Though there is only 10 percent difference in their respective rated outputs, the blades of the H80 sweep twice the area as the H40, since it is designed to perform optimally in lighter winds.

Of course, the only way to be absolutely sure if you have enough wind is to monitor the wind at your building site over the course of a year with a computerized anemometer that keeps track of wind speed over time, so that you can produce a graph to compare to past weather charts. This way, you will be able to see if the wind blows mostly during sunny periods, or when the weather is stormy.

Or, you can fall back on the annoyance factor.

OLD TECHNOLOGY VERSUS NEW

Take a lengthwise coil of wire and rotate it between two oppositely-charged magnetic poles, and you will produce alternating current. Spin it at the right speed (frequency), and you will produce a usable current for running AC motors and appliances. But try to charge a battery with this generator, and it won't work. Somewhere along the line, the AC current has to be converted into DC.

The old-style wind generators (the kind that gave wind power such a sullied reputation) performed this conversion with the use of brushes and a commutator; mechanical contrivances that work by transposing the energy from one-half of each sine wave cycle, so the current always flows in the same direction. A clever idea, but one requiring parts that wore out and needed replacing, invariably at exactly the wrong time.

rex's maxims

WIND TAKES ON A WHOLE NEW CHARACTER once you need it to power your lights.

Modern wind generators have done away with brushes and commutators, replacing them with rectifiers, components that perform the same function without moving parts. This leaves nothing subject to wear except for the maintenance-free sealed bearings in the spindle and yaw.

The propeller blades were another weakness of the old-style wind generators. Made from wood—a substance that is not inherently weather-proof—the blades would eventually succumb to the elements, absorb moisture, and become unbalanced. At best, performance would suffer; at worst, bearings would fail.

Modern propellers are made from composite materials, or wood that is coated with composites. They neither wear out, nor absorb moisture, and their slick surfaces reduce friction to an absolute minimum.

Wind brakes—located either inside the house, or outside, or both—are another (very) helpful feature of modern wind generators. With the flip of a switch you can stop the blades from spinning. This is particularly handy during ice storms, or for periodic inspections.

Regardless of what you may have heard to the contrary, today's wind generators are significantly more efficient and maintenance-free than their predecessors, and can therefore boast a much longer life span.

AC OR DC?

Some wind generators—mostly (but not exclusively) those that are rated at 500, or more, watts—send 3-phase AC current through the lines and into a charge controller, where a series of rectifiers convert it into DC current, for storage in the batteries. Once it senses that the batteries are charged, the charge controller shunts excess power to a heat sink.

Other wind generators do the AC to DC conversion within the turbine, itself, and send DC current through the lines and into the house. Certain advanced models go a (giant) step further, incorporating electronics that sense the batteries' state of charge and adjust the rotor speed accordingly. On these models the propeller stops, completely, once the batteries become fully-charged, eliminating the need for both a separate charge controller, and a heat sink.

Southwest Windpower's Whisper H-40. *(photo courtesy of Southwest Windpower)*

Is one better than the other? Not really. While it is true that 3-phase AC current is a little more efficient that DC current, the system voltage is the most important factor when choosing a wind generator. As we've already discussed, a wire that is rated to carry 40 amps of 12-volt current (480 watts) a distance of 50 feet, with 2 percent line loss, will carry 40 amps of 24-volt current (940 watts) 100 feet. In other words, by doubling the system voltage, you can move twice the wattage, twice the distance, through the same wire, giving you a four-fold return on your investment. Bigger generators, then, that need to be placed farther from the house, should operate at higher voltages.

So what size of generator should you buy? This is a tough question that requires several, regrettably slippery variables to be considered before answering. Where we live in Colorado, the sun shines over 300 days per year. I estimate the average wind speed at our house to be between 10 and 11 mph. Our PV system is rated at 1140 watts, our wind generator at 1000. I have not metered the wind output (yet), but I would estimate that it is between 20 and 30 percent of the total (wind and solar) production. Though I wouldn't want a bigger generator, I certainly wouldn't want a smaller one, either.

Bergey XL.1 Turbine. *(photo courtesy of Bergey WindPower)*

If you live in the Southwest, where the sun shines high and often, wind may not be as much of a factor, and a smaller generator with a lower cut-in speed may be the answer for those days when the sun doesn't shine. If you're building in the northern Great Plains, where the wind is fairly constant, and the sun fairly isn't, then you would want wind to figure more prominently into your energy scheme.

Does anyone near you have a (reasonably new) wind generator? Knock on their door and ask them about it. No amount of hair-pulling, divination, blind-guessing or rough-calculating can outdo solid experience.

Cost is always a consideration. Bigger generators are not that much more expensive than smaller ones, but there are greater peripheral costs involved. Bigger means farther (from the house), higher (off the ground), and sturdier. While some small generators can be mounted on the roof (provided the roof is built with standard trusses—which most log homes aren't—for mounting the mast), large generators need to be mounted atop towers.

Many people sidestep the tower issue completely by mounting two or more smaller generators along the peak of the roof, or next to the wall, of a barn or workshop. They pay more per watt for the generators, but make up the difference with what they save on the tower.

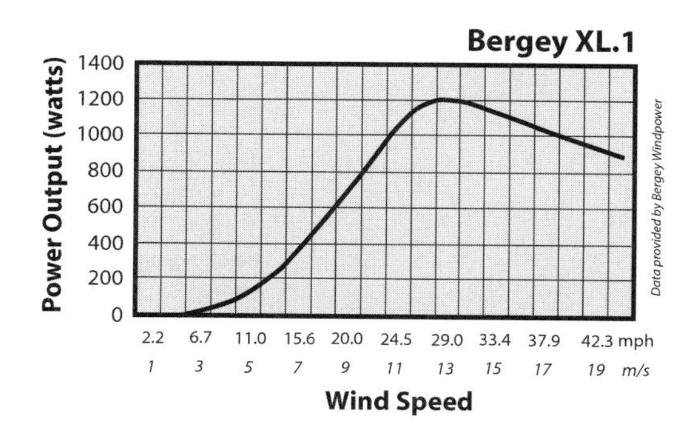

As with any major purchase, you want to buy your generator from a reputable manufacturer that stands by its products. Shop around and ask lots of (pointed) questions. Any salesperson worth his or her salt should be able to answer all of your questions about the various models, and help you make an informed decision. Besides the pros and cons of different generators, you will also want to know all the warranty details and how difficult it is to obtain warranty service. Who do you call with questions about installation and wiring? Or who do you call, once the unit is installed? Can you talk to a human without running through a computerized maze? It's good to know these things *before* you buy.

After deciding that you can afford both the generator and the tower to mount it on—and the extra wire—you need to consider how much work will be involved in getting the tower from the ground to the sky. Is it something you can do yourself, with careful planning, or will there be extra costs involved in erecting the tower? (Considering that you have just built a house with tons of heavy logs, you should be able to answer this question without too much consternation.)

Our tower rises at least 25 feet above the trees.

TOWERS

Before deciding on a tower, it's a good idea to check with the county, to see if there are any applicable regulations. Many counties have codes restricting the height and placement of towers of any kind. Other counties require that the foundation and support system be engineered (a good idea, in any event). Show them the manufacturer's recommendations, for both the generator and the tower you plan to erect. It may be that you can reach an equitable compromise.

FINDING THE RIGHT LOCATION

The higher you can mount the generator, the more wind you can catch, and the more power you will produce. Though it may not always be possible, the generator will perform best if it is at least 20 feet higher than any trees or buildings within 300 feet of the tower.

The tower should also be a safe distance from the house. At a bare minimum, the tower should be several feet farther from the house than it is high; at least you'll be a little safer if it crumples under the force of a 200 mph microburst. But farther is better. The owner's manual for our Whisper 1000 model suggests a minimum distance of 15 times the propeller diameter, which works out to 135 feet for that particular machine (with a 9-foot propeller).

An Air 403 turbine is mounted next to an exterior wall, and guyed to the roof. *(photo courtesy of Southwest Windpower)*

Types of Towers

Note: *Wind tower grounding is covered on page 248.*

There are two basic types of towers: lattice (either guyed, or free-standing), and fold-over pipe towers. Lattice towers can be assembled on the ground and raised as a unit, or erected piece by piece. Fold-over towers must go up as a single unit, with the generator already installed on the top.

Fold-over towers are far less expensive than lattice towers, and can be raised without too much trouble, provided you have enough navigable, open ground at your building site. The most common method is to support the top of the tower several feet off the ground (once the base is secured to its pivot point), and install the generator and the backside guy wires. The tower can then be raised by running a wire rope from the top of the tower, over a gin pole, and down through a pulley firmly anchored in the ground. Either a pickup, or a winch, can be used to provide the pulling power needed to stand the tower vertical. (Personally, I'd opt for the steady control of a winch.)

In principle, lattice towers can be raised in the same way, though the weight of a large tower increases the level of difficulty—and danger—severalfold. It's nothing you want to try on your own, unless you've got all the equipment and know-how to make it work.

Raising a lattice tower piece by piece is another option, albeit the most dangerous. It's a project best undertaken with a boom truck and qualified personnel, well versed in all the proper safety procedures.

I prefer a lattice tower for the simple reason that it's easy to climb when I want to conduct periodic inspections. I can also climb the tower to wipe ice from the propeller blades, after a freezing rain, rather than waiting a day, or more, for the sun to come out and melt the ice away.

Rex assembles our lattice tower using his home-made "safety donut".

Our lattice tower is a 50-foot 1950's affair, that stood un-guyed for 40 years—with a radio antenna mounted on top—before I took it apart and hauled it up the mountain. It now rests in a 3-cubic yard block of concrete, set on solid bedrock. It's nine 1/4-inch wire rope guys are likewise anchored in bedrock. I'm pretty sure it could ride out a hurricane with a Volkswagen parked on top, though I doubt I'll ever find out. (As much as I'd like to tell you how I raised it, you're probably better off not knowing.)

Any tower kit you buy should come with complete instructions for erecting and anchoring. The instructions will likewise tell you to consult an engineer and/or a rigger, to ensure that it's raised, and secured, safely. This is good advice. While it may seem that a preponderance of steel and concrete obviates the need for engineering, it never hurts to be sure.

LOOKING DEEPER

In this chapter I have tried to address every aspect of wind power that I deemed necessary for you to consider before coming to a decision on what type of generator to buy, and where—and on what—to mount it. At the very least, it should help to steer you in the right direction. I know that LaVonne and I came to our decision with far less information than is presented here.

At the same time, I realize that the information contained in this chapter is, at best, a shallow scratch on the skin of a very deep body of knowledge. There are volumes upon volumes of literature available on the subject of wind power. Hundreds of incredibly brainy people have devoted their lives to the study of harnessing the wind for the purpose of providing reliable, renewable, non-polluting energy. Yet, for all of that, it remains an elusive, empirical science. No matter how efficient an airfoil one person designs, someone else will always find a way to make it better. The same goes for turbines, and the associated electronics. There will forever be room for improvement, and that's the way it should be.

The wind is, after all, just so much air.

LaVonne's

LOGBOOK 18

December 2000

While Rex finishes the stairwell, Dave tiles the bathroom and pantry floor, and I try my hand at texturing the walls. I want an earthy, hand-troweled look. Silly me, I think, after many, many days of texturing massive amounts of drywall.

The holidays are approaching, but we will be spending another season in the little cabin. I was so hoping to be in the new house by now, but the cabin is cozy. Rex, however, is getting tired of chopping wood to heat both places.

My only wish for Christmas is to soak in a tub. With the floor finished in the bathroom, I paint those walls first. The plumber will come up soon to install the toilet, sink and clawfoot tub. The rest of the house is still a disastrous construction zone, but I'll get my Christmas wish after all.

It's mid-December when Rex starts the challenging log stair to the loft [35]. With the chainsaw, he cuts large logs in half for the treads; then he planes them flat and sands them smooth. A large post, set in the corner of the L-shape stair, will support a landing and two log stringers. The hard part is calculating the exact rise and position of the each log tread, so all steps will be identical. Once this is calculated and re-calculated, each log tread is then scribed to fit snugly against the log wall. It will truly be a beautiful masterpiece.

While Rex crafts the stair, I paint and paint and paint. The interior doors arrive, and are stacked in a corner until the painting is done. I'm not one for a plain wall, so I sponge on other colors for a textured, warm look. After our last house, I will never have stark white walls again: when the ground is white with snow and the sky is white with cloud, nothing is more depressing than white ceilings and white walls. A neutral palette of creams and beiges complements the honey-colored log walls quite nicely.

35

LaVonne's LOGBOOK 19

36

January 2001

The log stair is finished after nearly 4 weeks of work, so now I can start staining it [36]. I choose a tough Varathane finish for the treads. Then it's time to chink (again)...around all the purlins, stair logs, floor beams, you name it. It just never seems to end.

February 2001

The loft is open to the great room below and we need a railing. We are both pretty tired of peeling logs, sanding and staining, at this point. Rex suggests that we incorporate copper tubing with the log spindles. It is a wonderful marriage of wood and metal. I patina the copper to give it that aged, dark look before we assemble two copper spindles in between every log spindle. We like it so well that we do the stair railings the same way [37].

37

Carpet will be installed in the loft and office after we finish trimming the windows and mop boards...a sizeable job! Then we add some tongue & groove boards to the lower half of the framed walls upstairs. We hang the interior doors, and give them two coats of clear finish, along with all of the trim boards.

A common misconception of those who are building a house for the first time is that once the drywall is hung, you'll be moving in soon. I guess that'd be true if you could sub-out all the finishing details, but it's taking us forever. And I refuse to move in until it is completely done. But that dim light at the end of the tunnel is getting brighter every day!

CHAPTER 

CHARGE CONTROLLERS

Processing Your Batteries' Diet

The first time I ever held a charge controller in my hands, I was far from impressed. What could possibly be so important about this moderately heavy, little white box, with the interesting black cooling fins on top? It wasn't until I set it aside and began to read the 48-page instruction booklet (written entirely in the language I most often speak) that I began to appreciate just what a marvel of electrical engineering a charge controller is.

OutBack's MX60 charge controller.
(photo courtesy of OutBack)

Xantrex charge controller.
(photo courtesy of Xantrex)

The purpose of a charge controller is to charge the batteries, without overcharging them (except during "equalization," when the batteries are purposely overcharged to "boil" the plates clean). Different controllers have different ways of achieving these objectives. Some work better than others.

A good charge controller will also disconnect the battery from the solar array after dark, to keep current from flowing out of the batteries and back into the modules as they sit idle.

BATTERY CHARGING

We put a Trace (Xantrex) C40 charge controller, with a C40DVM digital meter, in the frame cabin where we lived while building the log house. It charges the batteries in three distinct stages: first, it allows the full charge from the PV array to reach the batteries, until a preset voltage limit is reached. This period of unrestricted charging is called the bulk stage.

Once the bulk voltage setting is reached, the controller backs off the amount of current sent to the batteries, in order to hold the voltage at the bulk setting for a cumulative period of one hour.

After that, the controller enters the float stage, where the voltage is allowed to drop to a lower (preset) voltage, where it will be maintained until the sun sets, or the (AC) loads exceed the DC input. The bulk and float voltage settings are all set by the installer, inside the unit, to voltages most practical for the specific application, and the types of batteries used.

Why the complexity? Simply put, the various stages are needed to allow the batteries to "soak-up" a charge. If you use a multimeter to read the voltage of a battery as it's being quickly charged, and then disconnect the charger and take another reading, you will notice a significant voltage drop. If you let the battery sit for several minutes and take still another reading, you will see that the voltage has dropped even further. It may seem that the battery is mysteriously losing its charge, but it isn't; it's merely dispersing the charge throughout the cells. By charging the battery bank in stages, the charge controller ensures that the batteries reach an actual full charge, rather than an *apparent* full charge.

EQUALIZATION OF BATTERIES

Equalization is the second important function of a charge controller. Sulfates can build up on the batteries' plates over time, and affect their performance. If the sulfates crystallize on certain areas of the plates, those areas are no longer able to function. By bringing the batteries to a very high state of charge, most of the damaging sulfates dissolve back into solution, increasing the batteries' storage capacity.

rex's maxims

A CHARGE CONTROLLER set for automatic equalization will invariably initiate the process at the beginning of a long stretch of cloudy weather.

The C40 equalizes the batteries by holding them at one volt above the bulk setting

(2 volts for a 24-volt system, or 4 volts for a 48-volt system) for a cumulative period of 2 hours. The charge controller may be set to equalize automatically every 30 days, but that's probably too often for a battery bank that is never deeply discharged. Besides, I prefer to initiate the process manually. That way, I can pick a sunny, windy day when I know it will equalize quickly. It doesn't really matter that much, except that during equalization the status light blinks alternately green and red (rather than just green, as it does during normal charging) and after awhile—even though I may only look at the charge controller 2 or 3 times during the day—I find the red blinking light annoying. So, due to my irrational distaste for blinking red lights, the sooner it equalizes, the better.

A CHARGE CONTROLLER FOR THE WIND GENERATOR

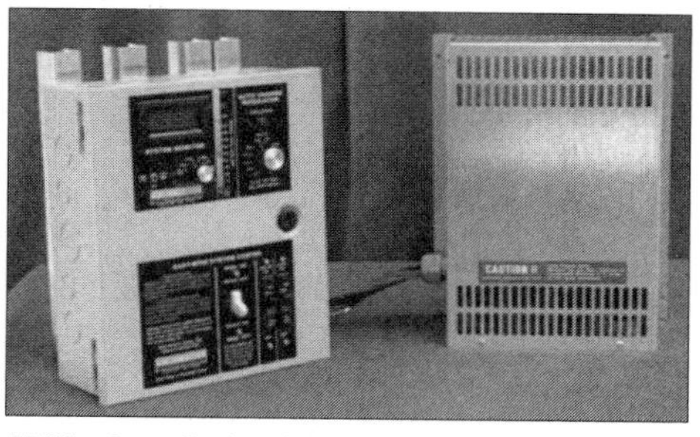

EZ-Wire Center for the Whisper H-40 and H-80 wind turbines. *(photo courtesy of Southwest Windpower)*

Since our Whisper 1000 wind generator sends 3-phase AC current to the house, it came with its own charge controller, one that uses a trio of rectifiers to change the AC current into DC. Because it also has leads for 40 amps of DC input from the solar array, we used this charge controller for both sun and wind at the new house.

Initially, I was quite impressed with it. It's big LED display offered a wealth of information, including separate readings for wind and solar amps, battery voltage, and a "volts per cell" feature (per each 2-volt battery cell, that is) that was internally averaged over time to provide a fairly accurate "fuel gauge" for the batteries.

With this type of charge controller, battery charging is regulated by a relay that sends excess amperage to a heat sink, once a preset volts-per-cell limit is reached. Equalization is achieved by setting the volts-per-cell dial to a higher (equalizing) limit, and leaving it there for a day or two, or until all the individual battery cells test the same with a hydrometer. It was a tedious process that made me long for the sophisticated simplicity of a C40 solar charge controller.

After 4 months of living in the new log house, we added 440 watts of solar modules. Because the combination wind/solar charge controller was not rated to handle the additional solar load, we bought a Trace (Xantrex) C60 charge controller and diverted the entire solar input through it. Now we are able to regulate battery charging and equalization with the C60, while using the wind charge controller's regulating features only to ensure the batteries don't become overcharged in high winds. Each controller senses the batteries' state of charge and adjusts it output accordingly. We've had no problems using the two controllers together.

OTHER USES FOR CHARGE CONTROLLERS

Some charge controllers have been designed to do more than regulate battery charging and equalization. Specifically, they may be used as either diversion load controllers, or as DC load controllers (though not at the same time as they are being used as charge controllers). Most of us have little need for either of these extra functions, but a short explanation of each may save you a moment or two of bafflement as you read the manufacturers' operating manuals.

DIVERSION LOAD CONTROL

What's the purpose of a diversion load controller? Well, let's say you have an old-style DC wind generator wired directly to the batteries. If the wind blows hard enough and long enough, the batteries could be overcharged and possibly ruined.

Big deal, you say. Why not just run the wind generator through the charge controller, and let it deal with the excess charge the same way it does with a solar array? The reason you can't do this is because a solar charge controller will simply disconnect the source from the batteries when the voltage gets too high; do this with a wind generator and the propeller will spin far faster than it was designed to spin.

By placing the charge controller (turned diversion load controller) on the other side of the batteries from the wind generator, and using it to divert excess current to a heat sink, the wind generator remains attached to the batteries at all times, without overcharging them, since any excess sent to one side of the battery bank will be drawn off the other side.

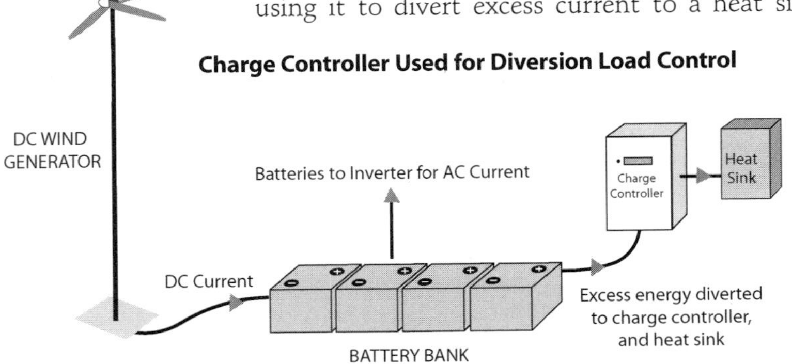

DC Load Control

Let's say you have a DC refrigerator that runs from current supplied directly from the battery. What happens when the batteries get too low to operate the compressor motor? It could damage the motor, and would certainly damage or destroy the batteries. If it were an AC appliance, the inverter would simply disconnect itself from the load, until the batteries were recharged sufficiently to once again supply ample current. But a DC load doesn't go through the inverter, and so is afforded no such protection. Unless, of course, some other regulating component is installed between the DC load and the batteries. That's the purpose of a DC load controller: when the battery voltage falls below a preset level, the load controller disconnects the load until the batteries again reach a safe level of charge. If the low-voltage condition persists for an extended period of time—as could happen if your array was buried in snow and you were away from the house for a few days—it may cost you a lot of food (and perhaps subject you to a memorable olfactory experience), but it's still a ton of money cheaper than a new high-efficiency refrigerator and a dozen or so batteries.

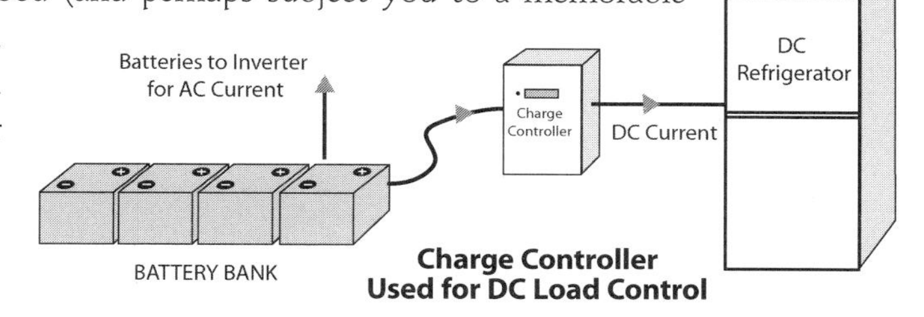

Charge Controller Used for DC Load Control

LOOK AROUND

Technology is changing all the time. Trace (now Xantrex) has been the industry standard for years, but it's not the only charge controller on the market. RV Power Products and OutBack Power Systems both have charge controllers that maximize the charge by converting excess array voltage into usable amperage. This can be particularly helpful during the winter months, when the modules are cold and therefore operating at higher voltages. OutBack goes one step further by offering a charge controller that uses 48-volt array current to power a 24-volt system. This can be very helpful for long wire runs.

And, as with everything else, buy a charge controller that will be big enough to handle the extra amperage, should you decide to add more solar modules at a later date. Or design your solar setup in such a way that it can be split into two arrays, operating through a pair of charge controllers.

Finally, check out how a charge controller does its job, before you buy it. The more sophistication you can add to the processes of charging and equalizing, the better off you'll be.

LaVonne's
LOGBOOK 20

March 2001

With radiant floor heat, we must have a floating floor so it can expand and contract as it warms and cools. After much research and shopping, we choose an engineered floor from Sweden—Kahrs is the brand. An exotic wood is my first choice, but the price is too steep. We'll settle for a red oak with a super tough finish (for the dogs, you know).

First we make sure the great room floor is level and fill any spots that are not. The flooring assembles easily, and the best part of this job is that the boards are all stained and finished...no need to do anything else except install matching stair nosing and trim boards where it meets the tile and carpet. To cover the edges around the log walls (which are very irregular) and still allow for expansion, we chink. It looks better than I thought it would, when Rex suggested it.

I try my hand at tiling the odd-shaped hearth for the wood stove [38]. Rex then trims it with small log poles. It looks great.

38

39

The cabinets are tricky to hang; log walls are quite irregular. We use lots of shims to get them just perfect. The island is customized with T&G boards on three sides and log posts on each corner. Then we set the countertops, hang the microwave over the stove, and tile a backsplash [39]. A few closet rods to put up, and we can hang clothes. We hook up the front-loading washer and gas dryer. Now I don't need to drag all the wash to a laundromat, 45 minutes away!! These conveniences really make a woman happy!

I take a deep breath before attempting to tile the shower walls and bathroom countertop. It goes well. Now I can call the plumber to hook up the final fixtures.

Rex hangs the light fixtures, and wires all of the outlets and switches, after many hours of trying to figure out how the electrician ran the wires for our 3-way and 4-way switches, (many were mislabeled with the wrong color of tape).

CHAPTER 23

BATTERIES

Care and Feeding of the Beasts That Hold Your Sunshine

Wind generators whir, inverters hum, but batteries just grumble. And why shouldn't they? Compared to the workout the batteries are subjected to every day, the other components in your PV/wind system have it pretty easy. Sure, the wind generator is stuck up on a tower, being beaten around by stray updrafts and errant cross currents all day and night, but it's a feisty machine—it loves to be in the thick of the action. The batteries have to stay forever locked up in a dark box, with no idea what's going to happen

Trojan batteries, T-105 and L16H. *(photo courtesy of Trojan Battery Company)*

Be Careful! Batteries are dangerous! They vent hydrogen gas, which is highly explosive. (Ever see footage of the Hindenberg disaster? Same gas). As if that weren't enough, they are filled with a caustic brew known as sulfuric acid. Always vent batteries to the outside, and don't let them anywhere near sparks or flames. And never, ever, allow a conductor (such as a wrench) to come in contact with terminals of opposite polarity. It could cause an explosion!

next. They alternate between being overstuffed with amperage, to wondering where their next meal is coming from. They're in a constant state of indigestion.

Believe me—if anything in your system deserves a little pampering, it's the batteries.

THE RIGHT BATTERIES FOR THE JOB

What is the best thing you can do for a battery? Never ask it to do more than it was designed to do. Only certain batteries can be used successfully in residential PV/wind applications. These are true, deep-cycle, lead-acid batteries. Because they have thicker plates (made of lead and lead dioxide), with less surface area than automotive batteries, they are made to be charged slowly, and discharged deeply.

The first time you reach down and lift a deep-cycle solar battery, you will be surprised at how much it weighs, compared to a car battery of comparable size. That's because car batteries are made with thin plates (with lots of surface area) so they can be charged and discharged quickly. The battery in your car (or duty-hardened pickup) is rarely discharged to less than 90 percent capacity, before it's quickly recharged by the alternator. A car battery has it pretty easy, compared to what you are going to put your solar batteries through.

A battery that fall somewhere in between a 6-volt deep-cycle battery, and a 12-volt automotive battery, is a 12-volt RV (or marine) deep-cycle battery. You might think that you can use this type of battery and save yourself a few dollars and some confusing terminal connections, but you won't be happy when the batteries wear out in a couple of years. They have thinner plates than the 6-volt deep-cycle battery, and are not made for the rigors of a PV/wind system.

Sealed, maintenance-free batteries (either liquid lead-acid, or gel type) are becoming more popular for PV/wind systems, largely because you never need to check the water level. Couldn't, even if you wanted to. And that's the rub: if they should ever accidentally become overcharged, they would lose part of their water and/or electrolyte through the safety vent, and it couldn't be replaced. Moreover, batteries that have been deeply discharged and left in that condition for a period of time need to be deliberately overcharged to cook the lead sulfate from the plates, but it can't be done (without dire consequences) when the batteries are sealed. So, while they may be less messy, sealed batteries do not allow any remedy, should the plates ever become

Concorde Sealed Batteries

If you insist on sealed batteries, check out the Concorde AGM series. They can be charged to a higher voltage than most other sealed batteries, and can even be equalized under controlled conditions.

fouled. You'll be buying new batteries, instead of restoring the ones you have.

For a reliable, moderately price PV/wind system, there are two good battery choices: either the "T-105," 220 amp-hour golf cart battery, or its big brother, the heavy-duty "L-16," 390 amp-hour battery. These are the two types of batteries most widely used in residential PV/wind applications. (There are several variations of these batteries on the market. Some come with warranties of 7 years or more, with commensurately weighty price tags.)

We went back and forth, trying to decide which style of battery to use for our house. In the end, we decided that the smaller T-105 was more economical, even though it meant more batteries and more connections. It would also allow us to add batteries to the system (four at a time, with a 24-volt setup) without such a tremendous outlay of cash.

After running T-105's in the cabin for 3 years, and the house for nearly 2 years, I have not noticed any difference in their performance from when they were new. On the other hand, all of our friends with L-16's are equally as pleased with the performance of their batteries, so in the end it boils down to which battery better fits your system, your available floor space (L-16's, though taller, have about the same footprint as the T-105, meaning more amp hour capacity in the same space), and your pocketbook.

How Many Batteries?
See *Chapter 19: Sizing The System*, as well as the *Battery Sizing Worksheet* on page 291.

PAMPERING YOUR BATTERIES

Batteries are like draft horses: treat them well, and they will reward you dutifully; treat them badly and they will tire out (or up and die), just when you need them most. And like horses, batteries don't require much to keep them happy; just a warm, dry place to rest, a little water now and then, and the security of knowing they will never go hungry. Nor does either object to being put to work, as long as they're not overworked.

CHARGING AND DISCHARGING

As was pointed out in the last chapter, a good charge controller will easily handle the chore of charging your batteries from wind and solar sources, as long as you give it plenty of amperage to work with. But when your batteries become greatly discharged after a few days of heavy loads and/or cloudy weather, you may need to charge them with a fossil-fueled generator. In this case, the charging will be done through the inverter, not the charge controller. *(See the next chapter on Inverters, for a full discussion of battery charging.)*

How low can you let the batteries get, before you need to drag out the generator? Lead acid batteries can suffer permanent damage if they are ever discharged more than 80 percent of their capacity. This should never happen in a properly-sized PV/wind system. Moreover, a good, well-calibrated inverter with built-in safeguards will shut down the AC loads, before allowing the batteries to discharge to such a dangerous degree. (For large DC loads, a DC load controller should be used as an automatic disconnect. See the previous chapter, for more information.)

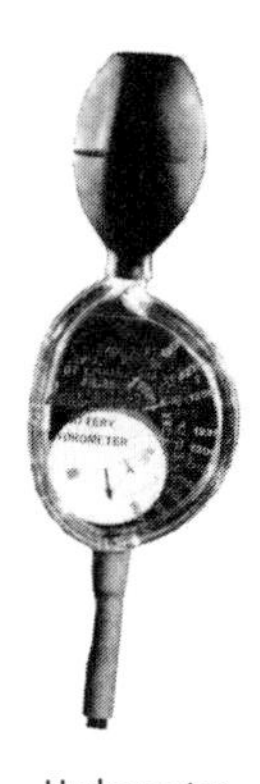

Hydrometer for measuring the specific gravity of each battery cell.

To keep your batteries truly healthy (which translates to a long life expectancy), you should never allow them to discharge to below 50 percent of their rated capacity. The trick, of course, is in knowing at what point they have reached this level, so you can either turn off all the loads connected to the batteries, or use a generator to charge them.

The easiest way, by far, to assess the batteries' state of charge is to install a meter that keeps track of amp hours in, versus amp hours out. At a glance, you can tell how many amp hours below full capacity the batteries are, by subtracting the "amp hours from full" from the battery bank's rated capacity. (Our meter, a TriMetric from Bogart Engineering, does the math for us, and displays a "fuel gauge" which shows the state of charge as a percentage.)

Another, far more tedious method, is to "weigh" the electrolyte in each battery, to determine what percentage of the sulfates are in solution (good) compared to what percent are trapped on the plates (bad). The heavier the electrolyte, the greater the batteries' state of charge.

To accomplish this task, a hydrometer (an apparatus somewhat similar in appearance—though not in function—to a turkey baster) is used to measure the specific gravity of each cell of every battery in the battery bank. (Specific gravity is a ratio that compares the weigh of a given volume of a substance to an equal volume of pure water.) A reading of around 1.172 indicates a 50 percent charge. (This is corrected to a battery temperature of 80 degrees Fahrenheit, so subtract .004 for every 10 degrees less than that.) A higher reading indicates heavier electrolyte with more sulfates in solution, and therefore a more highly charged battery. A lower reading indicates the opposite. A reading of 1.277 indicates the batteries are fully charged, while a reading of 1.098 tells you the batteries are at 20 percent of capacity and in need of immediate charge. When using a hydrometer, beware that it's an inherently messy process. Spilled electrolyte weakens the

A **hydrometer** measures a battery's state of health; a **volt meter** measures its state of charge.

batteries and wreaks havoc with your clothes. Consequently, it should be used sparingly.

To avoid testing every individual cell, you should be able to get a fair reading by first checking the voltage of each battery with a volt meter, making sure the loads and the charging rates do not vary throughout the procedure. If all the batteries test the same (to with a few hundredths of a volt), test a few random cells with the hydrometer. Significant variation, in either voltage or specific gravity, probably indicates sulfation of the plates, meaning that it's time to equalize.

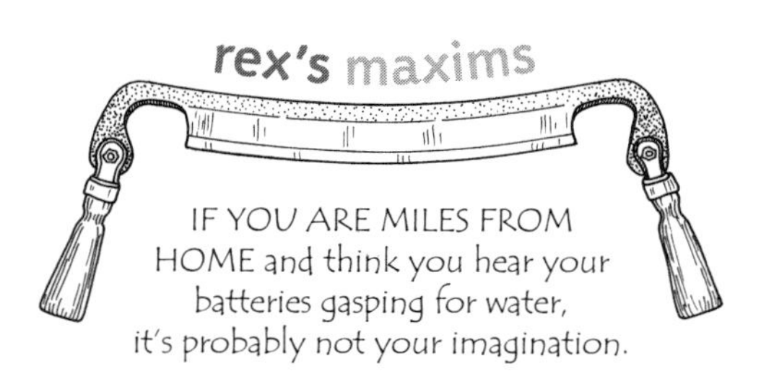

EQUALIZATION

Note*: Equalization should only be performed on vented, liquid electrolyte batteries—the kind you add water to, in other words. If you have gel type and/or sealed maintenance-free batteries, you won't need to read this section!*

Equalization is really just a fancy term for the process of overcharging your batteries. The purpose of equalization is "cook" any sulfates from the plates that may have crystallized there, and also to "stir up" the electrolyte, which tends to become stratified if the batteries go for long amounts of time without being fully charged.

How often should you equalize your batteries? Expert opinion varies from once a month, to one or two times a year. The Trojan Battery Company (who really *should* know, if anyone does) recommends equalizing only when low specific gravity is detected, or if the specific gravity varies widely (plus or minus .015) from cell to cell, and battery to battery.

Most people, however, will probably not bother to take hydrometer readings at regular intervals. In that case, "better safe than sorry" is the best rule of thumb. Batteries that are brought to a full state of charge often, and rarely (or never) allowed to drop below 50 percent of capacity, should easily be able to go six months to a year without equalization. Batteries that lead a rougher life will need comparatively more attention.

As mentioned in the last chapter, a good charge controller will initiate and monitor the equalization process. It's all automatic and nothing that requires your attention. There is one detail, however, that I should point out, because it just might save you a lot of hair-pulling later.

The Trace (Xantrex) C-series charge controllers take the battery voltage

1 volt higher than the bulk voltage setting (2 volts on a 24-volt system, 4 volts on a 48-volt system), and keeps it there for a cumulative period of two hours. So if, for instance, the bulk voltage on a 24-volt system is set at 29.2 volts, that means the batteries will be brought to 31.2 volts during equalization. There is no problem with this, of course, *unless* the "high battery cut out" setting on the inverter is *below* 31.2 volts. If it is, the inverter will shut down, once the voltage reaches the preset point, and leave you in the dark. You can believe me; I speak from experience.

Don't Forget The Water!

Most batteries that land in the recycling heap before their time have simply died of thirst. And most of those batteries come from homes owned by people who have never used alternative energy before. That's unfortunate, because there is really very little work involved in keeping the batteries topped off.

The amount of water your batteries use will depend upon how often they are brought to full charge, and how often they are equalized. To begin with, you should check the level at least once a month, and after each equalization. After a few months you will develop a feel for when you will need to add water. And after a couple of years a little built-in alarm will probably go off in your head whenever the batteries might be thirsty.

A procedure as simple as pouring a little water down hole should not need much explanation, but a few pointers will get you started on the right foot.

- **Use only distilled water.** Any other type of water will contain minerals that can reduce a battery's effectiveness.
- **Bring the battery to a full charge before adding water.** Why? because the electrolyte expands as the state of charge is increased. If you fill a battery with water and then charge it, acid will dribble out from under the caps. This creates a smelly, corrosive mess and also dilutes the electrolyte, since some of it will have escaped. If the battery is greatly discharged and the plates are exposed, cover the plates with water before charging.
- **Don't overfill the battery.** Adding water to a level just below the bottom of the fill well is sufficient.
- **Never let the water level drop below the tops of the plates.** Exposed plates quickly begin to corrode. At a bare minimum, the plates should always be covered by at least $^1/_4$-inch of water.

Any auto parts store will have a (turkey baster-like) tube with a rubber bulb on the end for filling batteries. It's well worth the money.

And by the way; if anyone has ever told you that you will dilute the electrolyte by adding water, don't believe them. The only gasses that escape a vented battery are hydrogen and oxygen, the constituents of water.

THE BATTERY BOX

It is neither necessary, nor desirable, to store your batteries outside. The optimum temperature for most batteries is between 75 to 80 degrees Fahrenheit. Efficiency falls off as they become colder, and outgassing increases as they become warmer. So, short of a climate-controlled room, the best place to keep your batteries is in a box within your house.

The box doesn't need to be fancy: I built both of mine from 1/2-inch CDX plywood. Many people use large plastic tool boxes. The only requirements are that the box be sealed, vented to the outside, and **not** placed under the inverter (according to the NEC). Door and window weather stripping works fine to seal the lid, and 1-inch PVC pipe is sufficient for the outside vent. A plastic kitchen scrubber stuffed loosely inside the outdoor vent opening will prevent insects and little furry varmints from exploring the inside of the vent pipe.

If the box is going to be placed on a concrete floor, it's a good idea to support it with treated 2 x 4's. This will allow air circulation under the box and avoid rot.

WIRING THE BATTERIES

Note: *The NEC (National Electric Code) does not allow welding cable to be used for battery connections, though many individual inspectors have no problem with it. Before you spend a lot of money, find out what your inspector will accept.*

Before you build the battery box, lay out different arrangements for your batteries on paper, because there is more than one way to do it. The object of the puzzle is to keep all the cables—especially those going to the inverter—as short a possible.

The best way I've found is to lay out the batteries in rows, with each row being equal to the number of batteries

Color-Code Your Battery Cables

Knowing positive from negative at a glance is helpful, safe and easy. Before wiring the batteries, lay out all the cables, separating the serial cables from the parallel. Wrap a piece of red tape around one end of each of the serial cables, and both ends of half the parallel cables. These will be your positive connections. It will help you avoid confusion later, and will probably impress the electrical inspector.

in a series (2 for a 12-volt system, 4 for a 24-volt system, and 8 for a 48-volt system.) If they will fit the space you have allotted, it makes wiring a simple task.

Let's say you are running 12 batteries in a 24-volt system. You will have 3 rows (series) of 4 batteries each. If you lay the batteries out in a 4 x 3 grid, then each row of 4 batteries will be wired in series (positive to negative), to bring the voltage to 24 volts per row. After you do this with each row, you will find all the remaining negative terminals will be on one side, and all the positives on the other. These terminals will be used to make the parallel connections that combine the amperages from each series (rows), without increasing the voltage. Connect all the positives together, and all the negatives, then take the shortest route to the inverter with one (very heavy) cable from each side.

The batteries will require more care and maintenance than all the other components of your wind/PV system, combined. Even so, they don't ask for much, in comparison to what they give back. And after a few months, you'll find that adding a little water, and checking the connections, now and then, is no more of a hassle than taking out the garbage, or shoveling snow off the deck (or giving your wife her nightly foot rub).

Just think of your battery bank as your own private herd of short, compact Clydesdales. Batteries may not be as much fun to watch, but you'll get more work out them, and they're a whole lot easier to clean up after.

Wiring the Batteries

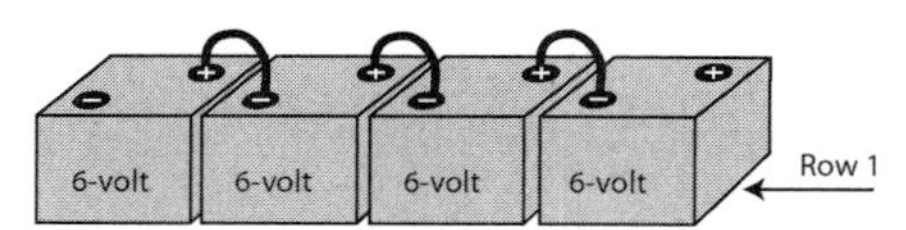

Step One: Connect each row of batteries in series (positive to negative)

Series Connections increase voltage: add voltage of each battery for total system voltage (6+6+6+6=24 volts)

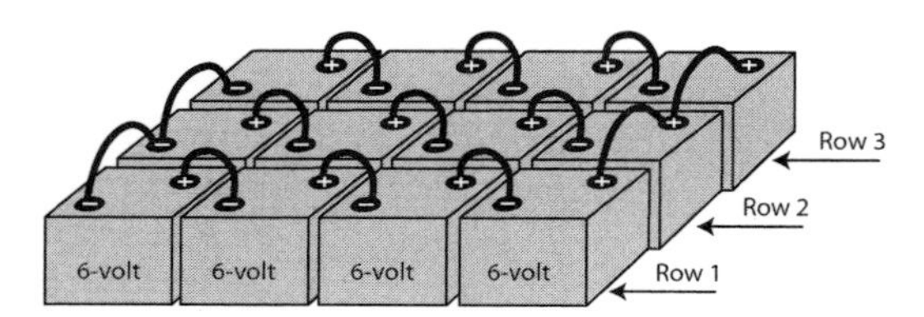

Step Two: Connect rows 1, 2 and 3 in parallel
(positive to positive to positive on one side;
negative to negative to negative on other side)

Parallel Connections do not increase voltage

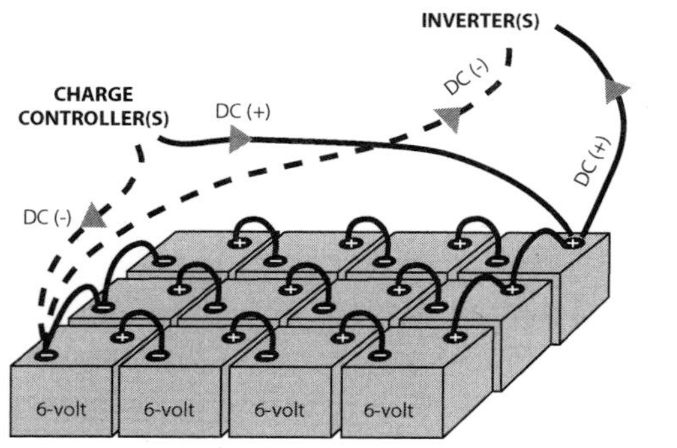

Step Three: Connect incoming current to the bank of batteries, and then run one positive and one negative connection to the inverter

Parallel and Series Connections

Connecting batteries in series and parallel may seem confusing, at first, but it's really logical and quite easy. The trick is to make all of the series connections first. That way, the remaining terminals *must* be for parallel connections.

INVERTERS

The Last Stop on the DC Trail

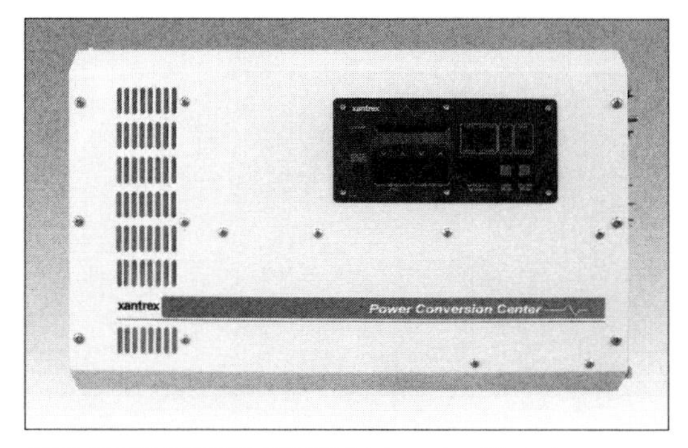

Trace (Xantrex) Inverter SW4024. *(photo courtesy of Xantrex)*

Before it gets to the inverter, the energy that will power your house goes through quite a ride. Energetic electrons knocked out of their orbits by particles of sunlight have charged through the wires at breakneck speed into your batteries, where they were pressed into service to convert lead sulfate into sulfuric acid. The sinusoidal positive/negative waves produced within the wind generator have been clipped and flipped and transformed into pulsing positive waves of direct current, before joining the current from the solar array in the batteries' chemical energy storehouse. There is enough potential energy sitting in the batteries right now to run your house for several days, but until it goes through one final transformation inside the inverter, you can't even use it turn on one measly light bulb.

The inverter is the magic box inside of which DC current from the sun and wind (and batteries) is converted into usable AC current. Some inverters perform this task better than others.

SINE WAVES AND INVERTERS

If Thomas Edison had gotten his way, no one today would be using AC current, and inverters would be no more than step-up DC converters. But, since it's easier and more economical to send AC current long distances through power lines, sophisticated DC to AC inverters are a must for anyone wishing to live off-the-grid and still use standard electrical appliances.

AC current is delivered in the form of a sine wave. This is a smoothly pulsing wave that gracefully arcs from a peak of positive voltage to an identical negative peak, and back again. Essentially, the current reverses flow with each crest and trough. And it does it very quickly; in the United States, AC current, and the myriad things that run on it, have been standardized to run at 60 hertz, or 60 positive-negative cycles per second.

As we saw in the chapter on Wind Generators, a sine wave is the natural form an electrical current takes when it is produced by a coil of wire being rotated between oppositely-charged, magnetic poles. But how do you take low-voltage DC current—a flat, old boring stream of electrons—and teach it to do the high-voltage tango?

Mind-numbing technicalities aside, suffice it to say that it can't be done in one fell swoop. First the low-voltage DC is converted to low-voltage AC, and then stepped-up, through a series of transformers, into 120-volt AC house current, operating at 60 hertz. Ultimately, the purity of the waveform will be determined by the number, and sophistication, of the steps the DC current is put through.

SINE WAVE INVERTERS

State-of-the-art sine wave inverters, such as the Trace (Xantrex) SW-series, will produce a current as clean as the smoke-belching utility company on the far side of the mountain. If there is anything that won't run efficiently on the current they produce, we have yet to find it. As you might imagine, such technology doesn't come cheap.

We bought a Trace SW4024 sine wave inverter when we first moved to the mountains. Initially, we installed it in the cabin, then moved it to the house, once we had the rest of system installed. Except for one incident that wasn't really the inverter's fault (I'll explain what happened, later in the chapter) it has performed flawlessly. In over three years of service, the only problems we have had have resulted from my own programming errors, or oversights, rather than the inverter's design.

Modified Sine Wave Inverters

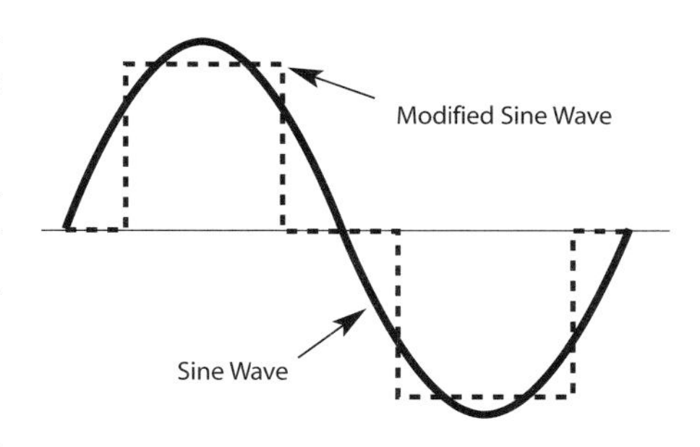

For a lot less money, you can equip your house with a modified sine wave inverter, such as one of the Trace DR-series. I would advise against it, however. These inverters take certain shortcuts, producing a stepped waveform that is really just a choppy approximation of a sine wave. For lights and toasters and vacuum cleaners, it may be good enough. But for certain other appliances, problems can arise.

After moving the sine wave inverter to the house, we bought a Trace DR 2524 modified sine wave inverter for the cabin. We were told by some people that it would eat an HP LaserJet computer printer in a hot minute. Others agreed, but said it would take a month or two to do it. I'm happy to say that we're still using that printer, after running it for more than a year with power from our modified sine wave inverter, though there were times when the printer would stall for several moments, before printing. The one appliance it would not run—at all—was LaVonne's Pfaff serger, which is a fancy sewing machine that cuts fabric as it stitches. Probably it has more to do with the rheostat that runs the machine, than the machine itself.

At the back of my manual for the DR series inverters, Trace compiled a list of devices that may experience problems running from a modified sine wave inverter. These include (but are not limited to) microwave ovens, clocks, ceiling fans, dimmer switches (which is to say, rheostats), and rechargeable devices. I quickly discovered that I could not let my DeWalt 12-volt drill batteries sit in the charger for very long after they were charged, or they would begin to overheat.

The bottom line? If you are building a weekend cabin, a modified sine wave inverter will probably work fine. But if you are building a house with all the modern conveniences you have come to rely on, don't scrimp: a good sine wave inverter is the only way to go.

Comparison of Slow Cooker Cooking

LaVonne had noticed a time difference when slow cooking a pot of stew at the cabin with a modified sine wave inverter versus here at the log house with a sine wave inverter. So we tested the usage with a Watts-Up? Meter and found it used the following wattage continuously:

	LOW	**HIGH**
Sine Wave	178 watts	241 watts
Modified Sine Wave	171 watts	234 watts

After many hours, the difference adds up!

INVERTER FUNCTIONS

What else can an inverter do, besides change low-voltage DC current into usable AC house current? Plenty; a top-of-the-line inverter will have more features than you will ever use. Here are a few to look for:

High and Low Voltage Shut-Off. This is the inverter's way of protecting your appliances, the batteries and—most importantly—itself. There should be one programmable setting for low voltage shut-off, and another for high voltage shut-off. The factory defaults are probably fine, unless (as previously mentioned) the high voltage shut-off is set lower than the voltage allowed by the charge controller during equalization. If this happens, the inverter will turn itself off.

Battery Charging. You will need an inverter that also doubles as a battery charger. It should have settings for bulk and float voltages, and they should be set the same as on the charge controller.

Generator and Grid Tie-ins. If you are completely off the grid (as we hope you are), then the second feature will be of no interest to you. But if you are connected to the grid, a good (sine wave) inverter will stay in sync with the outside power source, cutting in when there is a power outage, or selling power back (at wholesale, unfortunately) to the utility when there is an abundance.

There is no question, however, that you will need a tie-in for your generator. Some inverters will start the generator for you—providing the generator is wired for remote start—when the batteries get too low (though you really should size your system so the batteries don't get that low). Mostly, you will use the generator after a few cloudy days when you want to run a heavy load, like a washing machine, or a dishwasher. One thing to watch out for: make sure the "maximum charging amps" on the inverter is set within a range that the generator can handle; otherwise, it will trip the breaker on the generator. Even if it doesn't trip the breaker, the inverter might draw the generator voltage down below an acceptable level, and disconnect itself. Something to keep in mind, so you'll know what happened, if it happens.

rex's maxims

IF THE INVERTER does not seem to function properly, there's a 99% chance it's just doing what you told it to do.

Search Function. This is a feature we used—and still use—at the cabin, but not at the house. It is designed to save power, but it can cause problems. Essentially, the inverter in search mode is at rest, but it sends out a pulse of current every second or so (this pulse-rate is adjustable) to see if anything gobbles it up. If it does—such as when you turn on a light—the inverter will come to life and power the load. This is all well and good, until it finds a load that takes more than the preset search wattage to start, but less that the search wattage to run.

Usually, this is just annoying. But if you are not careful, it can get expensive and even dangerous. For example, I was charging a DeWalt drill battery with the inverter at the cabin set in search mode. (This is a different story than the previous one. Most of my inverter problems seem to revolve around drill batteries.) As long as the battery was charging there was no problem. After it finished charging, however, and the inverter went back into search mode, the battery charger interpreted each pulse of current as a signal to start up again and sent a surge of power to the drill battery. Then, sensing that the battery was already charged, it would shut down, only to go through the whole cycle again. The result was a $50 battery bursting at the seams, and too hot to handle.

Other Functions of an Inverter

- High and low voltage shut-off
- Battery charging
- Generator and grid tie-ins
- Search functions
- Stackable (for greater voltage or amperage)
- Computer interface

Once we moved to the house, we simply left the inverter in the "ON" mode. At absolute rest, our house consumes 45 watts of power. The loads include: the inverter itself; three smoke detectors (required by the county to be hard-wired into the power supply); the displays on two charge controllers and one amp meter; and the clocks on the gas range and the microwave oven. All other appliances that might draw a ghost current (television, satellite receiver box) are plugged into surge protectors with disconnect switches.

Stackable Inverters. No matter how big you think your inverter is, make sure it can be "stacked" with another, identical inverter. If your house has a number of heavy loads that might run simultaneously, or if you one day discover that the inverter you bought is too small for your growing needs, it may be wise to get two inverters and stack them, so that they operate, in phase, as a single inverter. The inverters may be wired in parallel, providing twice the amperage at the same voltage (120 VAC), or they can be wired in series, to double the voltage (240 VAC). A transformer can then be used to step-down, or step-up, the voltage for certain loads, such as a 240-volt well pump.

With renewable energy growing in popularity, people are building bigger houses with more appliances that can often tax the resources of a single inverter. For that reason, Trace (Xantrex) Engineering now manufactures power panels.

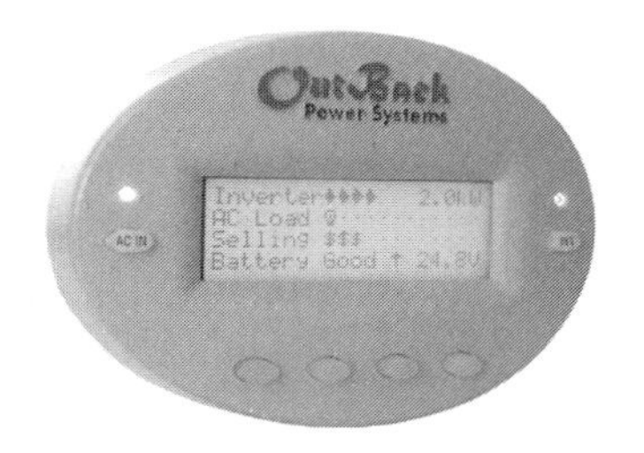

These are pre-assembled units with one or two inverters, along with a charge controller(s), DC disconnect, transformer, and whatever else you may require. As you might imagine, power panels are expensive, so shop around for the best price.

Taking a new approach, OutBack Power Systems has recently introduced the FX2000 inverter module. Up to eight 2,000-watt inverter modules can be stacked (in series, parallel, or both) and all run from a single remote system controller, The Mate—a small unit that simultaneously runs their MX60 charge controller(s) while serving a number of other useful functions. This stacking function of OutBack's FX2000 inverter means that you can add modules as you need them, without having to replicate the expensive programming electronics.

The Mate (top photo) and the FX2000 inverter by OutBack Power Systems. *(photos courtesy of OutBack Power Systems)*

Computer Interface. Most high-end inverters can be monitored and programmed by computer, as long as you have the interface and the software to run it. I haven't tried it myself, mostly because I really enjoy accidentally pushing the wrong button and shutting down the whole house, once in awhile. Still, I'm sure it would be handy to have sometimes; it's got to be better than resting on your knees on a concrete floor, pushing buttons with the hand that isn't holding the user's manual.

I know I've said it before, but I'm going to say it again, anyway: don't scrimp on the inverter! For a full-fledged house, a programmable sine wave inverter is a must. Get a big one, if not two. That way, when the well pump is simultaneously pumping water for the washing machine, you can still run your table saw without causing your own personal power outage. It will save you a few moments of button pushing, *after* several more moments fumbling around in the dark, trying to find a flashlight. And it may spare you a derisive comment, or two.

LaVonne's LOGBOOK 21

March 2001

March 26: the county inspector gave us the okay to move in with a temporary certificate of occupancy. Only 3 more inspections to go (wildfire, electrical final and then the FINAL).

We are ready to clear out that storage unit in town. And wouldn't you know it, the day we move the piano, couch, bed, and tons of other stuff, it starts snowing a few miles out of town. It snows and snows. We barely make it up the mountain with our trailer, but that's a story in itself. The mountain really has a way of testing anyone who wishes to live here.

April 2001

A month for sleeping and unpacking, and thoroughly enjoying our obsession of the past 3 years. The spaciousness and conveniences most people take for granted (like indoor toilets) are appreciated daily.

The high point of April: the state electrical inspector finally says the wind and solar systems (and all of the AC wiring) are up to code, and we can really live here.

May 2001

The deck construction begins in earnest. Since we really dislike staining redwood or cedar every other year, we choose a composite board made of oak and plastic. The weathered gray color complements the tan/grey chinking. Visiting family members, from Costa Rica [40] and North Dakota, are put to work—framing up the joists, pouring concrete piers, screwing down the decking, building the stairs and putting up the log posts for the railing.

41

Once again we use the copper pipe/log spindle design, choosing to make all of the spindles ourselves; 78 log spindles and 171 pieces of copper tubing and we are done! The crowning touch is a natural archway made with a very twisted, multi-branched tree limb [41].

June 2001

Flag day, June 14th, is a great day to celebrate. After 19 inspections, we have the final signature from the last inspector. Yea!

LaVonne's
LOGBOOK 22

Summer 2001

I declare absolutely no more building for many months. We hang the hummingbird feeder and lounge in the hammock, keeping a wary eye out for wildfires. It's time now for long hikes, and maybe we'll even see a movie in town.

September 2001

The last two 50-foot logs have been gnawing away at my crazy husband all summer. Finally he can't take it any more, and declares that we will have a rope swing "like none other" in the meadow below the house. I withhold any really serious comments, but he can sense my skepticism. Ummm. This will be interesting.

We drag the remaining two logs with chains hooked to the pickup and get them in their horizontal position. Hey, more logs to peel and stain. What a deal! Rex bolts the contraption together. I'm still skeptical.

Deep holes are dug in the meadow, and the log ends are treated so they won't rot. Erection day is conveniently scheduled while I'm in town. Neighbor Lane, who's sense of adventure matches Rex's, agrees to help [42]. Well, the first attempt didn't go so well, but the 2nd try, with more guy wires firmly anchored to the tractor, works [43]. Phew! Concrete is poured in the holes around the logs, and four piers anchored in bedrock hold the 4 guy wires. Soon a platform is built. And between you and me, it's the biggest blast. I should never have doubted my husband's sense of fun. It is quite a ride to swing on a 40-foot rope, over a meadow that drops away! [44]

42

43

44

CHAPTER 

PUTTING IT ALL TOGETHER — SAFELY

Protecting You and Your System from Nature, and Each Other

Imagine that lightning never wandered beneath the clouds. Imagine that you could be absolutely assured that every part of your system would work perfectly at all times—never requiring service or replacement parts or components—and that no one would ever try to draw more current through a wire than the wire could safely carry. If these three conditions were always true, then there would be no need for fuses, breakers, disconnects, ground wires or lightning surge protectors.

But this is planet earth, we're all humans here, and even when nature is on good behavior, components still wear out, and we still end up doing things with electricity that we shouldn't, even though we claim to know better. Since this is the way of the world and there's nothing we can do about it, we—sentient beings that we are—can, and most assuredly should, take precautions against the inevitable.

In this chapter I'll discuss grounding, over current, and lightning protection, and how important each procedure is to your home, especially to a *log* home.

I will then go through a typical system, beginning with the solar array and wind tower, and ending with the inverter. At each step along the way, I'll describe the minimum precautions you should take to protect your system and yourself from the forces of nature, and any inherent dangers that might be present when replacing, repairing, or reworking any part of the system.

The recommendations I give are sound practices that have worked for me, and other people I know, with our particular systems—and the two or three by-the-book electrical inspectors that roam these parts. Your system (and maybe your inspector) may differ in subtle, but significant ways, which means that your system might require additional safeguards that are not mentioned here. As in all things electrical, the inspector has the final say. Nor is the National Electric Code a static thing. It grows, every year. What passes code today may not pass code tomorrow. That's why electricians get the big bucks and the homeowner wires his house at his own peril.

It is not especially difficult to wire a PV/wind system, but it does take a clear, logical mind, an appreciation for detail, and a lot of time. If you think you can put together your own system, you probably can. If you have doubts, it might be better to leave it to a professional.

This chapter is intended to be a discussion of safety components, and where they should be located in relation to the working parts of your PV/wind system. Logistics, in other words. If you are hoping for specific information on wire sizes and types; conduit sizes and types; fuses, breakers, boxes or fittings, don't hold your breath, cuz you ain't gonna find it here. There's simply not enough room to cover that much ground in so few pages. Besides, it's boring stuff.

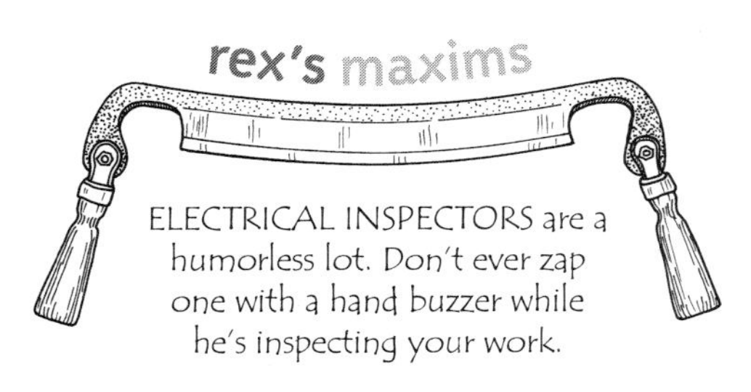

GROUNDING

The purpose of grounding a system is to provide an alternate path for current to flow, should a current-carrying conductor (the positive lead from a solar array, for instance) ever come into contact with a metal surface (such as a fuse box) that you might touch. With a good, unimpeded path to the earth, where the charge can quickly dissipate, the current won't have to try and seek ground through you, because (unless you're wearing a coat of arms) you are not as good a conductor as copper wire.

On the AC side of your system, the (white) neutral wires, and the (green) ground wires will all ultimately lead to a copper ground rod, outside the house and to the copper pipes leading to the well. They may also lead to a Ufer grounding system, if you installed one before the foundation was poured (see Chapter 6). In turn, every light fixture, outlet box, fuse box, junction box, and PV/wind component encased in metal will have a path to ground. Your electrician should know all about proper grounding of the AC side of things.

Grounding of the DC side is similar. All the negative leads from the wind and solar sources will ultimately be connected at the batteries, and all should have a path to the same ground rod as the AC side.

BONDING

The point where the AC neutral and ground wires join with the DC negative lead is called the point of bonding. This should be done at exactly one point within the system. It may be done at the ground rod, the AC service panel, or even the inverter. All that matters is that it is done *somewhere*.

Where is somewhere? Local codes vary on this issue. To be safe, explain to the electrical inspector that you wish to bond the DC negative to the AC neutral and ground leads, and then do whatever he or she suggests.

LIGHTNING

Anything above ground is subject to the effects of lightning. Solar arrays are particularly vulnerable. During one especially worrisome storm at the cabin, our charge controller went into overload protection mode three times, due to lightning hitting our array. Fortunately, the only damage was a few frayed nerves.

Lightning occurs when there is a massive disparity in charge between the clouds overhead, and the ground. The idea of a lightning rod is to provide a path

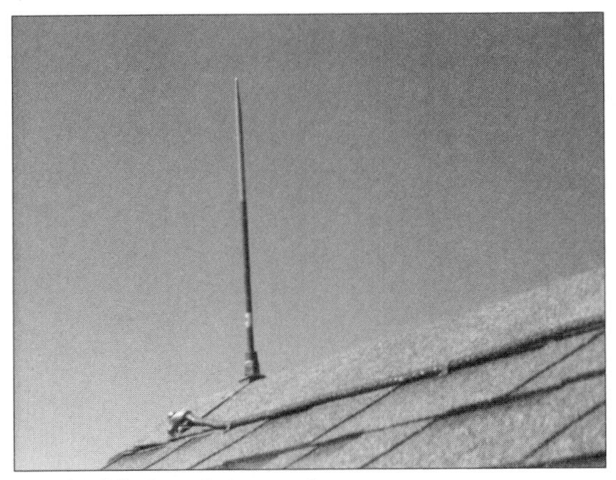
One of six lightning rods on our roof.

for positive charges from the ground to cancel out the negative charges in the air. In that way, a lightning rod helps to keep lightning from occurring, in the first place, since it serves as a bridge between the sky and the ground where the needs of the former can be offered up by the latter. But if the clouds demand more than the ground is willing or able to give, then a lightning rod provides a path to ground that does not run through your house.

In many ways, solar arrays and wind towers act as lightning rods. This means that they help equalize the electrical potential that exists between the ground and the sky. It also means that they will both attract lightning if the electrical potential becomes too great. There is nothing you can do to change that fact. But there is a lot you can do to mitigate the effects of lightning.

Well Casings

Heavy metal well casings are notorious for attracting lightning. If lightning is a problem in your area, you may want to consider asking your pump installer to wire a lightning arrestor into the system, to help prevent a damaging surge of electricity from zapping your inverter.

Log Homes versus Framed Homes

Being on top of a hill, we thought it would be a good idea to have lightning rods installed on our log house. Since lightning protection is something of a secretive art, we hired a professional installer to ensure that it was done right.

When he saw that we had a log house, he told us how wise we were to install lightning rods, since log houses always sustain more damage from lightning hits than conventionally-framed houses. Often, he said, a log house will burn to the ground, from the excess heat it absorbs from a strike.

With logs are laid horizontally, rather than vertically, a log wall presents a difficult path to ground. This means that lightning has to try a little harder. Bad news for the house.

THE SOLAR ARRAY

FUSES AND BREAKERS

Each solar module is designed to carry only so much amperage. The bigger the module, the more amperage it can handle. When you wire modules in series, you are increasing the voltage, not the amperage, so you can safely wire 2, or 4 modules in series without concern for overloading the module wiring.

But as soon as you wire one series of modules to another series of modules, in *parallel*, then you *are* increasing the amperage, and it is imperative that you isolate each individual series with a fuse or a breaker to protect it from a reverse electrical surge, as could happen with a short circuit somewhere in the line.

A combiner box showing a breaker for each series of modules, and a lightning arrestor in lower left corner.

Typically, a combiner box is used for this purpose. (OutBack Power Systems makes a good one.) The leads from a series of modules enter the box and run through a fuse (or a breaker), before its amperage is joined with the amperage from other series of modules.

In addition, there should be one common disconnect for each array, *after* all the current is flowing into a common feed. This is so the array can be shut down quickly and easily, either because of an emergency, or simply to service "downstream" components. A breaker box with a single properly-sized (DC-rated) breaker works well for this purpose.

GROUNDING AND LIGHTNING PROTECTION FOR YOUR SOLAR ARRAY

Note*: At the time our PV/wind system was inspected, the National Electric Code had no regulations regarding lightning protection. I have a feeling this is due to change. If it does, any recommendations I make here could be rendered moot.*

The array must be grounded. Period. Every module to every panel frame, every panel frame to the entire array, the array to a copper ground rod via a heavy copper ground wire. Obviously, the shorter the route to ground, the better. A buried ground rod beside the array, connected to the common house ground is ideal.

The ground (and the fuses and/or breakers) will protect your array from electrical accidents or oversights, and most ambient electrical surges from nearby lightning. If you have a good charge controller, it will disconnect from the array, even before the fuses and breakers can react. For more energetic strikes, a lightning arrestor is a very good idea. This is small device that "absorbs" excess voltage, then slowly dissipates it. It should be mounted close to the array; either on the combiner box, or on the main disconnect. Most have three leads: positive (red), negative (black), and ground (green). The ground wire may be connected to the disconnect box (if its metal), and the box should have a path to the heavy copper ground wire running from the array to a common ground.

THE WIND GENERATOR

The Wind Brake

Whether your wind generator sends 3-phase AC current to the house, or DC current, the electrical inspector will want some sort of disconnect outside the house. This will be a switch that stops the propeller from turning (a wind brake), and may or may not be supplied with the generator package. If it isn't you can order it separately.

Grounding and Lightning Protection for Wind

It may seem that a wind tower, set in solid concrete and guyed to the ground with heavy steel cables, would be well grounded. Unfortunately, it may not be. Since your wind tower will be the tallest thing around, you should take extra care to protect it from lightning.

To help avoid a lightning strike —and to minimize its effects, should it occur—drive a copper ground rod next to the tower and connect it to the tower with heavy copper ground wire. To be *really* safe, drive one ground rod next to the tower pad, and another rod at each of the guy wire pads. Connect all the ground rods together with heavy copper wire (#6, or bigger), connect them to the tower and each of the guy wires, and then run a ground wire to the common house ground. Bury all the wires at least 6 inches in the ground. Use heavy copper connectors, and make sure there is good contact (no rust, or paint). Expensive? In the grand scheme of things, not very. Worth it? If it's needed even once, yes.

A lightning arrestor should also be installed at the outside disconnect box, to help disperse any excess voltage that manages to get inside the lines. Since wiring differs from one type of wind generator to the next, you should ask the manufacturer what type of lightning arrestor to buy. Most likely, they will be happy to sell you one. Buy it.

CHARGE CONTROLLERS

With outside disconnects for both the wind and solar charging sources, there need be no other breaks in the lines, until the current moves past the charge controller(s). There should be some type of over-current protection between the charge controller(s) and the battery bank. A properly-sized inline fuse will work, though a (DC rated) breaker will make it easier to isolate the battery bank from the DC sources, and is more likely to bring a smile to the electrical inspectors face.

Some wind charge controllers come with their own disconnect. It is less common with solar charge controllers. Plan accordingly. The breaker, or fuse, should be rated for slightly more amperage than the surge amps the charge controller is designed to handle.

DC DISCONNECT

The DC disconnect is a very large, DC-rated, breaker that lies between the battery bank and the inverter. It is designed to protect the batteries—and the inverter—should a short circuit occur somewhere within the battery bank. It also makes it very convenient for shutting down the power to the inverter, and therefore the entire house, whenever you need to. The DC disconnect is sized for the inverter, and is designed to trip only when it senses far more amperage in the lines than the inverter could ever hope to use.

Trace (Xantrex) makes a 175-amp and a 250-amp DC disconnect. Both can handle more than their rated amperage for a short time, so they don't trip when the inverter surges to higher amps. Our Trace SW 4024 inverter has never tripped our 250 amp DC disconnect, though it has certainly drawn more than 250 amps from the batteries for very short intervals.

Xantrex DC Disconnect. *(photo courtesy of Xantrex)*

WIRING IT SAFELY

With properly placed breakers and disconnects, you will be able to wire most of your system without the threat of electric shock, or a component-destroying short circuit. The solar array and the batteries are two exceptions. To avoid the possibility of damaging the solar array by accidentally crossing the wrong wires, it's a good idea to cover the array with a blanket or tarp, before trying to perform the delicate and somewhat complex task of wiring the modules together in series and parallel.

Multimeter tester.

The batteries are another matter. By nature, they are full of electrical potential, and need to be wired with the utmost care. Know what you are going to do, before you do it. Never work on the batteries without first isolating them from every other component within the system. This means flipping the disconnects (breakers) that lead *from* the charge controller, and *to* the inverter.

There are basically two ways to coax a spark out of a battery: either by shorting together the positive and negative terminals on a single battery (wrenches and screwdrivers are the usual culprits), or touching the positive and negative leads from a series or parallel string of batteries (usually this requires negligence or confusion of purpose).

DC Wire Coding Colors

POSITIVE = Red

NEGATIVE = Black

NOTE: *The NEC now states that* ***black=positive*** *and* ***white=negative*** *on DC systems, though in practice, this new coding is rarely used on DC-AC systems.*

AC Wire Coding Colors

Black = HOT

White = NEUTRAL

Green = GROUND

Know which cable is which! Color code all the cables with tape (positive = red; negative = black) before connecting them—either to the batteries, or to the terminals of the charge controller, breaker boxes, or disconnects. It may be that you know exactly what you are doing at the time you're doing it, but come back 2 or 3 months later, and any wiring without color coding is going to look incomprehensible, especially on the AC side (where black = hot, white = neutral, and green = ground). At that point, you'll have to pull out the multimeter to decipher what you did.

A friendly word of advice for procrastinators: hide the multimeter under rolls of red, black, green and white tape. The tape will remind you of why you are looking for the multimeter, in the first place.

CHAPTER 26

HEATING OF HOUSE AND WATER

Staying Warm Without Busting the Energy Bank

By the time LaVonne and I began planning the new log house, I had logged seven years of living in a cabin with no other heat than a wood stove. Before and after the cabin interlude—except for the years spent in my parents' house, which was heated with hot water circulating through baseboard registers—I lived in dwellings with forced air (a.k.a. forced dust) heating systems.

Between the two, I far preferred the wood stove; it was quieter, easier to control, and cheaper to operate. But, after a day or two's absence in the middle of January, it took a steely constitution to come home in the dead of night.

Though LaVonne, poor girl, had missed out on the earlier cabin years—chopping holes through the ice in the creek for bath water is one my fondest memories—she was all too familiar with forced air heating. We were united in our loathing for it. Owing to that fact, we were able to quickly focus our heating options when it came time to build the house we'd been dreaming about since our courting days.

Obviously, electric heat was out; the PV/wind system needed to run it would rival the cost of the house. Propane wall heaters are a good, cheap, solution for cabins but quickly lose their practicality in a large, multi-room house. That left us with the hot water option. Baseboard or in-floor? It was a no-brainer: definitely in-floor.

But I'm getting ahead of myself. Before I let *all* my biases dangle in the wind, I'd better do a little explaining.

PROPANE WALL HEATERS

Propane wall heaters are small, inexpensive propane-fired units that can be mounted on a wall. They can be purchased either with a blower fan, or without one. As backup heat for a cabin or small house with a wood stove, they're terrific. We have several friends that use them. The heaters save them the trouble of having to stoke the fire in the middle of the night, and keep their houses adequately warm if they're away for extended periods.

But a propane wall heater is really pretty much of a brainless animal, with little hope of ever getting any smarter. It senses how cold it is in one location, then heats that location until it decides it's warm enough. It doesn't give a hoot how much heat makes it to the bathroom, or the far bedroom, which is unfortunate, because it's doubtful the building inspector would allow one to be mounted there to keep the chill out of your bones in the cold, winter nights.

So, for a very small house on a no-frills budget, a propane wall heater may suffice, but for a larger, comfortable house, you will need something more.

LaVonne's Verities

If you ever want to take A WINTER VACATION, invest in a good heating system that won't require a house-sitter to feed the woodstove.

FORCED AIR HEAT

Most houses in America—both old and new—are heated with warm, forced air. The air is warmed in a furnace (usually gas-fired), then pushed through a labyrinthine system of ductwork with the aid of an electric blower—a squirrel-cage fan—into the different rooms of a house through vents cut into the floor.

It's fairly inexpensive to install, and we know people who use this system in their PV/wind homes with reasonable success. But we don't know anyone, off the grid, or otherwise, who *likes* it.

Energy-wise, forced air heat is less efficient than hot water heat, requiring more propane *and* more electricity to heat a house. This is mostly due to the fact that air is thinner than water. It goes places we don't want it to go and therefore requires more energy per unit mass to heat.

Many of the problems with forced air heat are due to poor system design. Anyone who has ever lived in a house heated with forced air knows how easy it is to throw the whole system out of kilter, just by shutting a door or two. Some rooms get too hot, while others get colder. Often the only way achieve any degree of equilibrium is to leave open all the doors to all the rooms—not always a satisfying solution.

This problem can be alleviated, somewhat, by providing properly-placed cold air return ducts, so that the air can re-circulate throughout the house without building up pressure gradients in certain areas, pushing warm air out of house in some places, and drawing cold air in, in others. But, as long as the entire house is run off a single, centrally-located thermostat, the problem of uneven heating will persist.

Zoning is the obvious solution. By dividing the house into three or four distinct zones, each on its own thermostat, forced air heat becomes almost comfortable. Zoning comes with a price, however. Besides upping the original cost of the system by at least a couple thousand dollars, each zone requires a small motor to operate a zone damper within the duct, in addition to the main 5 amp (600 watt) blower motor, located inside the furnace. It can add up to lot of wattage at the time of year you can least afford to use it. And you'll still have to deal with dry, dusty air blowing up through the floor at incalculable intervals, a noisy blower, and severe limitations on how you can arrange your furniture.

Of course, any system that requires fans or pumps will tax your (electrical) energy budget; there's no way around it. But, if there were a system available that used less electricity and propane; a system that took up zero floor space while providing even, comfortable heat, wouldn't it make sense to use it?

HEATING WITH HOT WATER

Hot water heat has been around, in one form or another, much longer than propane has been available to fire the boilers that produce it. This is evidenced by the cast iron radiators we see in many older houses, school buildings, and court houses. A lot of those old coal-, wood- and oil-fired systems are still in use (now mostly converted to natural gas or propane), but their day is done; evolution has taken its course. Today's hot water heating systems come in two basic incarnations: baseboard registers and in-floor radiant heat.

Of the two, in-floor radiant heat provides the most even heat throughout the house. It is also the most logical choice for a log home, for the simple fact that log walls—being round by nature—do not have flat baseboards to which you can attach the registers. (Okay; I'll concede that any enterprising home builder could find a way to make a flat, vertical surface along a log wall beset with bumps and knots, but I defy anyone to make it look like it belongs there.)

But don't despair—if you install radiant floor heat in your log home, you won't be disappointed. In fact, I believe it's the perfect way to heat a long home, for reasons that will quickly become apparent.

Radiant Floor Heat

The idea of radiant floor heat is to make the entire floor one huge wall-to-wall radiator. To accomplish this, a continuous length of extremely tough (PEX) plastic tubing is snaked back and forth across the subfloor, stapled down, then embedded in a special type of lightweight (gypsum) concrete that is pumped over the floor in a soupy slurry that hardens in two or three hours.

You can have as many, or as few zones, as you need, without need of a nightmarishly complex system of ducts. Each zone runs on its own thermostat, which controls the pump for that particular zone. We have five zones in our house: one for the garage, and another for the workshop and electrical room. On the main floor we have our great room on its own zone, and the office and bathroom on another. The pantry is unheated. A single zone in the loft heats the upstairs bathroom; the rest of the loft stays plenty warm from the heat below.

Since we heat the great room and kitchen primarily with a wood stove (whenever we're around to stoke it) we set the thermostat lower there, than in the office and bathrooms. It's a very comfortable house, even during the coldest winter nights.

Special Considerations for Radiant Floor Heat

An oft quoted limitation of radiant floor heat is the amount of time it takes to warm a room, once the thermostat is turned up—there is no instant heat, as there is with forced air. This is because no additional heat can be felt until the hot water running through the PEX tubing raises the temperature of the medium in which the tubing is embedded.

If you lived in a drafty, poorly-insulated, stick-built house (of which there is no dearth in this country) this could be a real problem. But you don't. You live—or will soon, anyway—in a tight, solidly-built log house possessing tremendous thermal mass. When the house is warm, the log walls soak up heat, then release it as the inside air temperature cools. In effect, the walls of your house act as heat radiators, just as your floor does, so you never feel the temperature swings so evident in conventional houses.

You will be limited, however, in your choices for the finished floor. Carpet is feasible, though a thick, plush carpet above a standard, airy carpet pad won't work very well. You'll need a dense rubber carpet pad (not foam) to allow for the passage of heat. Considering the growing popularity of radiant floor heating, any reputable carpet distributor should know what will work and what won't.

If you elect, instead, to go with a wood floor, you will need to install an engineered floor, one that "floats" on the surface of the gypsum concrete, with no points of attachment. A floating floor can expand and contract, without warping or buckling, as it heats up and cools down. There are a few brands of engineered floors (not the thin, laminated variety) on the market; we went with one manufactured by Kahrs, out of Sweden. We're very pleased with it; it was easy to install and it's proving to be a very good heat conductor.

The third option, and probably the best, is tile. Not only is tile a good conductor of heat, it does not need an insulating underlayment of rubber or plastic, as is required for carpeting or wood flooring.

We used tile on our bathroom floors, wood in the kitchen and great room, and carpet in the office. Every room in the house stays plenty warm, even on the coldest days, but the system does have to work a little harder to heat the office. Just the same, I enjoy the feel of a carpeted office, so—for me and the dogs at least—it's worth the small loss in efficiency.

Helpful Hints When Installing Radiant Heat

- Increase your ceiling height to allow for the thickness of the gypcrete.
- Double plate the bottoms of your framed walls.
- Make sure your floor joists can support the extra weight.

Installing Radiant Floor Heating

There are three ways to install radiant floor heating. I have already discussed the most efficient method, wherein the PEX tubing is stapled to the subfloor, then embedded in 1-$^1/_2$ inches of gypsum concrete (or in the case of a garage or basement floor, 4 inches or more of regular concrete). Since the heating tubes are in direct contact with a considerable thermal mass, the transference of heat from the circulating water is optimized.

If you use this method—and I highly recommend that you do—there are three further considerations to bear in mind. First, you will have to allow for an extra 1-$^1/_2$ inches of ceiling space to accommodate the thickness of the Gypcrete®. Second, any framed walls will have to be double plated on the bottom, so that you have a nailer for wallboard and baseboard. And third, you may have to beef up your floor specifications to support the extra weight. Usually, increasing the thickness of the floor joists by one size (from 8 inches to 10 inches, for instance) is sufficient. Your local building department will be happy to tell you what you need to do. You may find, as we did, that your floor is strong enough without modifying the design.

But what if you've already built the floor, and discover that it is not strong enough to support the weight of the gypsum concrete? What do you do, then? Well, short of shoring up the floor from beneath to hold the extra weight,

Gypcrete® is poured over radiant heat tubes on our main floor, and leveled to the height of 2 x 4 sleepers.

you can always screw (or nail) a series of plywood sleepers to the subfloor, leaving just enough room between each one to push the heat tubing snugly into the groove. Setting the tubing down into a preformed, flanged aluminum sleeve will help to direct the heat upward, where its needed.

The last—and positively the worst—method is to run the PEX tubing beneath the subfloor, through holes drilled in the floor joists. The tubing is stapled to the underside of the subfloor, and then covered with aluminum heat transfer plates to reflect the heat into the subfloor. Insulation should then be installed beneath the heat tubing to further prevent heat loss. The shortcomings of this system are obvious, since all the heat must pass—and therefore, disperse—through the subfloor before it can even be felt on the floor above. For folks on a strict energy budget, this may not be acceptable.

Incorporating Solar-Heated Water Into Your Heating System

An added advantage to heating your home with hot water—aside from the extra comfort and energy savings—is the fact that your heating system can be adapted to use free energy from the sun to augment its efficiency.

Typically, water (or, in colder climes, a freeze-proof glycol solution) is heated by the sun in a series of solar collectors—weatherproof, glass-covered panels through which snake loops of black copper tubing. Though usually mounted on the roof, the solar collectors can be located anywhere near the house, as long as they have unimpeded access to direct sunlight, and a path to run tubing into the house.

The water heated in the solar collectors is circulated—via an electrical circulating pump—through a tank located near the boiler in the mechanical room of your house. Water from the house heating system is run through a heat exchanger inside the tank, where it's preheated before reaching the boiler. A second heat exchanger within the tank can be used to preheat domestic hot water.

The efficiency of such a system is dependent on many factors. The most important, the daily hours of solar radiation, is probably the least of your concerns if you're using sunlight for your electrical needs; if you have enough sun to drive your PV array, you should have enough to heat your water.

As with your PV array, the angle of the solar collectors in relation to the sun is important. Since it is highly unlikely that you will make seasonal adjustments of the hot water solar collectors, set them for winter, when you will need most of your hot water (an angle of latitude + 15 degrees, you will remember, is

CURT AND KELLY'S EXCELLENT SOLUTION

One of the nicest things about writing this book is our proximity to like-minded people who have engineered their own solutions to producing and saving energy. Curt and Kelly, our nearest neighbors, have come up with an ingenious—and cost-effective—solution for heating both their 1300 square foot house, and their domestic hot water.

To begin with, they use five 4-foot x 10 foot roof-mounted solar collectors to heat the water. Curt managed to pick up this impressive array from the classified ads, for a fraction of its original cost, from a person who needed to re-roof his house and had decided not to re-install the collectors after the job was complete.

To provide storage capacity for such a bountiful harvest of hot water, Curt and Kelly installed—which is to say, built their house around—a highly-insulated 500 gallon rectangular steel tank. Water from the tank circulates through the solar collectors and back, gradually raising the temperature inside the tank as the day progresses. On most sunny days they are able to bring the water to—and hold it at—a temperature near boiling. A differential temperature thermostat, hooked to a pair of temperature sensors (one inside the tank, another inside one of the solar collectors) activate a pump that circulates the water through the system as it's heated by the sun. Whenever the panels are cooler than the water in the tank, the pump shuts off, causing the water to drain back down into the tank. This is a handy feature to keep the water from freezing inside the copper loops within the solar collectors at night, and on cold, cloudy days. It also eliminates the need for antifreeze (glycol).

Our neighbors, Curt and Kelly, with daughters Jaclyn and Jessica, in front of their home. The large solar collectors on the roof (left side) heat their water; the PV solar modules (on the right) provide electricity.

A single coil of copper tubing running through the tank serves as a heat exchanger for both the radiant floor heat, and the domestic hot water. Being so massive (and efficient), Curt and Kelly's system does not require an expensive boiler, or even a standard hot water heater, to supply additional hot water during off-hours (or off days). Instead, the heat-exchanging coil runs from the tank through a propane-fired, on-demand hot water heater. It's all they need to heat their home and domestic water.

ideal for capturing winter sunlight). If this isn't feasible, they should, at the very least, be within 15 degrees of latitude, one way or the other.

The surface area of the solar collectors is important. The bigger they are, the more water they can heat—that much is intuitive. But the solar collectors will also need to be sized for the tank through which runs the heat exchanger. If the tank is too big, or the collectors too small (or too few), the water may not heat up sufficiently to do you much good. On the other hand, if the tank is too small in relation the solar heating capacity of your collectors, you will end up wasting valuable solar radiation because the water in the tank will be quickly heated to capacity during the day, but will soon lose all of its heat at night.

The best thing you can do before spending a lot of money on an improperly sized system is to seek advice from someone in your area who routinely installs solar hot water heating systems. Even if they charge you a consulting fee, you'll still be money ahead, in the long run.

WOOD STOVES

A fireplace is a wonderful, romantic setting for relaxing on cold winter nights, and if you plan to put one in your new home, I think it's great. There's nothing like the sight of jumping flames to excite the imagination and soothe the spirit.

But if it's heat you want, you will be much better off with a centrally located, wood-burning stove. It might not be as aesthetically pleasing as a fireplace, but it may save an argument or two over the cost of heating your home.

Although it's an ancient technology, burning wood for heat is still sensible and cost effective. Wood, like wind and sunshine, is a non-depleting source of power, since most firewood is standing dead, or culled from overgrown forests that need to be thinned. And, with the new, efficient stoves on the market, wood is a much cleaner fuel than ever before.

The greatest thing about using a wood stove in an off-the-grid, log home setting is the availability of fuel. If you build your own log home, it's likely that you can heat your home for at least a season just with the cut log ends, and log sections, removed from door

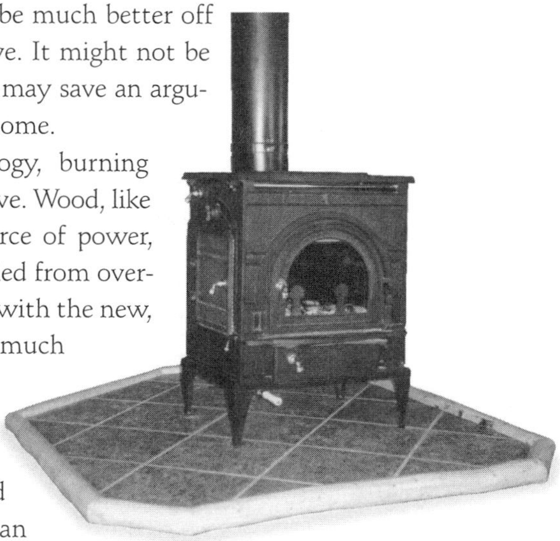

Our Vermont Castings wood stove (with side door and ash drawer) sits in the middle of the great room for efficient whole-house heating.

and window openings. After that—unless your home is in a most unusual place—you should have plenty of wood on, or near, your property. Even if you have to buy it, it will be cheaper than it is for folks in town, since you'll be much closer to the source.

If someone offers you a great deal on an old, pre-1988 wood stove, you should respectfully decline the offer. Why? Because 1988 was the year that wood stoves entered the modern world. Concerned about the growing problem of air pollution, and wood stoves' contribution to it, the EPA sat down with wood stove manufacturers and kindly asked (as only a government agency can) that all new wood stoves be designed to meet strict emission standards. The result was a pair of new designs that dramatically reduced emissions and greatly increased efficiency, in the bargain.

One of the new designs utilizes a catalytic converter, similar to the one in your pickup, that enables the stove to burn compounds within the smoke that would normally go up the flue and into the atmosphere, unburned. The extra combustion means cleaner air, more heat with less wood, and a stove that can hold a fire longer than any of its predecessors.

Another EPA-approved design, that accomplishes pretty much the same thing as a catalytic stove without the converter, simply circulates the gasses back through the stove to be burned a second time, before exiting up the stove pipe. Called "secondary combustion" stoves, these stoves boast the advantage of eliminating a costly element—namely, the catalytic converter—that will have to be periodically replaced.

rex's maxims

IF YOU DISCOVER all the secrets of your wood stove in a single season, you have either a complex mind or a simple stove.

Which kind of stove should you buy? Though specifications vary from one manufacturer to the next, as a general rule, catalytic stoves are more efficient, cleaner and more expensive than secondary combustion stoves.

Our catalytic stove easily holds a fire all night long, even with fast-burning pine in the fire box. The key is to keep the stove pipe free of creosote buildup—we clean ours every couple of months, just to be sure—and the doors adjusted so they close tightly.

Will a wood stove save you money? At $80 per chord, $200 worth of wood burned in the stove will save us around $500 worth of propane burned in the boiler. Besides, chopping wood is much better exercise than writing out checks to the propane company.

Who can argue with that?

FROM WHENCE FLOWS MY DOMESTIC HOT WATER?

Realistically speaking, you have three choices for your domestic hot water supply. The most common of these is the good old glass-lined tank with a gas burner on the bottom. They're cheap, and they use no electricity, which is good, but they're all bound to fail in a few years, which is bad. You also end up heating a lot of water that's going to cool off and have to be reheated before you get around to using it, which makes it wasteful.

An indirect water heater is another option. These units are heated with water from the home heating system, by way of a heat exchanger. On the plus side, they last far longer than conventional hot water heaters and, though the initial cost is greater, they will probably save you money over the long haul. On the minus side, they have the same problem of leaking heat while in standby mode, and they also require an electric pump to run the heat exchanger.

AquaStar Model 125B, a tankless, on-demand heater for domestic water heating. Other models will supplement solar hot water heating. *(photo courtesy of Controlled Energy Corporation)*

Tankless, on-demand water heaters are your third, final, and probably best choice. These units heat water in a compact, gas-fired burner as you use it. Formerly suited to nothing grander than a weekend cabin, on-demand heaters have gained a lot of sophistication, and well-earned respect, in recent years. Although the larger models (5 plus gallons per minute) are expensive, they last practically forever and can pay for themselves in a few short years, on the energy savings, alone.

Options for Heating Your Hot Water

- Stand-alone, propane- or natural gas-fired hot water heater
- Indirect water heater connected to the heating system boiler
- Tankless, on-demand water heater (gas-fired, not electric)

LaVonne's
LOGBOOK 23

October 2001

The weather is turning, so we'd better get going on the last big project—stonework. It's freezing this October day when we hang the metal mesh on the foam walls. We've never done this before, but I keep saying, "It can't be that hard."

45

The biggest moss rocks go on the bottom row and, like a puzzle, we build up from there. Day after day we mortar and set rocks. Someday I'll count the hundreds of rocks we set after 3 weeks of physically exhausting work. I have a new appreciation for anyone who does this, or any of the other trades, for a living. Rex will tell you I was not a happy camper at the end of every day, but I'm very proud we did it ourselves. The rough, dark, irregular stonework is the perfect compliment to the round, golden logs and light-colored stucco.

It **is** what I had pictured so many months and years ago. I am home, at last.

August 2002

Looking back over the past few years, I can easily recall the thousands of hours of work we put into our home (and believe me, it redefined my idea of 'work'), but the rewards far outweigh the sore muscles. Of course we take pride in our home; it is more than we hoped it would be. But more than just a happy home, we are rewarded by the nature that surrounds us, and provides for us. Being self-sufficient is a powerful, yet humbling feeling. Never again will we take for granted the conveniences of running water from the tap, the brightness of a light bulb, the ease of cooking and laundry... just to name a few.

Nature becomes very real when you live in the midst of it, and depend on it. We have a new appreciation for the winds that carry the hawks, the rising and setting of the sun, the changing of seasons, and every drop of rain that falls. Life is as it should be.

PUMPING WATER

Getting It From the Ground to Your House, Without Overtaxing the System

Water is your property's most valuable asset. Electricity you can make; propane can be brought in by truck. But if your land doesn't have sufficient, potable water, your life will revolve, to a large extent, around the transportation and storage of this life-giving elixir.

In some places, water is abundant; in others it's a crap shoot. Our neighbor to the west got a good well (3 gallons per minute) at 340 feet, while our neighbor to the east got a trickle (5 gallons per *hour*) at 700 feet. We had no idea what to expect, but after watching the driller sink a hole 480 feet through impermeable rock with no water in sight, any optimism we earlier felt quickly dissolved. Then, like magic, the morphology of the rock changed and water appeared. Lots of it. By the time the drill bit reached 540 feet, we had a well producing 5 gallons per minute. We let

(photo by Ken Jessen)

out the breath we'd been holding for several days, and uncorked a fine Merlot.

Our problems were far from over, of course. Being off the grid, and therefore on a strict energy diet, we still had to figure out the best way to get the water from the bottom of the well to the house, but at least we were dealing with definable parameters. After what we'd just been through, it seemed like a manageable concern.

Just the same, we carefully weighed the options—numerous and varied as they were—before deciding what we'd do.

SHOULD YOU INSTALL A CISTERN?

Before deciding on a pump, you will need to decide if you are going to pump water into a cistern, and then pressurize the house water with a much smaller pump, or simply forget the cistern idea and pressurize the house directly from the well pump. There are three primary reasons people use cisterns: low producing wells; not enough energy to run the well pump; and water for fire protection.

Low Producing Wells — People who have wells with very low recharge rates use cisterns to provide a buffer between what the well can store within its casing, and the amount of water they might need to use within a short period of time. As an example, let's say that you have a well with a paltry 5 gallons per *hour* recharge rate. In one day, it will provide 120 gallons of water. Not much, but enough for two people, aware of the limitations. But if the well casing only holds 70 or 80 gallons, that's all that can be used in a short period of time. However, by pumping the entire contents of the well casing into a 1000 or 1500 gallon cistern every time the well is fully recharged, you will be assured of always having enough water, even though the well is a poor one. A really deluxe setup uses a float system within the cistern (similar to the one in a standard toilet) to automatically shut off the well pump, and turn it on (and also start a generator). A sensor within the well can shut down the pump when the water level falls too low.

Reasons for a Cistern

- Low producing wells
- Not enough energy to run the deep well-pump
- Water for fire protection

Not enough energy to run the well pump — There seems to be almost a paranoia about running an AC deep well pump with a PV/wind system. This is partly because many people don't want to commit that much precious wattage to running a high amperage pump, and partly because they don't want to push the limitations of their inverters. Whether their fears are well-founded or not, most people on PV/wind systems with deep well pumps choose to pump their water into a cistern with a fossil fuel-fired generator, or a stand-alone, direct solar-powered DC submersible pump. They then pressurize their house water line with a small AC (or DC) pump. I'll be the first to admit that these people are right, on both counts: it *does* take a fair bit of energy to run a deep well submersible pump from the batteries, but not all *that* much; and it does tax the inverter at times, though (in our case, at least) never enough to threaten the integrity of the system. We knew we were asking a lot from our PV/wind system by using it to pump water from 540 feet down with an 11 amp, 240-volt pump, but we had to try it, even though many people told us they doubted it would work. The reason we did it is simple enough: by automatically pressurizing the house water with a deep well pump, it's one less thing to think about, meaning that we never have to worry that we'll be soaped-up in the shower some morning, only to discover that one of us (namely, me) forgot to fill the cistern. Besides, we don't even like to listen to our neighbors' generator run every night from a half mile across the canyon; we like to listen to our own even less.

But don't despair; as you will soon discover, a good DC pumping system can bypass all of the above concerns, though it will open yet another can of worms. (Is there no end to the worms in this business?)

Water for fire protection — Being in the third year of a relentless drought, fire is on everyone's mind around here. Having been on the fringe of a massive fire two years ago, and within a mile of four lesser lightning-started fires last year, we think about fire a lot. The local volunteer fire department recommends that everyone have at least 2500 gallons of water stored for fire protection. A large cistern can accommodate a large part of that amount. Since we don't have a cistern, we have a 1500 gallon agricultural tank outside the house, then built a fish pond to hold an additional 1000 gallons. We figure after the sheriff forces us to evacuate (if he can find us), the firefighters will have a much easier time finding a pond and a big, conspicuous, above-ground green tank than they will an indoor, or below-ground, cistern.

WELL PUMPS

There are two broad categories of submersible well pumps: AC and DC. Both have their strong and weak points, and neither can be used successfully in every application. In most instances, I agree with Demetri, the venerated pump installer that services most of the wells in these hills, when he says that you should never ask a DC pump to do what an AC pump can do better. But I'm getting ahead of myself.

DC Well Pumps

DC-operated well pumps can withstand a range of voltage that would quickly destroy an AC pump. Because of this, they are used primarily in stand-alone systems. This means that you can wire them to their own solar array, or wind generator, and forget about them. They will pump water whenever the sun shines, or the wind blows. They are designed to work with whatever power is available to them (within limits, of course), so long as it's enough to start the pump turning. Many models can be run dry without sustaining damage, which makes them quite useful in wells with low recharge rates. With the addition of a charge controller, the pump can be wired into a float switch that shuts off the power when the cistern is full, and starts it again when the water drops below a preset level.

Admittedly, it's an attractive idea. With a big enough cistern, you'll never have to worry about having enough water, even during a cabin-fever-inducing run of non-productive weather. And, by having the pump hooked to its own power supply, you won't have draw from your household energy savings—or drag out the generator—to shower, or wash the dishes.

So, how much is it worth to you to never have to worry about water? (That's always the rub, isn't it?) A good DC pump is an expensive proposition. And the wire doesn't come cheap either. For example, a 48-volt DC pump, rated at a mere 20 percent the capacity of our 240-volt AC pump, costs twice as much, and requires wire 6 gauges heavier. And, while we can figure, on average, that our water pumping takes about 200 watts of our 1140-watt array, to power a DC pump rated for a well the depth of ours, we would have to dedicate an additional 120 watts (320 watts, total) of solar power.

rex's maxims

A GOOD WELL with a trouble-free delivery system is more comfort than a healthy bank account. That's because water will get you through times of no money, better than money will get you through times of no water.

But if money were the only problem, we still might have gone with an install-it-and-forget-about-it DC pumping system. Except that it's not exactly that easy. All DC motors have brushes that have to be periodically replaced. And, we were told, at our well depth we should expect certain pump components to fail earlier than normal. The thought of pulling up 540 feet of drop pipe at the whim of a fractious pump motor was enough to drive us firmly into the AC camp.

Had our well been shallower, say 200 feet, the pendulum might have swung the other way.

AC Well Pumps

In the race to supply your water, DC pumps are the tortoises: they plod along slowly and ceaselessly. That means, of course, that AC pumps are the hares—on steroids. They're lean and mean and tough. They eat a lot, but they produce even more. They can pump from virtually any depth the well driller can find water, and you can expect them to last for many, many years without service or replacement.

Since AC pumps move such a high volume of water (our 1.5 hp pump delivers 6 gpm, even at 540 feet) the total *amount* of energy they use is surprisingly small. As mentioned above, we figure, on average, 200 extra watts of solar capacity is enough to power our well pump. The problem is, an AC pump needs so much power *all at one time*. Specifically, we're talking about the amperage the pump demands in the split second when it goes from "off" to "on", which may be as much as 3 times higher than its rated amps.

For us, as I've said many times in these pages, it's not really a problem. But it may be for others. Our well pump operates nicely within the rated capacities of our Trace SW4024 inverter, as long as we're mindful of other loads that might be operating at the same time. To be running the clothes washer and gas-powered dryer, a stereo and a couple of computers the instant the pump kicks-in does not present any difficulty. But, if we were also running the dishwasher, we might be pushing the system toward the edge. And throwing a table saw into the equation would certainly cast it into the abyss. Viola! Our own personal black-out. (But really; how much stuff do you need to run at one time, anyway¿)

A larger inverter, or two stacked inverters would alleviate the problem, and if you go with a watt-gobbling AC well pump, your PV/ wind equipment supplier will almost certainly try to convince you to buy two inverters. The choice is yours. I'll be the first to admit that a lot of families have trouble trying to run a large well pump with a single inverter, but in all likelihood, the problem lies more with the pump, than the inverter.

This is because all AC well pumps are not created equal; some require more power to start than others *(see inset)*. Your pump installer should be made aware of the limitations of your inverter(s), and should be able to sell you a pump that falls within the parameters set by the inverter manufacturer.

Specifically, you will want a pump that requires a separate starting box outside the well (inside the mechanical room), rather than a pump that has the starting circuitry built into the motor casing. A simple relay-type starting box will work better with an inverter than an electronic one.

Also, if you use a 240-volt transformer to supply power to the well pump, it is less work for the inverter if you place the transformer between the pressure switch and the starting box, rather than between the inverter and the pressure switch.

Explain these things to your pump installer. He, or she, should know exactly what your concerns are, and how to remedy any potential problems. If not, there are always other installers down the road.

Grundfos Well Pumps

For a well pump that doesn't "slam" the inverter on start-up, check out the Grundfos SQ series high-frequency pumps. They have a soft start, and can be programmed to pump at various rates. For ultimate flexibility, the SQ Flex pumps can run on either AC or DC, across a wide range of voltages.

DECISIONS, DECISIONS

It's not easy to weigh all the pros and cons of all the different ways people have conceived to deliver water from the earth under your feet to the sink in your kitchen. Just when you think you have it all figured out, some intractable fact, lurking in the shadows, jumps out and trips you. Happens to me all the time.

Odd as it may seem, the best remedy for too many facts is more facts. Talk to people on every side of the issue, AC and DC. Talk to your neighbors. Talk to your well driller and your pump installer. Call the inverter manufacturer. Tell them all what your particular circumstances are.

Then follow your instincts. You can't go wrong that way.

CHAPTER 

FINISH WORK: MAKING YOUR HOUSE A HOME

Running the Final Mile, In Style

The log railing is being assembled around the deck.

Anyone who has ever built a home can tell you: the finish work is the most tedious, and the most rewarding, part of the project. Unlike the structural work, when at the end of the day, you can look at what you've done and feel a sense of accomplishment, with finish work it seems that all you see is what you *haven't* done. That's because finish work is more exacting, and therefore more time consuming. It is a fact that you can frame, sheath and shingle a roof in a fraction of the time it takes to insulate, hang, tape and texture drywall, then paint the ceiling inside. That's just the way it is. The good part is, when you're done, you're done.

It is not the intent of this chapter to teach you skills you do not already possess. That would be folly. Entire books have been written on many of the subjects touched on here. But there are numerous considerations unique to log homes, and I would be remiss if I didn't take the time to point them out, in the course of this whirlwind tour of the work that remains to be done.

HANGING AND FINISHING DRYWALL—WITHOUT LOSING YOUR MIND

I've never considered hanging and finishing drywall to be my idea of a good time, so here are a few tricks for hanging, texturing and painting drywall that may save you a lot of time and aggravation, a possible domestic spat over the mounting cost of ruined wall board, and may even make your house look better, in the process.

After insulating, Rex screws the ceiling drywall to the rafters. The center seam of drywall is visible near his elbow.

Fitting Drywall Between Purlins

LaVonne and I spent a lot of time butchering wallboard to fit between the purlins in the loft ceiling, until we hit upon the right technique. Since the purlins curved inward toward the rafters, it was impossible to get a tight fit between them. Any drywall sheet that would fit between the wide parts of the purlins was too narrow to hide the gaps between the edge of the sheet and the purlin, once it was in place.

Then we realized we were making our lives miserable, trying to do too much at once. Wouldn't an extra joint in the middle be preferable to large gaps at the edges? We changed our tactics, by first cutting a full sheet of drywall lengthwise down the middle. Then I chalked a line on the rafters, midway between two purlins, and measured the distance from the chalk line to the purlin at 8 or 10 inch intervals. LaVonne plotted these measurements on the cut edge of each half sheet, and then connected the dots. We cut off the excess, and had a perfect fit when we pushed the cut edge into the purlin and laid the long tapered edge against the chalk line. Repeating the process on the other side of the line gave us a tight fit at both purlins, and an easy-to-finish tapered joint in the middle. (By design, our purlins were less than 4 feet apart; less than a sheet of drywall.)

Scribing Drywall Into A Log Wall

If you've ever hung drywall before, you know that you should avoid butting a cut edge against a factory edge, if at all possible. But it isn't easy to make the factory edge break on a stud, if you have to scribe a cut edge to fit against a log wall (that is, a log wall *without* a slot cut (kerf) to hide the edge of the wall board). Here's how to do it:

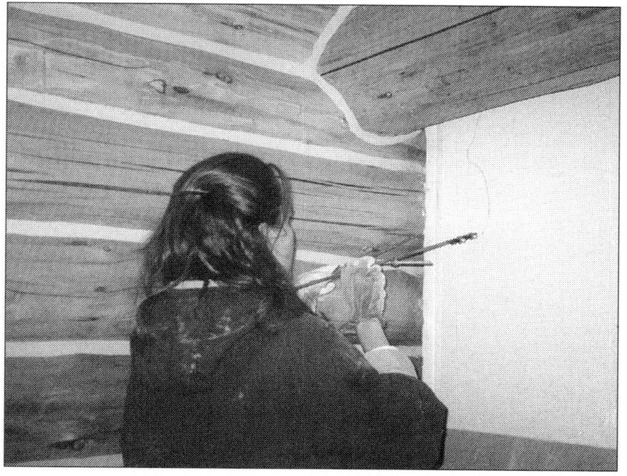

LaVonne scribes the drywall to fit around the log wall.

Measure the distance between the deepest crack on your log wall (between 2 logs) to the center of the stud where the drywall will be seamed. Cut the sheet at this length, and place the cut edge next to the log wall, so the tapered, factory edge is near the stud. Now scribe along the log wall, tracing the pattern of the logs onto your drywall. Cut along the scribe line carefully. (A small jigsaw, we learned, works much better for curvy cuts than a drywall saw, and is less likely to accidentally break off the weaker parts of the curve.)

Applying Texture By Hand

Once the drywall is taped and sanded, it's ready for texture. You could rent a texture machine, or use textured paint, but for a finish to truly accentuate the majesty of the logs, you might want to do it by hand.

This is a job better left to one person, preferably the artist in the family.

(In our case, that was LaVonne.) To begin, you'll have to determine the right mixture for your texture compound. We used off-the-shelf joint compound, silica sand to give it a gritty look and feel, and a little water. I attached a handle to a small square of plywood, which LaVonne used to hold the texture compound. She then applied it with a mason's finishing trowel, slapping random-sized globs against the wall (in a random fashion) and then smoothing it out with quick, slashing motions. She developed her technique inside a basement closet, then polished her skills in the electrical room. By the time she got to the areas anyone would actually see, she was admiringly proficient.

The result was even better than we'd hoped for: eye-catching in a subtle way. No two places on the walls or ceilings are the same, yet they all blend together into a cohesive whole. (And I'm beginning to sound like an art critic, so I'll move on to something else.)

Accents with Paint

The idea of covering her beautiful texture with a single, uniform color of paint was an insult to LaVonne's sensibilities. So, after applying a primer coat, and one coat of off-white paint, she went back with a sponge (a real sponge, like from the bottom of the ocean) and lightly (and, again, randomly) daubed on splotches of paint of a slightly different color. For the first go-round she used a light tan, then a light gray tint for the coup de grace.

She picked her shades well. The best way I can describe the effect is to say that you "feel" the contrasts, without actually being consciously aware of them. And yet it's as plain as day to anyone who knows what to look for. Good job, Hon!

WAINSCOTING

Even the most original of drywall finishes can get a bit monotonous, if it's not broken up with other elements. The same goes for logs, or any medium. So, to enhance the richness of the interior, we installed wainscoting in a few key locations: the stairwell leading to the basement, two interior walls of the office, the long wall outside the upstairs closet and bathroom, and around the kitchen island.

Rather than settle for the same thin boards as any do-it-yourselfer city dweller might buy at a huge lumberyard chain-store, we found a supply of 1 x 4 T&G, beetle-killed pine (with swirls of blue, grey and brown) at a local sawmill. It's a nice accent. Check around and see what you can find, before settling for the same wainscoting as the rest of humanity.

INTERIOR DOORS, KITCHEN CABINETS AND COUNTERTOPS

By this point you have almost certainly come to the realization that what looks good in a frame house in town is not what you had in mind for your log home in the country. This is especially true of doors. Even expensive, solid-wood, six-panel doors look out of place in a handcrafted log home.

LaVonne found a local door company that special ordered tongue & groove pine doors for the main floor and loft. They also ordered wrought iron door handles to complete the effect. Everyone asks us if we made the doors ourselves, which is exactly the look we wanted.

The closet and bathroom walls in the loft have a wainscoting of tongue & groove pine boards, and vertical log posts on the corners.

What holds true for doors is equally true for kitchen cabinets. Off-the-shelf cabinets in a log home are about as discordant as plastic seat covers in a Porsche. We got bids from several custom cabinet makers. Surprisingly, the only company willing to built the cabinets exactly as we wanted them (tongue & groove knotty pine, to match the interior doors) also came in with the best price.

Getting the kitchen cabinets to fit against a log wall is not nearly as difficult as you may think, though it will require a certain amount of time and patience. You'll find yourself chiseling in some places, and shimming in others. The nice part is, you won't have to worry about finding wall studs to sink your screws into. (See *Chapter 15: Settling Issues* when hanging cabinets on log walls that are still settling.)

We just couldn't put Formica countertops over our beautiful knotty-pine cabinets. Nor did we want to pay for granite or marble. Tile was an attractive option, but we didn't want to deal with cleaning grout lines over the years. We needed something simple and solid that didn't draw attention to itself. After a great deal of searching, we found a composite material; a dense, manufactured stone that seems to be impervious to anything that might happen to get spilled on it. (And believe me: when I'm in the kitchen, a lot of stuff gets spilled.) The solid, gray-black color emanates strength, and adds richness to the other elements of the house.

A CUSTOM LOG STAIR

Chuck from Rocky Mountain Stair assembles the spiral log stair in Benshoof's home.

I knew from the outset of our home-building project that the time would come when I would have to build a log stair. In my customary self-delusional manner, I told myself it would be easy, fun, and rewarding. I was right on one count: I love the stair, and therein lies my reward. But it certainly wasn't easy, and to say that it was "fun" is stretching things a bit.

Had it been a straight stair with a log stringer on either side it really might have been fun and easy; more than it actually was, anyway. But this stair wraps around a corner, with a landing at the midpoint. And, rather than using a stringer against the wall, I notched each step into the wall, for a cleaner, lighter look.

The treads were all cut from a single 13-inch log. I first cut it in half with a chainsaw, then cut up the halves into twelve 4-foot sections. That left me with one extra tread, for a single, solitary, mistake (which I obligingly made).

Using a table saw, I removed the sharp edges from each tread, and made them all a uniform width. I then used a hand-held power planer to smooth and level the surface of each tread, finishing with a belt sander and, finally, an orbital sander. After marking out the placement of each stair against the log wall (and checking, and rechecking, my measurements) I built the landing first with 2 x 6 planks, doweled and glued, over a 2 x 4 frame. Then I scribed and notched the treads into the log wall, securing each one with a pair of lag bolts angled into the wall through countersunk holes (which I later filled with dowels.)

Our finished stair to the loft.

Rather than trying to guess at the length, I let all the treads run wild, toward the inside of the room, and supported them with makeshift 2 x 4 stringers until they were all in place. I was then able to chalk lines and cut all the tread ends even, using a handsaw. After that, it was a fairly simple matter to push the log stringer against the cut ends, mark and chisel out the notches, then set the stringers into place and bolt them to the treads.

Then came the magic moment when, at last, I was able to remove the extension ladder that had provided access to the loft for over a year. That much, at least, was fun.

The Magic Number

For reasons no one fully understands, stairs with a combined tread width and riser height of 17-1/2 inches are the most comfortable. The Uniform Building Code sets the minimum tread width at 9 inches, and the maximum riser height at 8 inches. This adds up to 17, and is the steepest stair you can build and still meet code. If you've got the room, add another half inch to the tread width. If you've got lots of room, a 10-1/2 inch tread with a 7 inch rise makes a very easy stair.

THE DECK: HOW TO SAVE A TREE— AND A LOT OF WORK

When LaVonne told me she wanted to look at "designer" decking for our big wrap-around deck, I though she was spewing blasphemy. Didn't she know log homes required solid wood decking, cut from old-growth trees plucked from ancient forests? Apparently not.

Certain she would abandon her silly notion, once she saw how ugly the stuff was, I decided to humor her. We shopped around one morning, seeing what was available. I didn't like any of it. But she saw things I didn't, and finally settled on a product called ChoiceDek Plus, by Weyerhaeuser.

I had to admit it was a crafty idea, making a weather-proof decking material out of oak chips and old plastic bags and milk jugs, but I still wasn't sold. Then she reminded me of the yearly ritual we'd established at our last house at the farm: move all the furniture off the deck, barricade the stair to keep the dogs away, hose the deck down and let it dry, then spray $200 worth of sealant on the planks in two coats.

My thinking clouded by far-from-fond memories, I finally gave in.

Much to my surprise, it turned out to be a self-serving act of capitulation. Not only was the decking a joy to lay down (no twists or curves), it took fewer screws because it never warps.

Best of all, it *looks* good. After a couple or rainstorms, it mellowed to a uniform weathered-wood shade of gray that contrasts nicely with the stained log walls, deck supports and railings. And since it never has to be stained or sealed, we'll make up the extra cost in a few years, just by doing nothing.

LaVonne had other reasons. With a coy smile, she told me she likes it because it matches the chinking. As usual, she's right.

We've completed the decking on the west side, and continue working on the south side. We stagger the cut ends to break on different joists.

The log and copper spindles are ready to be fit into the top railings.

RAILINGS FOR STAIRS, DECKS AND LOFT

When you first see a deck, or look up at a loft, the one thing that catches your eye is the railing. To a lesser degree, this is even true of handcrafted log stairs. So, if you've built something you really want to draw attention to, finish it off with a stout, handcrafted railing.

What is a deck, after all, but a floor with gaps between the boards? It's plain and boring and it needs some help: a railing and support structure that belongs with your log home. Eschewing the common method of supporting the deck with 4 x 4's, and making the railing from 2 x 2 redwood spindles, we opted for heavy log supports, and hand-peeled poles for the spindles and handrails.

We used leftover 9-inch logs—resting on concrete piers—to support our deck, and peeled corral poles for the railing. Since the Uniform Building Code now requires all railings to be built so that a 4-inch sphere cannot pass through it at any point, we decided that the railing would look too heavy if we were to use all wood spindles. Besides, we were beginning to get a little tired of logs. Instead, we ran two sections of 3/4-inch copper tubing between each handmade pole spindle. It's a nice balance.

Usually, log railings are built in sections, then installed between the support posts, using mortise and tenon joints. It seemed to me like so much extra work for little or no gain. Why not just position the support posts toward the edge of the deck, and build the railing along the inside of it? It looks good, and it provides a continuous handrail along the entire distance.

We built the railings for the loft and the stairs using the same motif of two parts copper to one part wood. LaVonne put an aged patina finish on all the interior copper spindles, before assembly. Although Mother Nature will obligingly put her own patina on the exterior copper spindles, you'll avoid discoloration of the wood on the bottom rail if you do it yourself, then coat the spindles with a clear lacquer. It's also a good idea to drill a small ($^{1}/_{4}$-inch) hole at the bottom of each mortise, to allow rainwater to drain.

HOMEMADE SPINDLES

Mortise and tenon cutters are prohibitively expensive if you're only going to use them for one job, and the few local sawmills that sell hand-peeled, pre-made spindles only offer them in one or two lengths. Since we needed spindles and railing sections of various lengths and diameters, we decided to make our own.

We found that a Forstner bit works good for the mortise, even though it doesn't make a tapered, cone-shaped hole. The tenon cuts were a little trickier. First, we'd cut a peeled section of pole 3 inches longer than the space between the rails. This allowed 1-$^{1}/_{2}$ inches of tenon in each mortise joint. Next, we'd score the centers of the spindle ends with the same Forstner bit used to cut the mortise. Then we'd hand saw a ring around the spindle, 1-$^{1}/_{2}$ inches down from the end, and to the same depth as the score. To make the tenon, we'd chisel away the spindle end, starting from the score on the end, and stopping at the handcut groove.

After checking that the tenon fit the mortise, all that remained was to taper the thick part of the spindle down to the thickness of the tenon. I used a chisel at first, then advanced to pulling the pieces through a table saw from the backside, once we got into production. (If you're not confident of your table saw skills, you might want to stick with a chisel.)

In addition to spindles and railings, this method works good for building benches, beds, and all other types of log furniture.

LOG ACCENTS

A twisted branch finishes the stair rail.

We found so many other uses for logs, poles and tree branches inside the house, I couldn't possibly list them all. Log uprights, with a quarter section removed, work great for finishing off drywall corners. Similarly cut poles make a nice frame for a hearth. Half-poles (cut lengthwise on a table saw) worked splendidly to help trim the upstairs windows. To fill in the gap between the floor and the stair stringer going to the landing, I set tongue & groove boards in dado joints, cut around the inside of a triangular pole frame.

The most fun of all was in finding the free-form pieces to finish off the stair handrails, and the horizontal section to connect the log columns supporting the deck stair. We spent many hours wandering through the woods near our house, bringing home every oddly-curved branch that appeared to have some promise.

The archway to the deck.

Our searching eventually paid off. The stair handrails all terminate into eye-catching examples of naturally-sculpted forest art, and the beautifully twisted and gnarled branch that greets you at the bottom of the deck stairs looks as though it grew in place.

Let your imagination roam free. Don't be stuck thinking "straight" when "curved" might add an extra, pleasing dimension. You'll amaze yourself with your own cleverness, long before you've peeled the last log, pole or branch. Just remember: there is no reason to settle for the ordinary, when the extraordinary takes just a little extra reach.

MANY USES FOR TILE

Besides being a good conductor of heat for in-floor heating systems, tile is an attractive floor covering, offering a pleasing contrast to a home that also has carpeting and wood flooring. Its surge in popularity in recent years is good news for the home builder, because there is practically no end to the colors, styles and patterns you can use to make a one-of-a-kind floor. But flooring is just the beginning of tile's many uses. Here are a few more:

- **Shower stalls and vanities**—LaVonne used glazed 6-inch tiles inside the shower and on the bathroom vanity. Though she'd never set tile before, she had a fairly easy of time of it, using a few simple tools and an inexpensive tile saw.
- **Backsplashes for countertops**—once the kitchen countertops were in place, LaVonne applied tile to a plywood backer, set into the log wall, then used the same tile on the frame wall behind the gas range. For the upstairs bathroom, she found a colorful, decorative tile to use as a backsplash for the vanity.
- **Hearths**—rather than pay hundreds of dollars for a hearth for the wood stove, we made our own. We first screwed a heat-resistant tile backer-board to $^3/_4$-inch plywood, then covered it with 12-inch tiles in a diagonal pattern. I used 3-inch logs (poles, in other words) with a quarter-section removed to form a border, which covered the edges of the tiles.

- **Architectural tile around the walk-in door**—While the basement door itself—an off-the-shelf steel door, made to withstand the elements blowing in from the north—is certainly nothing to brag about, the natural stonework surrounding it, is. To help the one blend into the other, we needed a bold transition between the stonework and the door. Our neighbor, Lane Dukart, *(see page 283)* provided it for us. The handcrafted architectural tiles he made for us boast a rich, three-dimensional leaf pattern, blending into a headpiece with the Latin phase "Montani Semper Liberi" (People of the Mountain are Always Free) prominent in bas-relief.

A closeup view of Lane's architectural tile next to our granite moss rock.

STONEWORK

The idea of doing our own stonework on the foundation walls on the north and east side of the garage was nothing we warmed up to overnight (or even over a year), but the bids we got—ranging from $15 to $20 per square foot (labor only; you supply the stone, please)—were enough to get us thinking in a stone mason's frame of mind.

The brick ledge to support the stone was the first order of business. To make it, I first cut away the 2-inch foam insulation (that had served as the form for the concrete wall) at ground level, in a 4-inch high strip. I then pounded short pieces of rebar into predrilled holes (filled with construction adhesive) in the foundation, spaced roughly one foot apart. A simple form— 6 inches by 4 inches—was filled with concrete to become the ledge.

That was the easy part.

All the stone—lichen-covered granite, or "moss rock"—came from the hillside on the south side of our house. LaVonne had spent many hours the year before gathering the stone into piles, which she marked with blue flags. It was my job to hump it all up the hill. But even after all of her piles of stone were depleted, we still had only half as much as we needed. "It's good exercise," I kept telling myself, as I roamed farther and farther down the hill in search of flat, interesting rocks. (It might have been 'exercise', but at the time the word "torture" kept gnawing its way through my overheated brain.)

After the stone was all gathered, it was time to prepare the wall. We used lightweight, expanded-steel mesh as a surface to grab the mortar, and to affix wires to hold the stone while the mortar hardened. Deck screws worked well to secure the mesh to the rim joist (which was first covered with felt paper), and to the plastic spacer ties that were used to hold the foam foundation forms together.

The metal mesh is mortared for the next rock.

At this point, we were inexplicably encouraged that all that remained to be done was to attach several tons of rock and mortar to the wall. It was late October when we began, and the

The rock is securely fastened with temporary wire ties, and then the mortar between rocks is tooled smooth.

sun had long since lost interest in the north side of anything, including our wall. Cold, yet motivated, we pushed on.

Any skilled stonemason would probably get a chuckle out of our methods, but since none of them, as far as we could determine, has ever written a book describing a better way to go about it, I'll explain what we did.

First, I'd lay the rock against the wall and mark around it with a felt marker. I'd then hook long pieces of wire into the mesh near the line, to later hold the stone. While LaVonne mortared the marked areas of the wall, I mortared the backs of the stones. (We found the "Type S Mortar Mix" made by Quickcrete to contain a workable mixture of sand, Portland cement, and lime.)

I'd then lay the stone against the wall, tap it with a rubber mallet, and secure it with the wires I'd earlier attached to the mesh. (Then, after the mortar was set, it was a simple matter to clip the wires flush with the mortar, using wire nips.) LaVonne used a small, $^1/_2$-inch trowel to smooth the joints between the stones, then cleaned off any excess with a sponge. We moved laterally whenever we could, to avoid placing too much vertical weight in one place on any given day.

It took us the better part of 3 weeks to cover 350 square feet of wall, but it was worth it. It may not be the best stone work we've ever seen, but it's better than most. And our total investment in materials and tools was under $200.

A winter view of the north and east sides of our home.

CLAY MASTER, LANE DUKART

Lane Dukart and his family began building their modest solar-powered house and studio, near the creek below our house, in 1990. Seeing the artistic detail that went into their home, it was clear that Lane's abilities would take him far.

Since then, Lane has earned a far-ranging reputation with his unique stoneware bells and chimes, which are featured in art galleries all across the country.

Eager to broadened his horizons, Lane has recently begun making custom stoneware tiles for, among other things, entrances and fireplaces. For our garage entryway, LaVonne and I gave Lane a few ideas spun around a central theme, then left him alone to create.

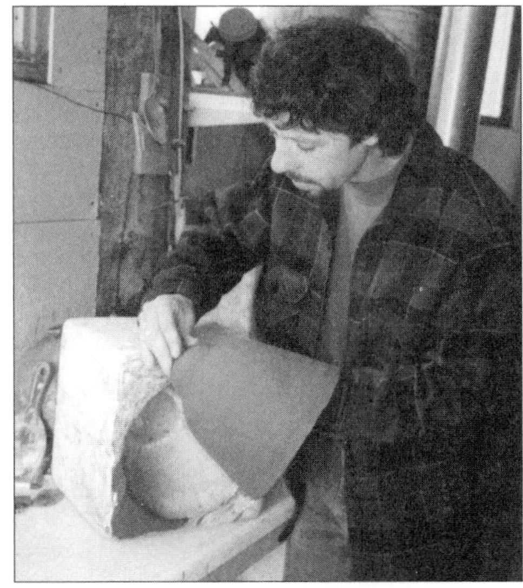

Custom architectural tile by Lane Dukart surrounds our walk-in garage door (and dog door).

We knew what Lane could do—we'd seen much of his work before. But it still took our breath away when he called us to his studio to examine the newly completed tiles.

Somehow, we knew he'd do that to us.

To reach Lane, write to Lane Dukart Studios, PO Box 34, Masonville, CO 80541 USA.

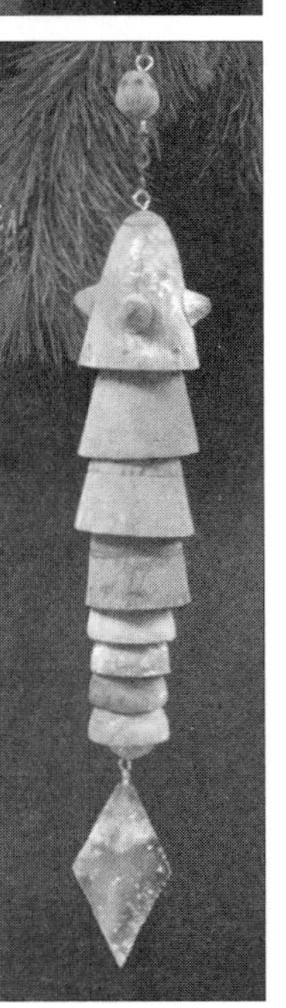

AND FINALLY.....

Mosaic tile on the bathroom floor.

The myriad details of finishing a home are the very things that *make* your house a home. And the more you do yourself, the more the house becomes *your* home. When it's all said and done, it is the little things that you'll notice; the beveled glass panel above the bathroom door, or the small stained glass window on the stair landing that reflects rainbow hues on the handcrafted stair treads. Every time you step out of the shower, you'll see the decorative mosaic tile pattern in the floor, and the special ledge you trimmed into the bottom of the bathroom window.

A stained glass window, created by Glee Grau, adds wonderful color to our stair landing.

It's the little things that warm your heart, and bring a smile to your face. And it's the little things that remind you that, at long last, you are through.

(photo by Mike Fox)

With that, LaVonne and I bid you adieu. May your new home be as grand as your dreams!

ACKNOWLEDGMENTS

thanks!

No book is entirely the work of its authors, especially one that covers as much ground as this one. We have relied throughout on the kind assistance of people who know far more about particular disciplines than we ever will. In this sense, the adage, "it's not what you know, but who you know," rings loud and clear. To the book's credit, we have been blessed by knowing a large number of very capable people. Here are a few of them who have helped us in various ways.

For reading the manuscript and finding ways to make it better: Dave Masaitis, the most exacting home builder we've every known; Joe Bolte, who's helped me with every house, garage, cabin, barn, outhouse, doghouse and loafing shed I've built since 1980; Doug Pratt, technical editor of Real Goods; Rex Bosworth, who builds homes in Montana with really big logs; Gary Schroeder, president of Schroeder Log Home Supply; David Petroy from RMS Electric; and Steve Iwanicki, a friend who shares our love for nature.

For having the good judgment to be building their log homes at the same time we were writing this book: Josh French, John Benshoof, and Gregg and Donna Kernes.

For all the cool crane rides, so we could get bird's eye photos of John Benshoof's house as it was being erected, a special thanks to "Light Touch" Roland Younghein, owner of Rocky Mountain Boom.

For taking part in our blind survey: Burnham-Beck & Sun, RMS Electric, and Backwoods Solar Electric. Thanks for all of your hard work and helpful input.

For providing photos and valuable information: all the fine companies whose products are mentioned in these pages, even though they didn't try to buy us off with freebies.

We'd also like to thank our friends Sara Tuttle, for her excellent animal illustrations (are mermaids animals¿); Mike Fox and Colorado history author Ken Jessen, whose photos, as always, are first-rate.

Nor can we forget everyone who helped with our home: neighbors, friends, family and subcontractors (at least the ones who finished the job).

And last, but certainly not least, we'd like to acknowledge two important family members: Inspector Micky, who dutifully monitored construction progress each morning, while Newt the Regulator made our work site safe by keeping the velociraptors and saber-toothed tigers at bay. They only asked for yummy dog food, a walk in the woods, and a few pats on the head each day for payment.

Appendix A
Costs To Consider

Financing Fees

Land
- survey fees

Building Plans

Building Permit(s)

Site Prep
- road work
- excavation

Foundation
- footings/piers
- walls
- floor (concrete)

Main Floor
- steel beams & posts
- lumber: rim joists, floor joists, subflooring
- supplies: nails, bolts, screws, glue
- backfill

Logs & Delivery
- special log tools
- supplies: spikes, drill bits
- chinking, backer rod, caulking
- stain/sealer: exterior and interior

Roof/Gables/Dormers/Trusses
- logs
- T & G ceiling (or drywall)
- rafters
- sheathing
- shingles, tile or metal roof
- insulation, vapor barrier
- subfascia, fascia
- soffits
- exterior finish: stucco, cedar siding, etc.
- supplies: nails, hurricane clips, vents, etc.

Additional Floors
- lumber: rim joists, floor joists, subflooring
- supplies: joists hangers, screws, glue

Windows / Doors (exterior)
- windows
- doors
- skylights
- flashing
- trim
- supplies: caulking, screws, stain for trim

Exterior Finish
- stonework
- landscaping / drainage
- deck: decking material, railing, posts, joists, joist hangers, supplies, stain
- gutters & downspouts

Plumbing
- labor (if subcontracted)
- piping: water, gas/propane, vents
- kitchen sink, disposal
- bathrooms: sinks, toilets, tub, shower
- laundry, utility sink
- faucets
- water heating: regular, indirect, on-demand and/or solar
- water softener

Septic System
- perc test
- tank & piping
- leach field

Water Well
- drilling & casing
- well pump
- piping to house
- pressure tank
- cistern

Metric Conversion Factors

1 foot = 0.3048 meters (m)	1 meter = 3.28 feet
1 foot = 30.48 centimeters (cm)	1 meter = 39.37 inches
1 inch = 2.54 centimeters (cm)	1 centimeter = .394 inches
1 inch = 25.4 millimeters (mm)	

Appendix A
Costs To Consider (continued)

Grid Utilities (if needed)
- hookup fees for water, gas, sewer, phone

Electrical
- permit fees
- labor (if subcontracted)
- **solar system**
  - solar modules & frame
  - inverter(s)
  - charge controller(s)
  - DC disconnect(s)
  - 240 transformer
  - meter
- **wind system**
  - turbine & charge controller
  - tower
- batteries & cables
  - battery box, venting
- wiring
  - interior
  - exterior (from solar and wind)
  - low voltage
- supplies: boxes, cover plates, etc
- fixtures (interior and exterior)
  - compact fluorescent light bulbs
- lightning protection

Heat
- heating system: radiant heat & gypcrete/ hot-water baseboard / forced air furnace / propane wall heaters
- fans: ceiling, bathroom, kitchen

Fireplace or Wood Stove
- hearth, chimney

Interior Finish
- frame walls & ceiling
  - framing lumber & insulation
  - drywall & tape
  - wainscoting
- paint & primer
- trim boards & stain
- doors & knobs
- kitchen cabinets & knobs
- countertops
- appliances: gas stove, refrigerator (propane or electric), microwave, dishwasher
- laundry: washer & dryer; cabinets

Stairs & Railings

Flooring
- carpet/hardwood/tile

Garage
- doors; openers

Landscaping

Other ______________________

____

____

____

____

____

____

____

____

Notes on Appliances

Remember: low-usage, high energy appliances (microwaves, hair dryers, coffer makers, etc.) are not much of a problem since they draw very little power when averaged out over time. You can also choose not to use them, if you're low on power. Electric refrigerators and freezers, on the other hand, run many hours a day, and night, and can't simply be shut down when the batteries need a respite from their continual demands. **Always use compact fluorescent light bulbs**...they add up to big energy savings. And a front-loading clothes washer is a must, as is a gas-fired clothes dryer.

Appendix B
Comparison of PV/Wind Quotations

We thought it would be an interesting exercise to request four renewable energy consultants/suppliers to estimate what our house would require, given the following information:

- A well-insulated home with 2 adults (no children)
- The house is 900 square feet on the main level (with radiant heat; temp set at 63 degrees); 600 square feet of open loft (no radiant heat); plus a 1st level basement/garage of 900 square feet (with radiant heat; temp set at 55 degrees).
- A wood stove will be used extensively for heating the main floor/loft.
- Propane used for radiant heat boiler, refrigerator, stove and clothes dryer.
- Hot water heated with indirect tank connected to main boiler.
- Average wind speed is 11-12 mph.
- Great southern exposure on a mountaintop, at 40 degrees latitude.
- A 24-volt system, please.

The PV/Wind system will power the following:

- water well (1.5 hp pump; 11 amps at 240 volts; to draw water from 540 feet at 5 gal/minute; no cistern; 40 gallon pressure tank)
- Radiant heat circulation pumps (4 zones)
- Front-loading clothes washer (3 loads/week)
- Dishwasher (2 or 3 cycles per week)
- Microwave
- 20" TV (4 hr/day)
- Computer, monitor & peripherals (6 hr/day)
- Laptop Computer (6 hr/day)
- Stereo (4-5 hr/day)
- All compact fluorescent light bulbs

We asked them to quote installation separately, and also to quote an option of adding an electric fridge, rated at 400 kWh/year.

Three companies promptly responded to our request; the 4th one (Company D) took a few weeks. Their responses varied greatly:

Company A gave a very general bid without specific equipment information or prices; they did ask additional questions before quoting (new or existing home, grid-tied or off-the-grid; what elevation; how far from home to solar array).

Company B sent very detailed information, including all misc. items and freight in their bid. They have continued to follow up, with more information, options and prices.

Company C asked many questions (how many gallons of water used per day, wattage of circulating pumps and hours used per day; how many light bulbs and usage per day; number of sunny days per week or month). Their bid was specific to equipment recommended and prices, but extra items and freight were not included.

Company D wanted a very detailed spreadsheet completed (which I did not do), but gave a general (high) bid. (Since they did not specify equipment, they are not included on the following page) They highly recommended a DC pump to save on PV/wind equipment costs.

We are not listing equipment prices nor total cost estimated, since these prices will change with the market. It is our intent to show that given identical specifications, each supplier/consultant recommended different equipment, and did not always include the extras (which can add significantly to the cost).
So you can see just how important it is for the homeowner to understand the complexities of a wind and solar system...what is necessary, what isn't; and what questions to ask. Basically, how to compare "apples to apples".

Appendix B
What They Recommended Versus What We Use

	Company A	Company B	Company C	*Our System*
Solar capacity	960 watts	600 watts	1440 watts	*1140 watts*
Wind Turbine	not specified	1000 watts (Bergey)	1000 watts (Whisper H80)	*1000 watts (Whisper 1000*)*
Inverter	dual inverters 48-volt system	dual inverters 24-volt system	dual inverters 48-volt system	*one inverter with transformer; 24-volt system*
Charge Controller	not specified	2-40 amps	1-40 amp	*1-60 amp (solar); wind is separate*
Meter	yes	yes	yes (TriMetric)	*TriMetric*
Batteries	1680 amp hrs *maintenance free*	1690 amp hrs (HUP)	2340 amp hrs	*1100 amp hours*
Installation	$2000-5000	need site visit	would suggest local installer	*we installed it ourselves*
Fridge Option	add $1000	add 2nd wind tower & bigger inverter	add 2 - 4 panels	

** discontinued model*

Solar Radiation Maps for Winter & Summer

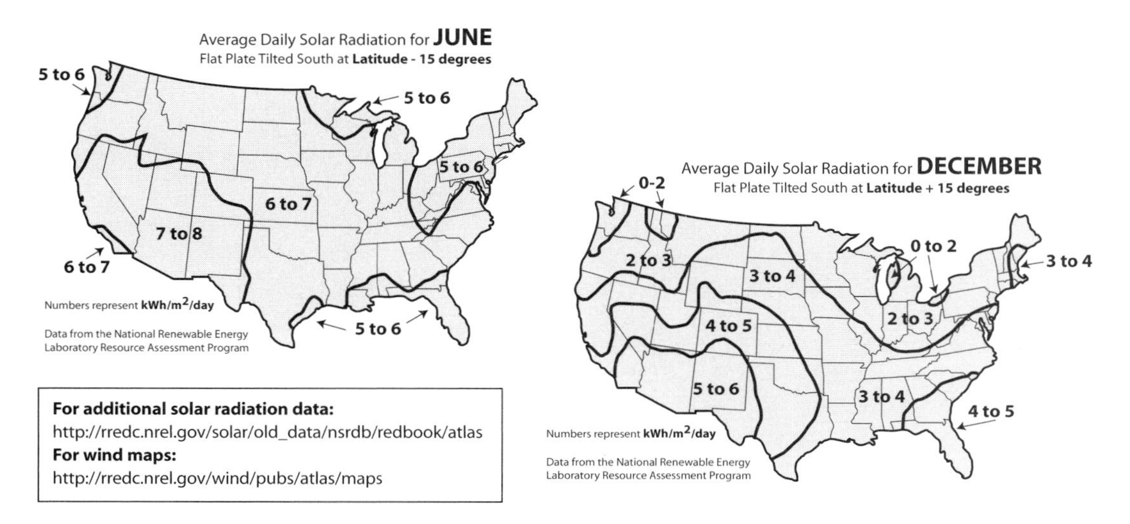

For additional solar radiation data:
http://rredc.nrel.gov/solar/old_data/nsrdb/redbook/atlas
For wind maps:
http://rredc.nrel.gov/wind/pubs/atlas/maps

Appendix C

System Sizing — Your Electrical Needs

Electrical Device	Wattage	x	Hours of Daily Use	x	Days Used per Week	÷	7	= Ave. Daily Watt-Hours
		x		x		÷	7	
		x		x		÷	7	
		x		x		÷	7	
		x		x		÷	7	
		x		x		÷	7	
		x		x		÷	7	
		x		x		÷	7	
		x		x		÷	7	
		x		x		÷	7	
		x		x		÷	7	
		x		x		÷	7	
		x		x		÷	7	
		x		x		÷	7	
		x		x		÷	7	
		x		x		÷	7	

Total Average Watt-Hours per Day	
15% Loss Correction Factor	**x 1.15**
Adjusted Average Watt-Hours per Day	

We recommend doing 2 calculations: one for December (winter), and one for June (summer).

Wattage Consumption We Measured with a WATTS-UP? Meter

Appliance	Watts
Computer, desktop	90
Computer, laptop	45
17" monitor	100
HP LaserJet printer	600
HP Inkjet printer	15
Dishwasher, cool dry	736
Microwave	1400
Coffee Maker	900
Toaster, 2-slice	750
Amana Range (propane)	
Burners	0
Oven	380
Blender	350

Appliance	Watts
Mixer	120
Slow Cooker (high/low)	240/180
Vacuum, Oreck	410
Vacuum, Dirt Devil Upright	980
20" Television	50
Stereo System	25
Stereo, portable	10
Table top fountain	5
Sewing Machine (Bernina)	70
Serger (Pfaff)	140
Clothes Washer (front-loading: per load)	145
Clothes Dryer (propane)	300

Appliance	Watts
Clothes Iron	1200
Hair Curling Iron	55
Hair Dryer (high/low)	1500/400

We have not listed refrigerators nor freezers since their efficiency is getting better every year. The EnergyStar.gov website will give you the latest ratings for many household appliances and office equipment.

For additional information on wattage consumption, see Real Goods' website and/or catalog.

Appendix C
System Sizing - Solar & Battery Sizing

Solar Array Sizing Worksheet

		June	*Example*	December
1.	Input your **Adjusted Ave. Watt-Hours per Day** from page 290.		*3000*	
2.	Find your site on the June and December Insolation Maps on page 289 and input the nearest figure.*See the website, page 289, for more specific information, and additional months.*		*6*	
3.	To find the number of watts you need to generate per hour of full sun, divide line 1 by line 2.		*500*	
4.	Select a solar module and enter the wattage it produces. *Example: enter 120 for a Kyocera 120 watt module.*		*120*	
5.	To find the number of modules needed, divide line 3 by line 4. *Remember that pairs of modules are needed for 24-volt systems; sets of 4 modules for 48-volt systems.*		***6***	

This worksheet assumes you will operate entirely on solar power. If you have sufficient wind speed, and add a wind tower, you can downsize the number of solar modules needed. We suggest to start conservatively, and add more solar modules as needed.

Battery Sizing Worksheet

		Average	*Example*	Winter
1.	Input your **Adjusted Ave. Watt-Hours per Day** from page 290.		*3000*	
2.	Input the number of days of battery storage you need (the number of cloudy days in a row).		*4*	
3.	Multiply line 2 by line 1.		*12,000*	
4.	Input the battery depth of discharge you are comfortable with: 80% discharge (.80) is maximum; 50% discharge (.50) is better.		*.50*	
5.	Divide line 3 by line 4.		*24,000*	
6.	To derate batteries for low temperatures (^{O}F), select a factor next to your lowest operating temperature and enter here : 80°F — 1.00; 70°F — 1.04; 60°F — 1.11; 50°F — 1.19; 40°F — 1.30		*1.11*	
7.	To find your total battery capacity, multiply line 5 by line 6.		*26,640*	
8.	Calculate the watt-hour capacity of your selected battery: **voltage x amp hour**. *Example L-16 is 6 volts x 350 amp hours*		*2100*	
9.	To find the number of batteries you need, divide line 7 by line 8. Adjust the number of batteries to fit your system voltage. *Example: 24-volt system requires sets of 4, 6-volt batteries.*		***12.7***	

APPENDIX D
ELECTRICAL FORMULAS & HELPFUL INFORMATION

Calculating Line Loss

For a long time, I have wanted to know what the exact voltage drop would be in the wires if I added two modules to the solar array. By looking at standard wire loss tables I could see that it would be more than 2 percent, and less than 5 percent, but that wasn't close enough. Finally, I found the formula in *Pocket Ref,* a tight little book with more tables and formulas than I ever knew existed.

Following is an abbreviated version. It will work for all DC wiring, and all single phase AC wiring, using copper wire below 121 degrees Fahrenheit. (For 3 phase AC, or aluminum wire, the complete formula can be found in the *Pocket Ref.*)

EXAMPLE:
You want to run 70 feet of #2 wire for a 1000 watt array, operating at 24 volts. What is the exact voltage drop?

First calculate the amps by dividing the watts (1000) by the volts (24) = 41.66 amps. Then find the Wire Area in the chart below for #2 wire (66,400). Plug the numbers into the formula:

$$\textbf{Voltage Drop} = \frac{22 \text{ x } 70 \text{ feet x } 41.66 \text{ amps}}{66{,}400}$$

The voltage drop is .966 volts. To find the percentage of loss, divide .966 volts by your system voltage (24 volts) = .040, or 4% loss.

If you used #1 wire instead, the calculations would show a 3.1% loss; 1/0 wire will bring the voltage loss down to 2.5% ... a more acceptable number.

Using the Wire Size/Line Loss Tables

EXAMPLE:
Your 1100 watt solar array is located 50 feet from the batteries. By referring to the Wire Size/Line Loss tables on the following pages, what size of wire do you need for a 2% loss?
48-volt System #4 wire
24-volt System 2/0 wire *(over 3 times thicker wire than #4; and proportionately more expensive)*

EXAMPLE:
You have a well pump that draws 10 amps at 24-volts DC, and is 90 feet from the batteries. What size of wire do you need, for a 2% loss?

By referring to the 24-Volt chart with 2% voltage drop, 10 amps going 90 feet would require #4 wire. If you settle for a 5% loss, you could use #8 wire, but the efficiency and life of the pump will be decreased.

Pocket Ref *states that "Voltage drop should be less than 2% if possible. If the drop is greater than 2%, efficiency of the equipment in the circuit is severely decreased and life of the equipment will be decreased. As an example, if the voltage drop on an incandescent light bulb is 10%, the light output of the bulb decreases over 30%!"*

watts = volts x amps

amps = watts / volts

Wire Area in Circular mils	
4/0	212,000
3/0	168,000
2/0	133,000
1/0	106,000
#1	83,700
#2	66,400
#3	52,600
#4	41,700

$$\textbf{Actual Voltage Drop} = \frac{22 \text{ x length of wire in feet x amps}}{\text{wire area in circular mils}}$$

Appendix D
Wire Size / Line Loss Tables for 12 Volts

12 Volt DC — 2% VOLTAGE DROP

Amps in Wire	Wattage at 12V	WIRE SIZE #14	#12	#10	#8	#6	#4	#2	1/0	2/0	3/0
1	12	45	70	115	180	290	456	720	-	-	-
2	24	22	35	57	90	145	228	360	580	720	912
4	48	10	17	27	45	72	114	180	290	360	456
6	72	7	12	17	30	47	75	120	193	243	305
8	96	5	8	14	22	35	57	90	145	180	228
10	120	4	7	11	18	28	45	72	115	145	183
15	180	3	4	7	12	19	30	48	76	96	122
20	240	■	3	5	9	14	22	36	57	72	91
25	300	■	■	4	7	11	18	29	46	58	73
30	360	■	■	3	6	9	15	24	38	48	61
40	480	■	■	■	4	7	11	18	29	36	45
50	600	■	■	■	■	5	9	14	23	29	36

12 Volt DC — 5% VOLTAGE DROP

Amps in Wire	Wattage at 12V	WIRE SIZE #14	#12	#10	#8	#6	#4	#2	1/0	2/0	3/0
1	12	113	175	275	450	710	-	-	-	-	-
2	24	56	87	138	225	355	576	900	-	-	-
4	48	25	43	68	113	178	288	450	725	900	-
6	72	18	30	43	75	119	188	300	481	600	760
8	96	13	21	36	56	88	144	225	363	450	570
10	120	11	17	28	45	71	113	180	290	360	457
15	180	7	11	17	30	47	75	120	193	240	304
20	240	■	8	13	22	36	56	90	145	180	229
25	300	■	■	11	17	28	45	72	115	145	183
30	360	■	■	8	15	23	37	60	96	120	152
40	480	■	■	■	11	17	28	45	72	90	114
50	600	■	■	■	■	13	22	36	57	72	91

To Calculate 10% loss, multiply the distance by 2.

■ **Exceeds ampacity; do not use wire sizes in this zone; it may cause overheating.**
\- **Over 1000 feet**

One-way distances listed: measured from point A (such as the solar array) to point B (the batteries).
The **VOLTAGE DROP** refers to the percent of power lost due to resistance.
All distances calculated in feet for copper wire.

Appendix D
Wire Size / Line Loss Tables for 24 Volts

24 Volt DC — 2% VOLTAGE DROP

Amps in Wire	Wattage at 24V	WIRE SIZE #14	#12	#10	#8	#6	#4	#2	1/0	2/0	3/0
1	24	90	140	230	360	580	912	-	-	-	-
2	48	45	70	115	180	290	456	720	-	-	-
4	96	20	35	55	90	145	228	360	580	720	912
6	144	15	24	35	60	95	150	240	386	486	610
8	192	11	17	29	45	71	114	180	290	360	456
10	240	9	14	23	36	57	91	145	230	290	366
15	360	6	9	14	24	38	60	96	153	192	244
20	480	■	7	11	18	29	45	72	115	145	183
25	600	■	■	9	14	23	36	58	92	116	146
30	720	■	■	7	12	19	30	48	77	97	122
40	960	■	■	■	9	14	23	36	58	72	91
50	1200	■	■	■	■	11	18	29	46	58	73

24 Volt DC — 5% VOLTAGE DROP

Amps in Wire	Wattage at 24V	WIRE SIZE #14	#12	#10	#8	#6	#4	#2	1/0	2/0	3/0
1	24	226	350	550	900	-	-	-	-	-	-
2	48	112	175	276	450	710	-	-	-	-	-
4	96	50	87	137	226	356	576	900	-	-	-
6	144	37	60	87	150	238	376	600	962	-	-
8	192	27	42	72	112	177	288	450	726	900	-
10	240	22	35	57	90	142	226	360	580	720	914
15	360	15	22	35	60	95	150	240	386	480	608
20	480	■	17	27	45	72	112	180	290	360	458
25	600	■	■	22	35	57	90	145	230	290	366
30	720	■	■	17	30	47	75	120	192	240	304
40	960	■	■	■	23	35	57	90	145	180	228
50	1200	■	■	■	■	27	45	72	115	145	182

To Calculate 10% loss, multiply the distance by 2.

■ **Exceeds ampacity; do not use wire sizes in this zone; it may cause overheating.**
\- **Over 1000 feet**

One-way distances listed: measured from point A (such as the solar array) to point B (the batteries).
The **VOLTAGE DROP** refers to the percent of power lost due to resistance.
All distances calculated in feet for copper wire.

Appendix D
Wire Size / Line Loss Tables for 48 Volts

48 Volt DC — 2% VOLTAGE DROP

Amps in Wire	Wattage at 48V	WIRE SIZE #14	#12	#10	#8	#6	#4	#2	1/0	2/0	3/0
1	48	180	280	460	720	-	-	-	-	-	-
2	96	90	140	230	360	580	912	-	-	-	-
4	192	40	70	110	180	290	456	720	-	-	-
6	288	30	48	70	120	190	300	480	772	972	-
8	384	22	34	58	90	142	228	360	580	720	912
10	480	18	28	46	72	114	182	290	460	580	732
15	720	12	18	28	48	76	120	192	306	384	488
20	960	■	14	22	36	58	90	144	230	290	366
25	1200	■	■	18	28	46	72	116	184	232	292
30	1440	■	■	14	24	38	60	96	154	194	244
40	1920	■	■	■	18	28	46	72	116	144	182
50	2400	■	■	■	■	22	36	58	92	116	146

48 Volt DC — 5% VOLTAGE DROP

Amps in Wire	Wattage at 48V	WIRE SIZE #14	#12	#10	#8	#6	#4	#2	1/0	2/0	3/0
1	48	452	700	-	-	-	-	-	-	-	-
2	96	224	350	552	900	-	-	-	-	-	-
4	192	100	174	274	452	712	-	-	-	-	-
6	288	74	120	174	300	476	752	-	-	-	-
8	384	54	84	144	224	354	576	900	-	-	-
10	480	44	70	114	180	284	452	720	-	-	-
15	720	30	44	70	120	190	300	480	772	960	-
20	960	■	34	54	90	144	224	390	580	720	916
25	1200	■	■	44	70	114	180	290	460	580	732
30	1440	■	■	34	60	94	150	240	384	480	608
40	1920	■	■	■	46	70	114	180	290	360	456
50	2400	■	■	■	■	54	90	144	230	290	364

To Calculate 10% loss, multiply the distance by 2.

■ **Exceeds ampacity; do not use wire sizes in this zone; it may cause overheating.**
\- **Over 1000 feet**

One-way distances listed: measured from point A (such as the solar array) to point B (the batteries).
The **VOLTAGE DROP** refers to the percent of power lost due to resistance.
All distances calculated in feet for copper wire.

Appendix E — Resources

The information listed below will give you a good start in the right direction. The internet is an excellent tool for finding for new information and resources in this ever-changing business of building and energy.

LOG HOME INFORMATION

Manufacturers of Chinking & Finishes

Perma-Chink Systems, Inc.
800-548-1231
www.permachink.com

Sashco
800-767-5656
www.sashco.com

Weatherall Company, Inc.
800-367-7068
www.weatherall.com

Suppliers: Log Tools/Supplies/Chinking/Finishes

Bailey's, Inc.
800-322-4539
www.baileys-online.com

Bosworth Tools
406-886-2500
www.bosworthtools.com

Log Home Store, Inc.
800-827-1688
www.aloghomestore.com

Schroeder Log Home Supply, Inc.
800-359-6614
www.loghelp.com

Van Dyke's Restorers
home hardware (hinges, door knobs, etc.)
800-558-1234
www.vandykes.com

Log Home Plans

Log home magazines (articles and advertisers) are an excellent source for ideas, in addition to these books:

Best Log Home Plans, Robbin Obomsawin
Log House Plans, B. Allan Mackie
Small Log Homes, Robbin Obomsawin
The Log Home Plan Book, Cindy Thiede with Heather Mehra-Pedersen

Log Home Building Schools

The following websites lists schools:
www.lhgic.com (article index; annual directory)
www.loghomelinks.com/build.htm
www.loghomelists.com
www.logassociation.org/directory/

Lasko School of Log Building
800-292-8043
www.laskoschooloflogbuilding.com

Log Home Shows

Country's Best Log Home Shows
www.loghomesinfo.net/loghomeshow.asp

Log Home Living Home Shows
www.loghomeliving.com/shows/index.html

International Log Home Show
www.log-home-show.com

Log Home & Timber Frame Expo
www.logexpo.com

RENEWABLE ENERGY

Manufacturers

Bergey Wind Power
405-364-4212
www.bergey.com

Bio-Sun Systems, Inc.
waterless, composting toilets
800-847-8840
www.bio-sun.com

Bogart Engineering
TriMetric meter
831-338-0616
www.bogartengineering.com

Concorde Battery Corporation
www.concordebattery.com

Controlled Energy Corporation
AquaStar tankless heaters
800-642-3199
www.controlledenergy.com

Grundfos Pumps Corporation
www.grundfos.com

OutBack Power Systems
360-435-6030
www.outbackpower.com

Southwest Windpower Inc.
928-779-9463
www.windenergy.com

Trojan Battery Company
800-423-6569
www.trojan-battery.com

Xantrex Technology
(formerly Trace Engineering)
360-435-8826
www.xantrex.com

***UNI-SOLAR®* Products**
Bekaert ECD Solar Systems LLC
800-843-3892
www.uni-solar.com

Consultants/Suppliers We Have Worked With

Backwoods Solar Electric Systems
208-263-4290
www.backwoodssolar.com

Burnham-Beck & Sun
970-482-6924
www.burnhambeck.com

Real Goods
an excellent website for information / products
800-919-2400
www.solar.realgoods.com

RMS Electric
303-444-5909
www.rmse.com

OTHER PRODUCTS & SERVICES NOTED IN THIS BOOK

Lite-Form International
800-551-3313
www.liteform.com

Kahrs International
engineered wood flooring
www.kahrs.com

Accent Media Group
low voltage wiring (audio, computers)
303-671-9053
www.accentmediagroup.com

ORGANIZATIONS

American Council for an Energy-Efficient Economy (ACEEE)
www.clean-air.org

American Solar Energy Society
303-443-3130
www.ases.org

International Log Builders Association
250-547-8776
www.logassociation.org

Log Homes Council
www.loghomes.org

The Institute for Solar Living
707-744-2017
www.solarliving.org

Rocky Mountain Institute
970-927-3851
www.rmi.org

REFERENCE WEBSITES

Energy Star®
EPA energy ratings of appliances
www.energystar.gov

U.S. Department of Energy's EREC
(Energy Efficiency and Renewable Energy Clearinghouse)
www.eren.doe.gov

U.S. Solar Radiation Resource Maps
http://rredc.nrel.gov/solar/old_data/nsrdb/redbook/atlas

Wind Energy Maps/Tables
http://rredc.nrel.gov/wind/pubs/atlas/maps
http://rredc.nrel.gov/wind/pubs/atlas/tables

BOOK SELLERS

Back Home Books
800-992-2546
www.backhomemagazine.com

Bailey's, Inc.
800-322-4539
www.baileys-online.com

Log Home Guide Information Center
Log Home Book Store
888-345-5647
www.lhgic.com

Log Home Store, Inc.
800-827-1688
www.aloghomestore.com

Mother Earth News Bookshelf
800-678-4883
www.motherearthnews.com

Real Goods
800-919-2400
www.solar.realgoods.com

MAGAZINES

Back Home
www.backhomemagazine.com

Country's Best Log Homes
www.loghomesinfo.net

Home Power
a good source for finding PV/wind suppliers
www.homepower.com

Log and Timber Style
www.logandtimberstyle.com

Log Home Design Ideas
www.lhdi.com

Log Home Living
www.loghomeliving.com

Log Homes Illustrated
www.loghomesmag.com

Mother Earth News
www.motherearthnews.com

Natural Home
www.naturalhomemagazine.com

Solar Today
www.solartoday.org

Appendix F — General Bibliography

Aldrich, Chilson D., with Harry Drabik. *The Real Log Cabin.* Minneapolis, MN: Nodin Press, 1994.

Burch, Monte. *Complete Guide to Building Log Homes.* NY: Sterling Publishing Company, 1990.

Feirer, John L., and Gilbert R. Hutchings. *Carpentry and Building Construction, 3rd Ed.* Encino, CA: Glencoe Publishing Company, 1986.

Gipe, Paul. *Wind Power for Home and Business.* Post Mills, VT: Chelsea Green Publishing, 1993.

Glover, Thomas J. *Pocket Ref.* Littleton, CO: Sequoia Publishing, 2001.

Gundersen, P. Erik. *The Handy Physics Answer Book.* Detroit, MI: Visible Ink Press, a division of Gale Research, 1999.

Mackie, B. Allan. *The Owner-Built Log House.* Ontario, Canada: Firefly Books Ltd, 2001.

Mackie, B. Allan, and others. *Log Span Tables.* Canada: International Log Builders Association, 2000.

Muir, Doris, and Paul Osborne. *The Energy Economics and Thermal Performance of Log Houses.* Gardenvale, Quebec, Canada: Muir Publishing Company Ltd, 1983.

Phelps, Hermann. *The Craft of Log Building.* Ottowa, Ontario: Lee Valley Tools Ltd, 1982.

Stewart, John W. *How To Make your Own Solar Electricity.* Blue Ridge Summit, PA: Tab Books Inc., 1979.

Threthewey, Richard, with Don Best. *This Old House Heating, Ventilation and Air Conditioning.* New York: Little, Brown & Company, 1994.

Tiepner-Thiede, Cindy, and Arthur Thiede. *The Log Home Book.* Salt Lake City, Utah: Gibbs Smith, Publisher, 1993.

The Solar Electric House. Worthington, MA: New England Solar Electric Inc., 1998.

U.S. Department of Energy. *Home Wind Power.* Charlotte, Vermont: Garden Way Publishing, 1981.

Appendix G — Suggested Reading

We also recommend the following books:

Natural Capitalism: Creating The Next Industrial Revolution, Paul Hawken, Armory Lovins, L. Hunter Lovins

The Independent Home, Michael Potts

Log Homes Made Easy: Contracting and Building Your Own Log Home, Jim Cooper

Log Spirit, Linda Arnus White

The Passive Solar House, James Kachadorian

A Primer on Sustainable Building, Diana Lopez Barnett with William D. Browning

Solar Living Source Book, John Schaeffer

There Are No Electrons: Electronics for Earthlings, Kenn Amdahl

Index

Italic numbers refer to photos/illustrations

A

access to site 26-27
air-conditioning 17
"An Unlikely Tale of a Pond Pump" 189-192
appliances, notes on 287
appliances, wattage consumption list 290
AquaStar water heater 261, *261*
architects 35
architectural tile 280, *280*, 283, *283*
arrangement of PV/Wind equipment *37*

B

batteries 19, 227-234
    charging & discharging 229-230
    color-code the cables 233
    don't forget the water! 232
    equalization 231
    gel-type or sealed, maintenance-free 228, 231
    how many? 196
    hydrometer 230, *230*
    pampering 229-232
    parallel & series connections 234
    system sizing worksheet 291
    testing 230
    the right ones for the job 228-229
    Trojan T-105 and L16 228-229
    wiring in series/parallel 233-234, *234*
battery box 19, 233
    venting 233
Benshoof, John 22, *22*, *45*, *106*, *107*, *116*, *138*, *140*, *152*, *159*, *164*, *166*, *170*, *207*, *274*
Bergey Wind Power 215, *215*, 296
bibliography, general 298
Bio-Sun Systems 296
blueprints 34-36
blueprints, concerns unique to log homes 35-36
bonding (*see* grounding) 245
book sellers, listing 297
Bosworth Tools 89, *89*, 296
Buckhorn Camp log home 23, *23*, *98*, *137*, *155*
building codes (*see* plans & permits)
buying a log shell versus doing it yourself 22

C

ceiling, finish options 21, 134-135
chainsaws 88
"Changing with the Weather, a metaphor" 187
charge controllers 221-225, 249
    battery charging 222
    DC load control 225, *225*
    diversion load control 224, *224*
    equalization of batteries 222-223
    for wind generators 223-224
checks/cracks of logs
    caulking 173, *173*
    placement of 105, *105*
chimneys 113
    settling 168
chinked versus chinkless style 93-95
chinking & finishing 171-177
    applying chinking 175-177
    cleaning the logs 173, *173*
    tools *175*
cisterns 264-265
cleaning the logs 173, *173*
collar ties 142, *134*, *142*
combiner boxes (electrical) *206*, 247, *247*
come-along 105, *105*
composting, waterless toilets 30
Concorde batteries 228, 296
concrete
    floors 69
    pumper 66-67, *66-67*
    roofing tiles 145
Controlled Energy Corporation 261, 296
converters 182, 195, 236
costs to consider 286-287
county planning department 34

D

damp-proofing 68, *68*
DC disconnect 249, *249*
DC converters 182, 195, 236
deck 276
designing for efficiency & comfort 15-16
doors
    exterior (see 'windows') 149-157
    interior 273
dormers
    design ideas 121, *121*
    framing *130*, *132*
drawknives *87*, 89, *89*
drip edge (flashing) 113, 144, 156
drywall
    fitting between purlins 270-271, *270*
    hanging & finishing 270-272
    scribing around log walls 271, *271*
    texturing & painting 272
Dukart, Lane - Clay Master 283, *283*

E

eaves
    construction 142-143
    design of 17
electric winch 82, *82*, 91, *91*
electrical current: AC & DC 189-192, *189*

electrical formulas & helpful information 292
actual voltage drop 292
calculating line loss 292
using wire size/line loss tables 292
wire area in circular mils 292
electrical needs, system sizing worksheets 290-291
electrical wiring
low voltage 160
of house 159-160, *159-160*
testing 250 *250*
electricity
high voltage and low voltage 189-192
sinewave graph 237
sinewaves 236-237
wind generated 213-214
EnergyStar program 297
equalization, batteries (see 'batteries') 231
excavation 53-56, *53*
dynamite 54-55, *54*
septic & well 56
the perimeter 55

F

finishes & finishing 174-175
fireplaces 259
flashing (drip edge) 113, 144, 156
counter-flashing 168
flooring materials 255
floors (*see* subfloor)
installing 2nd floor 112-113, *112-113*
log beams versus wood I-joists 72-73
main 71-77, *71*
floor plans, sources 296
foundation 57-69
anchor bolts 68, *68*
backfilling 68
batter boards 60, *60*
beam pockets 68, *68*
concrete pour 66-67, *66-67*
damp-proofing 68, *68*
footings 61-63, *62, 63*
height of 16, 172
making it level 61
making it square 59-60, *60*
polystyrene forms 64-65, *64-65*
walls 63-67
pier & off-the-grid considerations 36-37
frame walls, interior 18, 159, 164-166
French, Josh *85, 136, 173*
fuses & breakers, for the solar array 206

G

gables
design ideas 115-121
exterior finishes for framed ends 120-121
framed gable ends 120-121, *120, 123,* 137
full log gable ends 117, *117,* 138
vertical log gable ends 118-119, *118-119,* 137
gin pole 69, 81-83, *81*
grounding
bonding 245
solar array 207, 247
the system 245
Ufer Grounding System 67
Grundfos well pumps 268
gusset plates 119, *119*
gypsum concrete (for radiant heat) 256, *256*

H

heating of house 251-260
Curt & Kelly's Excellent Solution 258
forced air 253
incorporating solar-heated water 257, 259
propane wall heaters 252
radiant hot water floor heat 254-257
wood stoves 259-260
home design
blending elements 21
cooling of house 17
cross-ventilation 18
electrical room 18-19
extra (non-living) spaces 18
frame walls & plumbing 18
heat-efficient 15
mechanical room 18
orientation 58, *58*
protection for logs 172-173, *172*
sound vs. heat efficiency 19-20
hot water
domestic use 261
options for heating 261
on-demand water heater *261*
hydrometer, batteries 230

I

insulation, in roof 134, 136
interior doors 273
interior walls
drywall (see drywall)
wainscoting 273, *273*
internet via 2-way satellite 26, 160, *160*
inverters 19, 235-240
slow cooker comparison 237
functions 238-240
modified sine wave 237, *237*
sine wave 236, *236*

J

Johnson, Stanley, chainsaw wizard 102, *102*
joists (*see* subfloor)

K

Kahrs flooring 255, 297
keyways & splines for windows and doors 155
kitchen cabinets and countertops *20,* 273-274
settling 169-170

L

Lasko School of Log Building 23
lighting
- compact flourescent light bulbs 287
- natural 17-18

lightning 245-246
- rods 245-246, *246*
- log homes versus framed homes 246

lightning protection 243-249
- Ufer Grounding System 67
- well casings 246
- wind generator/tower 248-249

Lite-Form® *64*, 65, *65*, 296
log accents, finishing touches 279
log building schools 23
log cracks/checks 105
log home building school resources 296
log home plan resources 296
log home shows 296
log home tools & supplies, listing 296
log home, finish work 269-284
Log Homes Made Easy, by Jim Cooper 22
log homes with chinking 93
Log Knowledge, 22, *22*, 102, 170, *170*
log railings 277-278
Log Span Tables, by Mackie, Read & Hahney 35
log spindles, homemade 278, *278*
log walls & corners
- making it square 101-102, *101*
- door & window openings 108, *108*
- interior log walls 107, *107*
- maintaining even height 109-110, *109*

logs
- 1st log 96-97, *96*
- 1st notches 97-101
- 2nd & 3rd logs 97-101
- accent (non-structural) purlins 141-142, *141-142*
- boom truck 85
- buying 42-43
- calculating shrinkage for doors/windows 152
- checks/cracks 173, *173*
- chinking 175-177, *176*
- choose your logs well 104-105
- cleaning 173, *173*
- cribbing 44-45
- cutting the ends 158
- decorative uses 279, *279*
- delivery 39-42, *41*
- ends, trimming 158, *158*
- finishes (stains/sealers) 174-175
- getting to know your logs 45
- green or seasoned 43-44
- hand-peeled versus machine peeled 22
- height off ground 16, 172
- knots removed 105-106, *106*
- lifting 81-85
- lifting with gin pole 81-83

logs *continued*
- marking the floor for windows, doors 95-96, *95*
- moving with tractor 83, *83*
- peeling 44, *79*, 80-81, *80*
- preservatives 173, 175
- pressure washing 173
- purlins 135-138, *135-138*
- rafters 134-135
- ramp 84, *84*
- R-value of 15
- shrinkage 43
- spiking 107-108, *107*
- splicing 106, *106*
- square corners 95-96
- stained/discolored 173
- structural 35-36, 110
- structural purlins (*see* purlins)
- the last log 113
- thermal mass 15
- top wall logs 126, *126*, *127*
- twist 43, *43*
- tying-in floor beams 110-112, *110-112*

low voltage electrical wiring 160

M

Mackie, B. Allan 23, 35, 95, 153
magazines, listing 297
metric conversion factors 286
moisture content of logs 174
mortar for stonework 282
multimeter for testing 183, 250, *250*

N

notches
- around floor beams 111
- cutting 99-101, *99*, *100*
- round vs. scarfed 97-98, *97*
- saddle 97-101
- scribing 98-99, *98*

O

off-the grid 14, 181-186
Ohm's Law 193-194
on-demand water heaters 261
organizations 297
OutBack Power Systems *206*, 221, *221*, 240, *240*

P

passive solar design 16-18
peeling logs (*see* logs, peeling)
Perma-Chink 177, 296
permits (*see* plans & permits)
photovoltaic (PV) modules (see solar modules)
placement & orientation of the home 16
plans & permits 33-36
- solar & wind power considerations 37-38

plat of home & utilities *56*

plumbing
gas lines for refrigerator & stove 38
settling considerations 168, *168*
through frame walls 18, 159
preservative for logs 173, 175
pressure washing logs 173
propane wall heaters 252
pumping water 263-268
purlins (*see* logs, purlins)
PV/wind recommendations versus our system 288-289
Pythagorean Theorem 59, *59*, 128

R

radiant floor heat
installing 256-257
special considerations 255
rafter tails & rain gutters 143
rafters
frame (dimensional lumber) 129-134, *133*
log or timber 134-135, *134*
lookout & fly rafters 133-134, *133*
railings *269*, 277-278, *277*
rain gutters & rafter tails 143
renewable energy, the basic system 189-192, *183*
resources 296-297
rock, dynamite 30
rockwork (*see* stonework)
roof
asphalt shingles 145-146
basic (standard frame) 125-134
beams 140
concrete tile 145
constructing the eaves 132-133
cutting rafter ends & bird's mouths 129-130, *129-130*
eaves 142-143
framing 123-146, *130-131*
log purlins & framed gable ends 137
log purlins & full log gable ends 138
log purlins & vertical log gable ends 137
making it dry 143-144, *143*
material options 144-146
measuring for rafters and gable ends 127-129, *127*
metal 145
non-structural log purlins 141-142, *141-142*
overbuilt & loving it 124
pitch 124-125, *124*
pitch & angles 128, *128*
putting in the dormers 131-132
structural log purlins 135-136, *135*
truss designs 139, *139*
wall plate 126-127, *127*

S

safety components for electrical system 243-249
Sashco 174-177, 296
satellite communication (TV, internet) 26
Schroeder Log Home Supply, Inc. 296
screw jacks, for settling 168
scribing
a notch *93*, 98-99, *98*
considerations 105-106
drywall 271
septic system 30
settling issues 163-169
chimneys & stove pipes 168
frame walls 164-166, *165*, *166*
kitchen cabinets 169-170
plumbing pipes & vents 168, *168*
screw jacks 168, *168*
stairs 167
The Benefit of Experience 170
the big picture 164
vertical support posts & screw jacks 169, *169*
shrinkage of logs 152
site selection 25
sizing the system 193-196
solar array
fuses and breakers 206, 247
grounding 207
leaving room to grow 207
lightning protection 247
on roof, ground, deck 200-201, *200*, *201*, *207*
placement 27
system sizing worksheet 291
tilt angle 201-203, *203*
trackers 205
wiring 205-206, *205*
solar consultants/suppliers 296
solar heated water collectors 257, 259
solar modules *28*, 197-207
amorphous *199*, 200
mounting 204-205, *204*
performance in hot weather 199
polycrystalline 198-200, *197*
types of 198-200
solar radiation data
website listing 289, 297
June (comparison) *202*
June and December *289*
southern exposure 27-29
Southwest Windpower Inc. 212, *212*, 214, *214*, 217, *217*, *223*, 296
spindles, homemade log 278, *278*
stains & sealants for logs 174-175
stairs
custom log, design/build 274-275, *274*, *275*
settling 167
the magic number 275
stonework, exterior 281-282, *281*, *282*
subfloor
floor joists 75-76
plywood 76-77, *77*
rim joists 75, *75*, *76*
sill plate 73
supporting with steel 73-74, *74*

suggested reading 298
sun angle and tilt of the solar array 203
  3 seasons *202, 203*
  measuring 203-204, *203*
system sizing worksheets
  batteries 291
  electrical needs 290
  solar array 291
system voltage, 12-, 24-, or 48-volts? 194-196

T

television via satellite 26, 160
The Energy Economics and Thermal Performance of Log Houses 15
The Owner-Built Log Home, by Mackie 95, 153
tile, many uses for 280, *280, 284*
tool storage 51, *51*
tools for logwork 87-91
  chainsaws 88
  chisels 89-90
  drawknives 89
  log dogs & log cleats 90, *90*
  logger's tape *91*
  peavey & straight bars 90, *90*
  power planer 88-89
  scribers 90, *90*
tools for pre-log construction 47-51
  generator 48
  odds & ends 50
  sight level 61, *61*
towers (also see wind towers) 216-218
TriMetric meter 185, *185*, 230
Trojan batteries 228-229, *227*, 296
Trus-Joist 73
truss designs 139, *139, 140*

U

U.S. Department of Energy's EREC 297
Ufer Grounding System 67
UNI-SOLAR® products 145, 199-200, *199*, 296

V

Van Dyke's Restorers 296
Vermont Casting wood stove 259

W

wainscoting 273
walls (*see* interior walls)
water
  availability 29
  drainage 16-17
  drilling a well 29, *29*
  heating 261, *261*
  pumping 263-268
wattage consumption of various appliances 290
Weatherall Company, Inc. 296
well pumps
  AC 267-268
  DC 266-267
Where is North? 58-59, *58*
wind charts/maps (website listing) 289, 297
wind generators 209-218, *210*
  (*see also* Southwest Windpower, Bergey Wind Power)
  size to buy 215
  AC or DC? 214-216
  charge controllers 223
  lightning protection 248-249
  the wind brake 248
wind speed formula 211
wind towers *31*, 216-218, *216*
  finding the right location 216-217
  types (fold-over & lattice) 217-218, *217, 218*
wind, and your site 29-30
wind
  how much is enough? 211-213
  old technology versus new 213-214
  size of generator needed 215
  speed conversion formula 211
windows & doors
  adding trim boards 156-157, *156, 157*
  bucks & trim 150-151, *150, 151*
  calculating log shrinkage 152, *152*
  installing 149-157
  installing bucks & windows 154-155, *154, 155*
  keyways and splines 155, *155*
  marking & cutting the openings 153-154, *149, 150*
windows
  efficient/super insulated 17
  skylights 18
  south-facing 17
wire coding colors, AC and DC 250
wire size / line loss tables
  12-volts 293
  24-volts 294
  48-volts 295
wiring (*see* electrical)
wood stoves 259-260, *259*

X

Xantrex Technologies (formerly Trace) 221-222, *221*, 235, *235*, 249, *249*

About the Authors

Rex and LaVonne Ewing currently live and work from their solar- and wind-powered log home overlooking Colorado's expansive front range. After handcrafting two log homes in the 1980's, Rex spent several years as CEO of a well-respected equine nutrition firm, where he formulated and marketed numerous nutrition products worldwide. In 1997, he wrote a best-selling book on horse nutrition: *Beyond the Hay Days: A Refreshingly Simple Guide to Effective Horse Nutrition*, and has been published by several equine publications. Since leaving the corporate world, Rex has been hard at work building their dream home, and writing novels. LaVonne is owner of Image Resource, a graphic design firm that specializes in book design, art catalogs, and corporate identities.